'This account of 30 women who went with Mao Zedong and China's first Communists on the Long March is a new view: for it has realism without rhetoric, politics without propaganda, heroism without hyperbole, and sadness without sentimentality. But the authors show how soon the Communists who claimed to treat women equally fell back on traditional ways of exploiting them.'

Alison Broinowski, a former diplomat, has written or edited five books about Australia and Asia, including *The Yellow Lady*. She is a Visiting Fellow in the Faculty of Asian Studies at the Australian National University.

'The women were wives, lovers, political cadres and professionals in the Chinese Communist Party's great trek in the 1930s. Lily Lee and Sue Wiles draw on original sources to bring their unrecognised achievements to life.'

Jocelyn Chey, former Australian diplomat and trade official, Visiting Professor, University of Sydney.

ABOUT THE AUTHORS

LILY XIAO HONG LEE was born in China and has worked and studied in Hong Kong, Southeast Asia, USA and Australia. She lectures in Chinese language and literature at the University of Sydney, and is author of *The Virtue of Yin: Studies on Chinese women* and *Vignette of an Age: Shishuo xinyu—new sayings through the ages* (forthcoming). She has written numerous articles on Chinese women and the literature of the Wei-Jin period (220–580 AD) and is co-editor-in-chief of the biographical project *Biographical Dictionary of Chinese Women* (M E Sharpe).

SUE WILES is a researcher and translator who teaches translation at the University of Western Sydney. She is the author of *T'ai Chi*, a collection of her translations of instructions and advanced practical techniques, and is collaborating on the *Biographical Dictionary of Chinese Women* project. Her areas of research include the Qing revolutionary Qiu Jin, and female Daoist divinities of the Wei-Jin period.

Women of the Long March

Lily Xiao Hong Lee and Sue Wiles

ALLEN & UNWIN

Australia Council for the Arts

This project has been assisted by the Commonwealth Government through the Australia Council, its arts funding advisory body.

First published in 1999
Allen & Unwin
9 Atchison Street, St Leonards 1590 Australia
Phone: (61 2) 8425 0100
Fax: (61 2) 9906 2218
E-mail: frontdesk@allen-unwin.com.au
Web: http://www.allen-unwin.com.au

National Library of Australia
Cataloguing-in-Publication entry:

Lee, Lily Hsiao Hung.
  Women of the Long March.

  Bibliography.
  Includes index.
  ISBN 1 86448 569 8.

  1. Women and communism—China. 2. Women soldiers—China.
  3. China—History—Long March, 1934–1935—Participation,
  Female. 4. China—History—20th century. I. Wiles, Sue, 1940– .
  II. Title.

951.042082

Set in 10.5/13 pt Arrus by DOCUPRO, Sydney
Printed and bound by Australian Print Group, Maryborough

10 9 8 7 6 5 4 3 2 1

CONTENTS

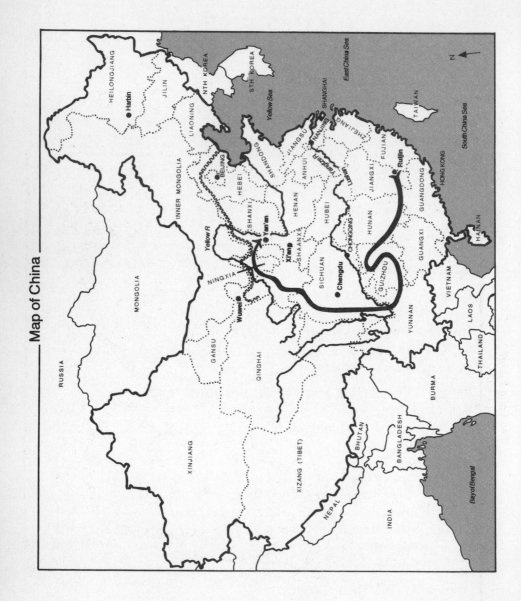

Map of China

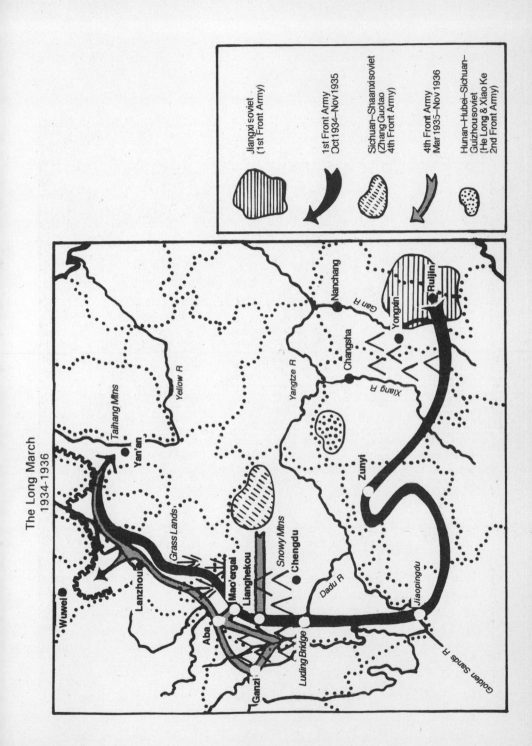

The Long March
1934-1936

Jiangxi soviet (1st Front Army)

1st Front Army Oct1934–Nov1935

Sichuan–Shaanxi soviet (Zhang Guotao 4th Front Army)

4th Front Army Mar 1935–Nov 1936

Hunan–Hubei–Sichuan–Guizhou soviet (He Long & Xiao Ke 2nd Front Army)

Wuwei
Lanzhou
Ganzi
Aba
Mao'ergai
Lianghekou
Snowy Mtns
Chengdu
Luding Bridge
Dadu R
Jiaopingdu
Golden Sands R
Yan'an
Taihang Mtns
Yellow R
Grass Lands
Zunyi
Yangtze R
Xiang R
Changsha
Gan R
Nanchang
Yongxin
Ruijin

PREFACE

Thirty women took part in the main Long March of the Chinese communists in 1934–35. Little is known in the West of these women, even though a handful of them rose to national prominence after 1949, when the communist People's Republic of China was established. The idealism of these women as well as their courage and endurance under cruel conditions inspired us to write this book. It is a natural corollary of our common interest in China and women's studies, and our years of research into Chinese women's lives over the centuries.

In the past fifty years women in mainland China have gained political and economic rights and social freedoms their grand-mothers never dreamed of. We must make clear at the outset, however, that our motivation to write this book came not from a desire to defend the Communist Party's claims of gender equality, which many Westerners have viewed with considerable cynicism. Rather, we are motivated by an admiration for those thirty young women of the Long March—the youngest was nineteen when they set out, the oldest thirty-four—who retained a lifelong commitment to their ideals despite the disappoint-ments, and sometimes betrayals, of reality. We have tried to recapture something of the spirit of idealism which moved them, and millions like them, to leave home and family and risk their lives over many years for the Communist Revolution. To do this, where we could we used contemporary sources to tell their stories. While we know that many of the statements, conversations and descriptions we quote will sound naive to late twentieth-century

Western readers, we ask them to remember that what they hear as propaganda those young women took to heart as a genuine message of hope.

Stoicism was second nature to these women. Born during the transition from traditional China to modern nation, they lived in a society that still devalued women. As children, they expected to be told who they would marry; some suffered footbinding; many were sold or given away as child brides to families who mistreated them. Education was denied to all but the privileged few. The Long March women sometimes spoke to interviewers and biographers of their sufferings, but rarely did they reveal their feelings. American journalists Helen Foster Snow and Edgar Snow, who lived in China during the period of the Long March, wrote repeatedly of how difficult it was to get the Chinese communists to speak of personal matters. Thus, we can never know how He Zizhen felt when she left her children behind, because she spoke of this publicly only once that we know of, when she admitted tearfully that she had never forgotten the baby she abandoned on the Long March. We do not know how Wang Quanyuan felt when she was betrayed and ostracised, because she steadfastly refused to accuse her tormentors. We can only guess at how Kang Keqing felt when she was made to leave the army, because she unflinchingly defended the decision as being for the good of the nation.

This brings us to the intriguing issue of what Westerners see as the blind obedience of Chinese communists in the face of the Communist Party's clear failure to fulfil many of its early promises. This is especially evident during controversial episodes such as the Hundred Flowers Movement of the late 1950s and the 1966–76 Cultural Revolution, but the lives of the three women whose stories we have told also amply demonstrate this trait. We wonder, however, how useful it is to ponder the concept of obedience in this connection. More useful, perhaps, would be to consider the context in which the communists sought and won millions of supporters from all levels of Chinese society in the three decades between 1920 and 1950.

To our minds, it was loyalty rather than obedience that bound the early communists, including the women of the Long March, to the Communist Party. The slogan under which Mao came to power was 'Great Unity' (*da tuanjie*), a powerful catchphrase that signified a coming together of workers, peasants and soldiers for the single purpose of overthrowing the oppressive traditional order. The Chinese word for 'comrade' is *tongzhi*, which literally means 'same ambition; common will'. This word symbolised the idealistic attitude of the early communists, who joined together not out of obedience but in the hope of creating a viable future. Having identified themselves as holding the same ambition, they then agreed that in order to realise their aims they must abide unquestioningly by the decisions of their leaders. Unity of purpose within the Confucian family system made China the world's longest continuous civilisation; unity of purpose made the Communist Revolution possible. Since traditional Chinese society was based on the concept of loyalty and responsibility to the family, the communists had no need to distort this traditional way of life; they simply adapted it, asking their followers to transfer their loyalty from a system they claimed had failed to one that offered hope.

Unfortunately, loyalty carries within itself the seed of betrayal, and the fear of being cast out will always play a larger or smaller part in close-knit societies where the community rather than the individual is most valued. Once the communists gained power, it became clear that the imperial leaders had been replaced by another set of leaders—the communist leaders. In the second half of the twentieth century China remained a country ruled by its handful of leaders, not by its people. Yet even this obvious failure of communism to guarantee equality did not destroy the hope of millions of Chinese, who remained patiently loyal to the party, confident that at some future time those early dreams would become a reality.

Strictly speaking, three separate armies were part of the Long March, which lasted from 1934 to 1936: the 1st Front Red Army left Jiangxi Province in October 1934 and reached Shaanxi Province in the north-west one year later; Zhang Guotao's 4th Front Red Army marched from Sichuan to join them on the Tibetan border in 1935; the 2nd Front Red Army under He Long and Xiao Ke followed the same route one year later as the 1st Front Army had, reaching Shaanxi in 1936. The women whose stories we have told all marched with the 1st Front Red Army.

This is generally considered to be the main body of the march because the marchers covered the longest distance and because it was during this time that Mao Zedong confirmed his leadership of the Communist Party, thus becoming the key figure of the revolution.

While this book is not about party politics, it is impossible to write about China without some reference to history and politics. Why these women did what they did, or even why they were included in the Long March in the first place, is unintelligible without a political context. We have therefore provided a short Prologue at the start of each Part, outlining the events of that period.

Chinese-language sources dating from the Long March are unavailable to foreigners. In their stead we have relied on several first-hand accounts in English of events in that period. Although written by American journalists from a Western perspective, they have the value of immediacy and are untainted by either hindsight or official political imperatives. *Red star over China*, written in 1937 by Edgar Snow, has long been regarded as a classic. *Inside Red China* (1939) and *Red dust* (1952), both written by Helen Foster Snow, who spent several months in Yan'an in 1937, provide information and insight on several of the Long March women. A third American journalist, Agnes Smedley, also spent time in Yan'an. In her *China fights back* (1938) and *The great road* (published posthumously in 1958), she reveals a clear bias towards the communists as well as a tendency to romanticise, but it is this very 'fault' that allows her to bring vividly to life the people she wrote about and to evoke the evangelical atmosphere of that time.

Many of our Chinese-language sources were written in the 1980s and were often concerned less with historical fact than with reflecting current Communist Party decisions on how the past should be viewed: this really brought us face to face with the problem of bias. We found Kang Keqing's memoirs, for example, extremely useful and interesting. We were reluctant to rely on them for the early periods of her life, however, because her experiences since then and the political climate of 1987 when she dictated the memoirs inevitably coloured her recollections of the events of 1927 and 1937. We must also acknowledge our debt to Guo Chen, a Beijing journalist who in the mid 1980s carried out valuable research on the Long March women. Guo Chen graciously granted us permission to quote liberally from his *Jinguo liezhuan: Hong yifangmian jun sanshiwei changzhen nü hongjun shengping shiji* (Biographies of brave women: Thirty women soldiers of the 1st Front Red Army), and was able to provide information on the present whereabouts of those women who are still alive. He also produced several rare photographs used in this book.

A few words on Chinese names and titles are called for. Chinese people go by their family name, or surname, followed by their personal names, or what Westerners used to call Christian names: for example, Mao Zedong's family name is Mao, his personal name is Zedong. Also, Chinese women traditionally keep their family name when they marry, children taking their father's family name. Thus, with our main characters, He Zizhen's family name is He, her personal name is Zizhen; Kang Keqing's family name is Kang, her personal name is Keqing. Wang Quanyuan was unusual in taking her husband's surname Wang when she married, but her personal name remains Quanyuan. We have consistently referred to our characters by their full names, a practice Western readers may find strange. We have done this because we felt it too personal (as well as un-Chinese) to call such historical personages by their given names, while to use only their surnames could lead to confusion. If we only used surnames, how could we avoid when writing of Mao's wife, He Zizhen, sentences such as 'He fell in love with Mao Zedong' or 'They lifted He onto a stretcher'? As with so many other things, Mao is an exception to this general rule simply because he is so well known that there is no risk of confusing him with anyone else.

Chinese names are notoriously difficult for Westerners to remember and distinguish one from the other, and for this we have no answer. We decided at the start, however, that to anglicise our characters' names would be too 'orientalist' an approach. We also decided, reluctantly, against providing a translation of the name of each character; reluctantly because many names are quite delightful and often rich in meaning. This is because of the characters used to write them as well as because people often choose the personal name they wish to be known by. A few examples will illustrate this: Kang Keqing's name means 'Healthy Unequivocal Vanquisher'; Cai Chang is 'Cai, the Unencumbered'; Han Shiying means 'Heroine Han'; Li Bozhao is 'Enheartening Li'; and Li Jianhua is 'National Reconstruction Li'.

We have used standard *pinyin* romanisation throughout, with two major exceptions. The name Jiang Jieshi means nothing to generations of Westerners brought up on the old spelling of Chiang Kai-shek, so we have chosen to refer to the Generalissimo as Chiang Kai-shek. Similarly, instead of the proper but lesser known spelling of Sun Zhongshan, we have used the Westernised version of his name for Dr Sun Yat-sen. Readers will find that Helen Foster Snow, Edgar Snow and Agnes Smedley used a different system of romanisation than that presently in use, but we have given in each case the modern equivalent. The Snows and Agnes Smedley also faced the problem of trying to unravel unfamiliar names pronounced by dialect speakers or written by barely literate colleagues, so that sometimes mistakes were made or confusion arose about people or places.

Chinese names for titles, departments, bureaus and units of many kinds are complicated and detailed; this makes them extremely unwieldy in English. So, apart from recurring terms such as the Communist Youth League, the Young Pioneers, the Convalescent Company, and certain ministries, we have not tried to translate titles with pinpoint accuracy. For those interested, such information can be found in reference works.

Lastly, our thanks. We would like to express our gratitude to Elizabeth Weiss of Allen & Unwin for recognising the potential of this project and for her good-natured support and encouragement throughout, and to Bernadette Foley for her expert and sensitive editorial hand. We also extend sincere thanks to those friends who read the manuscript in its various stages, but in particular to Sybil Jack and Zula Nittim. On a more personal level, Sue offers thanks to Nadège Lamy for giving her heart, as well as doing the maps, and Lily wishes to thank her family for being patient and understanding.

CHRONOLOGY

1905   • Tongmenghui (United League) founded in Japan

1910   • He Zizhen born in Yongxin County, Jiangxi
             Province

1911   • September: Kang Keqing born in Wan'an County,
             Jiangxi Province
        • October–December: Xinhai Revolution, overthrow
             of Qing dynasty

1913   • Wang Quanyuan born in Ji'an County, Jiangxi
             Province

1919   • May Fourth Movement

1921   • July: Chinese Communist Party (CCP) formed in
             Shanghai

1923–24 • Dr Sun Yat-sen's reorganised Nationalist Party
             (KMT) formed

1923   • First CCP–KMT Alliance formed

1925   • Dr Sun Yat-sen dies, Generalissimo Chiang
             Kai-shek assumes leadership of KMT

1927   • KMT and CCP split
        • Nanchang Uprising: Zhou Enlai, Zhu De, He
             Long, Lin Biao, Zhang Guotao and others
             attempt to wrest power from the KMT; although

the attempt fails, this marks the founding of the
Red Army
- Autumn Harvest Uprising, Hunan Province, led
by Mao Zedong, fails
- Mao retreats to Jinggangshan

1928
- Mao and He Zizhen marry, on Jinggangshan
- Zhu De joins Mao on Jinggangshan

1929
- Zhu De and Kang Keqing marry, on Jinggangshan
- He Zizhen gives birth to her first child, a girl, in
Fujian Province

1931
- Soviet Republic of China (the Jiangxi soviet)
formed

1932
- He Zizhen gives birth to her second child, a boy
(Xiao Mao)

1934
- He Zizhen gives birth to her third child, a
premature boy, who dies
- Kang Keqing leads troops into battle and is
dubbed 'the Girl Commander'
- October: the Long March begins from the Jiangxi
soviet
- December: Zeng Yu gives birth on Laoshan, baby
abandoned

1935
- January: Zunyi Conference in Guizhou
- January: Wang Quanyuan marries Wang Shoudao
in Zunyi
- January: Liao Siguang gives birth, baby abandoned
- February: He Zizhen gives birth to fourth child,
a girl, who is abandoned
- April: Chen Huiqing gives birth, baby abandoned
- Spring: He Zizhen wounded by bomb shrapnel
- June: 1st Front and 4th Front armies meet at
Lianghekou
- July–August: Mao'ergai meeting
- September: 1st and 4th Front armies split, Mao
heading north, Zhang Guotao returning south to
Sichuan, then Tibet

- October: Mao and 1st Front Red Army reach Wayaobu
- November: 2nd (He Long) and 6th (Xiao Ke) Front armies leave Hubei–Hunan soviet base

1936
- January: communists move to Bao'an
- June: Edgar Snow arrives in Bao'an
- June: 2nd, 6th and 4th Front armies join forces in Tibet
- October: He Zizhen gives birth to her fifth baby, a girl (Jiaojiao), in Bao'an
- October: Women's Vanguard Regiment led by Wang Quanyuan crosses Yellow River into Gansu Corridor; Western Route Army wiped out by Moslem cavalry
- December: Xi'an Incident (arrest of Chiang Kai-shek) leads to KMT–CCP united front

1937
- January: communists move to Yan'an
- January: Agnes Smedley arrives in Yan'an
- March–April: Wang Quanyuan captured by Moslems
- May: Helen Foster Snow arrives in Yan'an
- July: Sino–Japanese War begins
- July–August: Lan Ping–Jiang Qing arrives in Yan'an
- September: Agnes Smedley and Helen Foster Snow leave Yan'an, Kang Keqing goes to the front
- October: He Zizhen leaves Yan'an
- November: He Zizhen boards train to Moscow with Liu Ying

1938
- May: He Zizhen gives birth in Moscow to sixth baby, a boy, who dies

1939
- March: Wang Quanyuan escapes Moslems

1940
- Jiaojiao and Mao's two sons sent to He Zizhen in Moscow

1941
- Rectification Movement in Yan'an

1942
- Yan'an Forum on Art and Literature
- He Zizhen consigned to sanitorium in Moscow

- July: Wang Quanyuan returns home to Jiangxi

1945
- World War II ends; KMT–CCP civil war begins

1947
- communists leave Yan'an
- He Zizhen returns to China

1948
- Wang Quanyuan marries Liu Gaohua

1949
- March: All-China Democratic Women's Federation formed
- 1 October: People's Republic of China proclaimed
- He Zizhen living in Shanghai

1956
- Hundred Flowers Movement

1957
- Kang Keqing elected deputy chair of the Women's Federation, and is involved in anti-rightist campaigns and criticism of other prominent women

1958
- Great Leap Forward
- He Zizhen moves to Nanchang, Jiangxi Province

1959
- He Zizhen meets Mao, on Lushan

1964
- He Zizhen reported to be living in Shanghai

1966
- May: Great Proletarian Cultural Revolution begins

1967
- Kang Keqing paraded in streets and 'struggled'

1968
- Wang Quanyuan re-assigned work

1973
- Yang Yuehua, He Zizhen's first-born daughter, found living in Fujian

1976
- January: Zhou Enlai dies
- July: Zhu De dies
- September: Mao Zedong dies
- October: Jiang Qing arrested, signalling the end of the Cultural Revolution

1977
- Kang Keqing reinstated in Women's Federation; elected to Central Committee

1978
- Kang Keqing resumes position of deputy chair of

the Women's Federation; elected deputy chair of
5th Chinese People's Political Consultative
Conference

- He Zizhen elected to 5th Chinese People's
  Political Consultative Conference

1981   • Wang Quanyuan granted Red Army veteran
          privileges; she is portrayed as a heroine in film
          Echoes of Qilian Mountains

1984   • 19 April: He Zizhen dies in Shanghai

1985   • Wang Quanyuan re-admitted to CCP

1987   • Wang Quanyuan's party credentials restored

1989   • 4 June: Red Army tanks crush democracy
          movement in Tiananmen Square

1992   • 23 April: Kang Keqing dies in Beijing

1996   • Wang Quanyuan celebrated in interviews as Long
          March survivor

Cai Chang	蔡畅	Liu Ying	刘英
Chen Huiqing	陈慧清	Qian Xijun	钱希均
Deng Liujin	邓六金	Qiu Yihan	丘一涵
Deng Yingchao	邓颖超	Wang Quanyuan	王泉媛
Han Shiying	阚士英	Wei Gongzhi	危拱之
He Zizhen	贺子珍	Wei Xiuying	危秀英
Jin Weiying	金维映	Wu Fulian	吴富莲
Kang Keqing	康克清	Wu Zhonglian	吴仲廉
Li Bozhao	李伯钊	Xiao Yuehua	肖月华
Li Guiying	李桂英	Xie Fei	谢飞
Li Jianhua	李建华	Xie Xiaomei	谢小梅
Li Jianzhen	李坚真	Yang Houzhen	杨厚珍
Liao Siguang	廖似光	Zeng Yu	曾玉
Liu Caixiang	刘彩香	Zhong Yuelin	钟月林
Liu Qunxian	刘群先	Zhou Yuehua	周越华

PART I
THE LONG MARCH
1934–1936

PART I PROLOGUE

China's is the world's longest unbroken civilisation. For over 2000 years that country's sheer size in terms of geography and population meant that it had little to fear from its smaller Asian neighbours. Secure in their cultural and military superiority, it is little wonder the Chinese believed their world to be the centre of all under heaven. Their complacency was not shaken by the periodic disruptions that took place within China, for these quickly fell into a predictable pattern. Dynasties sprang up one after another, with some lasting hundreds of years (such as the Han, Song, Tang, Ming and Qing dynasties), and others holding power for less than a generation (as did the first dynasty, established in 221 BC by Qin Shihuangdi, Inaugural Emperor of Qin, which collapsed after fifteen years).

Following the collapse of a ruling dynasty, after a period of chaos varying in violence and length, one strong man would restore order by founding a new dynasty and declaring himself Emperor, the Son of Heaven. The personal vigour of this founding emperor never survived beyond his grandsons, however; any trace of originality in young emperors was stifled by a vast bureaucracy that baffled all but the most insistent attempts at change. The men who ran this bureaucracy belonged to the educated gentry class that paid no taxes, since a man and his entire family were exempt from taxation once he passed the civil service examination. The gentry's was a comfortable life, elegant and expensive, financed entirely by the taxes exacted from landlords, peasants and merchants. But the system that made this possible was corrupt in other ways. The peasants' taxes destined for public works would go instead into the sleeves of tax collectors and officials, leaving roads, bridges and dams unrepaired. Waterways thus left derelict exposed the land to the devastation of floods, while droughts exhausted the people. When the government increased taxes to raise revenue to combat these natural disasters, landlords evaded their taxes by passing the burden on to their peasant tenants; sometimes they demanded the payment of rent and taxes up to forty years in advance. Families were forced into astronomical debt which was passed on for generations. Peasants starved, bandits roamed the countryside, unrest and disaffection spread until the government finally lost control. When this happened the incumbent Son of Heaven was deemed to have lost the mandate of heaven to rule. The dynasty would collapse and from the military conflicts that followed one man would emerge to fight his way to the top and found a new dynasty.

The fate of the last of China's traditional dynasties, the Qing (1644–1911), was clouded by two complications. First, it was a foreign dynasty superimposed on the Chinese system, its emperors not Han Chinese but Manchu invaders from the north. Second, the inevitable decline of Qing coincided with Europe's aggressive expansion into Asia in the mid-nineteenth century, thus compounding the Chinese people's resentment against foreigners. Antagonism towards their non-Chinese rulers exploded in the peasant-based Taiping Revolution (1850–64) and crystallised by the end of the century during the de facto reign of Empress Dowager Cixi into a quest for Chinese renewal under the slogan 'Overthrow the Manchu rulers and restore the Han Chinese'. Three years after the death of the Empress Dowager, the last emperor of Qing, a six-year-old boy, was dethroned by the 1911 Xinhai Revolution. Within four years the dynastic cycle was set to re-engage when General Yuan Shikai dismantled the fledgling republican government and prepared to ascend the throne in Peking. The all-too-human General Yuan Shikai found, however, that not only did he lack the mystique of a genuine Son of Heaven, he had absolutely no military or political support. The 1911 Revolution had been nearly twenty years in the making, and the nation's leaders wanted a republic, not a return to outdated monarchy. Provincial leaders turned against him and

several provinces declared their independence; warlords conscripted peasants into their private armies and declared their
sovereignty over entire provinces; the south seceded and set up
its own government in Canton.

By this time an expanding West had collided with China,
which became an object of desire for the international community.
The British dominated the trade centres of Hong Kong and
Shanghai. The Japanese controlled vast areas of north China,
including the province of Shandong, birthplace of the venerated
sage Confucius. The British, French, Germans and Italians
retained rights to 'concessions', special areas of privilege in which
foreigners were immune to the laws of China. There they re-cre-
ated the social and administrative structures of their native
countries. As the foreigners steadily appropriated Chinese territory, the humiliation of the Chinese people grew.

China's desperate situation came to a head during the peace
negotiations at the end of World War I when, instead of returning
to China the concessions Germany had held in Shandong, the
Allies handed Shandong to Japan as part of the 1919 Versailles
Peace Treaty. News of this betrayal by the West spawned the May
Fourth Movement, a series of anti-Japanese demonstrations and
wide-ranging boycotts that began on 4 May 1919 and are now
regarded as part of the New Cultural Movement of 1917–23.
This was a period when intellectuals rejected traditional Confucian values, seeing them as the root cause of China's obvious
weakness. Young men and women from wealthy families travelled
abroad to work and study, bringing back the new ideas that were
sweeping the West: liberalism, utilitarianism, individualism,
socialism, pragmatism, materialism, Darwinism, anarchism and
Marxism. Writers rushed into print to discuss these exciting new
theories, personifying them as 'Mr Democracy' and 'Mr Science'.
Intellectuals preached an end to the 'moral philosophy' of Confucianism that demanded the sacrifice of individuals' needs,
desires and happiness to the rigid hierarchies of what they now
regarded as an oppressive social fabric.

The family was widely condemned as 'a despotic institution
that perpetuated the odious practices of footbinding, concubi-
nage, arranged marriages, women's illiteracy, seclusion, and female
submission to male authority'.[1] Feminism became a focus in the

writings of intellectuals in their fight for a rejuvenated China at the same time as women in the West were agitating for female suffrage and emancipation. Women founded journals and published articles on education for women, birth control, women workers, factory conditions and strikes.

Two key revolutionary forces took shape in this period: the Chinese Communist Party and the Kuomintang (the KMT, or Nationalist Party, now romanised as Guomindang).

Communism in China grew out of a thirst for new ideas to save the nation. Intellectuals formed study groups to discuss the ideas flooding into China through books, journals and translations: Henrik Ibsen's play *A Doll's House*, for example, became popular at this time. While the appeal of Marxism was that it was 'scientific', Marxism–Leninism had proven itself in Russia with the success of the 1917 October Revolution. Of great significance in finally convincing intellectuals of the justice of communism was the new Russian Government's gesture in 1919 of relinquishing its territorial rights in China. Patriotism, fuelled by disillusion with the West over the Versailles Peace Treaty, played no small part in turning many to communism. In 1921 twelve men gathered in a girls' boarding school in the French Concession of Shanghai to form the Chinese Communist Party; one of the junior members of this group was a tall young library assistant named Mao Zedong.

The KMT grew out of the Tongmenghui (United League) founded in Japan in 1905 by Chinese students and revolutionaries intent on transforming China into a republic. The KMT remains synonymous with Dr Sun Yat-sen, still today revered equally on Taiwan and on the mainland as the father of the Chinese Revolution, and it was he who in that crucial year of 1919 began to revive the KMT. By 1924, his reorganisation of the KMT was complete and as the party's leader he loosely defined its ideology as 'Three Principles of the People'—nationalism, people's rights and people's livelihood; he dedicated the KMT to national unification and reconstruction.

The Communist Party and the KMT had several things in common. Both were structured as political parties supported by their own politically-indoctrinated armies. Both viewed as enemies the Chinese warlords and the foreign imperialists, in particular Japan, whose stated ambition it was to conquer China. Both also saw their goal as creating a China that belonged to the Chinese people.

Despite these commonalities, however, their basic philosophies were diametrically opposed and they quickly became mortal enemies. The straw-sandalled, rag-tag Red communists were led by intellectuals committed to Marxist–Leninist class struggle and social revolution. They wrote of feminism, criticised the family, rejected arranged marriages and entered into common-law marriages; they formed a women's bureau, recruited students and illiterate peasants; they styled themselves as the party of the rural poor, who were the vast majority of the Chinese people. The well-armed White KMT, mostly of landlord and gentry stock, stood for national unity and specifically opposed class struggle. While intent on reforming the outmoded imperial system, the KMT were at heart traditionalists: they had no place for women or peasants in their organisation, and retained the old hierarchy of the educated and wealthy ruling as by right over the toiling masses. They remained the party of the urban well-to-do.

The Russian Communist Party, as the first to overthrow the old order and establish a socialist state, stood in relation to the tiny Chinese Communist Party as an elder brother. The Russians soon chose, however, to throw their weight behind the KMT machine as the pivot of the Chinese Revolution. The Russians insisted that the Chinese communists and the KMT unite in a military push to bring down the warlords and expel from Chinese soil all foreign influence, most urgently that of the Japanese moving in aggressively from the north. This military exercise occurred at the midpoint of what came to be known as the Nationalist Revolution of 1923–28.

Dr Sun Yat-sen, whom Lenin described as possessing 'inimitable, one might say, virginal naiveté', also encouraged the communists and the KMT to work together. When he died in 1925, however, his successor Generalissimo Chiang Kai-shek surrendered to an innate distrust of the communists. Within two years he had initiated the massacre of tens of thousands of known and suspected communists and brought the urban labour movement to its knees. Generalissimo Chiang Kai-shek became the leader of the Chinese nation in 1928 when he was made President of the Republic of China. He turned a blind eye to Japan's invasion of Manchuria in 1931 and its subsequent occupation of Shanghai, choosing instead to concentrate his considerable military resources on a series of five 'encirclement and extermination' campaigns against the main communist enclave in Jiangxi Province in southern China. He stockpiled the massive financial and military support his American-educated wife garnered from the United States of America and became obsessed with liquidating every last Chinese communist.

This is the story of three of those communists: He Zizhen, whose love for Mao Zedong destroyed her; Wang Quanyuan, the ugly duckling peasant girl who got left behind and shut out; and Kang Keqing, the 'Girl Commander', who wanted only one thing of life—to be a soldier.

1

LOVER, MOTHER, WIFE

He Zizhen was seventeen when she and Mao Zedong became lovers, although no-one quite knows when and where this momentous event took place. In most accounts she appears as if by magic at Mao's side shuffling papers and acting as his personal secretary some time in 1928. Some say they met in her hometown of Yongxin in Jiangxi Province, others that their meeting took place in the mountains of Jinggangshan.

The official reticence to clarify how and when their relationship began may be due to a lack of precise information. It might well, however, have more to do with a reluctance to admit that within months of being temporarily parted from Yang Kaihui, his first and said to be his great love, Mao had no hesitation in publicly forming a liaison with He Zizhen, then a young partisan. Given Mao's now acknowledged sexual appetite and He Zizhen's hero worship, it would be reasonable to suggest that they became lovers early in 1928, not long after they met on Jinggangshan.

He Zizhen was born at the time of the mid-autumn festival into a family of minor officials whose fortunes had soured in tandem with the Qing dynasty's. She was the second of four children and the year of her birth is recorded as 1910, the same year International Women's Day came into being. Her parents named her Guiyuan (meaning 'longan') because her skin was as translucent as the fruit of the longan, a cousin of the lychee.[1] Her oval face with its high forehead and thick, shapely eyebrows grew beautiful as she matured. She was a lively, happy girl who didn't like her birthname Guiyuan because she thought it was sissy. So, as was the habit for an intellectual, when she went to school she chose a name for herself: He Zizhen (Congratulatory Little Treasure).

Yongxin, where she was born, was a walled town of some importance in the area and the county seat of Yongxin County. It was tucked away among fish ponds and rice fields in rugged mountains close to the Jiangxi–Hunan border, and peasants ferried their produce to market there along the Yongxin River. The river swept around the town in a great slow curve, and wide slate steps cascaded down to it from the warehouse at the foot of Long Street. Water carriers dipped wooden pails from bamboo poles into the river and carried the water through the handful of streets for certain sale. In good years, white peaks of rice gleamed in huge wooden barrels in the rice shop, not far from the grocery shop with its sharp smells of pickled turnip and salted fish.

What was left of He Zizhen's family's land holdings, eaten away by taxation over the generations, were confiscated when the authorities imprisoned her father for speaking out in support of the local peasants after the 1911 Revolution. Following his release from prison her father managed to scrape together enough money to open a teahouse on South Street near Yongxin's south gate, and men gathered there to talk of the weather, the crops and the taxes. Her parents had experienced injustice; they had also watched as year after year local peasants sold everything they grew to pay taxes, sinking into poverty while landlords and officials grew fat. In the intellectual turmoil of the 1910s and 1920s wealthy boys studying in the cities sent new books and magazines back to Yongxin, and talked on their visits home about democracy, independence, nationalism and communism. He Zizhen's parents encouraged their children to explore these new ideas and allowed them to attend the meetings held by roving communist propaganda teams.

He Zizhen did not receive a classical education, as the wealthy boys did, but attended the free missionary school in Yongxin. There, along with other local girls, she was taught to read and write and showered with Sunday school stories of Jesus. She responded eagerly to the patriotic call to sweep away repressive Confucian attitudes: she is credited with being one of the first students in the school to cut off her thick plait, thus signalling her equality with men and her rejection of the old values, which included refusing to submit blindly to an authority she did not respect.

One of the tales of her youthful exploits that are told to demonstrate her revolutionary fervour is that when Dr Sun Yat-sen died in 1925 and the missionaries refused to allow their students to attend a proposed memorial service, He Zizhen gathered her fellow students outside the whitewashed chapel.

'Dr Sun Yat-sen is the father of our new nation,' she told the girls solemnly. 'It is our duty to show our respect. Will we Chinese let foreigners tell us what to do? We must go to the memorial service for him.'

The schoolgirls followed He Zizhen to the memorial service, and the foreign principal ordered them the next day to kneel beside the black pews to ask God's forgiveness for their disobedience. 'We've done nothing wrong. We will not kneel,' He Zizhen retorted on behalf of her meeker fellow students.[2]

The early communists professed commitment to the liberation of women, seeing it as an essential element in strengthening China and becoming part of the modern Western world. They criticised the traditional practices of footbinding, of women's exclusion from education, and of the seclusion of gentry women from public life. They also rejected arranged marriages and the double standard which allowed men to take many concubines while demanding that women be chaste: this meant that young women were required to remain single if their fiance died, and that even very young widows could not remarry but were expected to remain celibate for the rest of their lives. So strong appeared the support of these men for gender equality that educated women were attracted to communism not so much because of its political stance but because they saw it as a sympathetic 'subculture' in the traditional male world.[3] It was many years before it became clear that communist men were as deeply entrenched as their fathers had been in the belief that it was the natural right of men to rule, and their commitment to gender equality revealed itself as purely theoretical.

A separate women's bureau was formed to mobilise women of all classes, and women were permitted to hold office only in this bureau. The men thus effectively excluded women from the power structure of the Communist Party by creating a female ghetto, and women werc able to gain access to party decision making only through the informal avenue of their office-holding husbands. Father, brother and husband taking precedence within the family, and the sexes leading largely separate lives were so much a way of being in China that it was taken for granted that the party would reflect this tradition in its structure.

In 1925 the party responded to an insistent call from Xiang Jingyu, the first head of the women's bureau, to recruit more women. Organisers visited schools and went out into the community to talk to individuals and to organise groups to discuss the fallacy of the inferiority of women. In direct opposition to the traditional view that girls should receive only the most elementary education and should always be respectful and submissive, they urged girls to seek education, to reject arranged marriages, whether as wife or concubine, and to go out into the world as equal partners with men in order to overthrow Confucianism and lead China into the modern world.[4]

He Zizhen joined the Communist Youth League in 1926 and soon became a full member of the Communist Party, sitting with her older brother He Minxue and her younger sister He Yi on the Communist Party Committee of Yongxin County. She was made head of the county women's bureau and became assistant secretary of the youth bureau which, like the women's bureau, existed outside the formal power structure of the party. She went about the countryside on propaganda trips, travelling alone because as a young female it was easier to mingle with the peasants and not arouse the suspicions of KMT soldiers and militiamen. She would explain to the peasants the ways in which the traditional landlord system—personified by members of the KMT—exploited them and how the landlords became rich and powerful through the labour of others.

In the summer of 1927, the year in which the joint KMT–Communist Nationalist Revolution fell apart, she was away from home in another county doing propaganda work. Obeying a nationwide order to flush out communists, KMT soldiers rounded up all Communist Party members in Yongxin township, imprisoning He Minxue. He managed to escape but their younger brother, just barely into his teens, was executed when he was caught carrying messages for the communists.

The local people rose up and wrested Yongxin from KMT control in an incident commemorated as the Yongxin Uprising. When news of these disturbances reached He Zizhen, she walked for three days from Ji'an to help defend her hometown from the KMT troops. With the gates of Yongxin closed against the enemy, He Zizhen and thirty or forty others climbed onto the walls of the town to station themselves above the south gate. They were issued with a couple of guns and a few rounds of ammunition between them, and told to hold the gate. In the melee He Zizhen shot and killed two enemy soldiers as they tried to scale the walls of the town. The stories that circulated later of her galloping on a horse through the hills, a pistol in each hand, shooting at the enemy are an exaggeration and she later described herself as 'not a good shot', saying of the south gate battle: 'It was pure luck that I killed those two men.' The townspeople held the south gate and the town was saved, but only until the next attack.

By the time the KMT eventually re-took Yongxin, He Zizhen had fled to the lush mountains of Jinggangshan, whose dense pine and bamboo forests provided shelter for wild pigs, monkeys, tigers and leopards as well as communist bandits and outlaws. Occasionally its fogs lifted, revealing volcanic peaks covered in flowering creepers and steep ravines littered with huge boulders. The Hakka clans who lived in its secret valleys did well to coax vegetables, herbs and tea from the red earth. From time to time they would rush out of the mountains on marauding expeditions for supplies of rice but otherwise kept very much to themselves. Although not an ethnic minority, the Hakka people were not considered to be exactly Chinese either; their name, Hakka, means 'guest people, strangers'. In these inaccessible mountains He Zizhen joined a group of partisans led by two illiterate peasant bandits, Wang Zuo and Yuan Wencai, who had recently converted to communism. Theirs was a harsh existence and she often went hungry, but there was no going back, because she was on the KMT's wanted list.

In the autumn of that year the communists won a major, if temporary, victory when they seized Nanchang, the capital of Jiangxi Province. Shortly afterwards, Mao Zedong, who was then a young party dissident, led an uprising of peasants on the city of Changsha, capital of his native Hunan Province. When this Autumn Harvest Uprising also failed, Mao retreated into the Jinggangshan mountains that stretched along the Hunan–Jiangxi border for 100 kilometres. The isolation of Jinggangshan, with its scattering of small towns and villages linked only by foot tracks, made it an ideal hide-out. Mao, at thirty-four years of age, had already gained a reputation as a strong believer in the revolutionary potential of the peasants and he won the loyalty of Wang Zuo and Yuan Wencai. By winter they had allowed him entry to the heart of Jinggangshan, to the secluded valley of five villages, each with its own well, that gave the area its name: Ridge of Wells Mountain. There he set about establishing a maverick communist base on a plateau that could be reached by only five steep passes.

He Zizhen says she met Mao on Buyunshan (Mount Walking-on-clouds).[5] Recalling their meeting many years later, after his death, she said that at the time she had not fully recovered from a bout of malaria but was curious to have a closer look at this newly arrived communist leader whom Yuan Wencai held in such esteem. Mao was very tall and very thin, with long black hair falling around his face, tanned and gaunt from weeks of fighting on the run. She noticed his faint surprise at seeing a young woman among the local party representatives who were there to greet him on the mountaintop. When Yuan Wencai introduced her as a party official from Yongxin, Mao smiled and said: 'I thought she was your daughter, or a member of someone else's family!' He shook her hand, murmuring: 'Good, good. Let's fight on together.' Mao soon moved down the mountain to the village of Maoping where He Zizhen was living and where he established his headquarters in an old octagonal-shaped building. Still weak from malaria, He Zizhen often sunned herself outside her hut and Mao would stop and pass the time of day.

In these recollections, after talking at some length about Mao's ability to inspire his followers, his patient guidance in such matters as land reform, note-taking and research, and his brilliant report writing, He Zizhen says: 'These things aroused in me a reluctance to be away from him. At long last we married. There was no ceremony, Yuan Wencai just cooked some vegetables for everybody and we had a bit of a party.'

This innocent account of a charming rural romance is difficult to take seriously, no matter how sincere He Zizhen's perception of it may have been. The American journalist Agnes Smedley wrote of Mao, whom she met in 1937 and disliked on sight: 'Sensitive and intuitive almost to the point of femininity, Mao nevertheless possessed all the self-confidence and decisiveness of a pronouncedly masculine man.'[6] He must have been very attractive to a seventeen-year-old country girl filled with the fire of revolution, and it is not likely that Mao would have wasted much time in seducing such a willing admirer.

A more credible version of how they met was made public many years later by a man who had by then transferred his allegiance to the KMT. While the facts of this version may not stand up to scrutiny and its author's motives are highly suspicious, it is perhaps closer in spirit to the sexual modus operandi of Mao Zedong than He Zizhen's official sanitised version. According to this man, He Zizhen and Mao met in the following manner.[7]

When Mao visited Yongxin in the first half of 1928, He Zizhen was among the local comrades who welcomed him; she was then Secretary of the Youth League. She chatted to Mao for some time and that evening took him two chickens and two bottles of wine, which he invited her to share. The following night, after a public meeting that lasted until eleven o'clock and at which she spoke forcefully and intelligently, he called her aside: would she have a few minutes to discuss an important matter with him? She went to his room and stayed until the early hours. She returned to his room straight after breakfast the next morning and worked by his side all day. That night she didn't go home. At nine o'clock the following morning Mao finally appeared, with He Zizhen standing shyly by his side. Beaming with satisfaction he announced: 'Comrade He Zizhen and I have fallen in love! Our comradely affection has changed to true love and from now on our life together will be devoted to the revolution.'

Mao Zedong already had a wife and three sons when he took He Zizhen as his lover. His wife's name was Yang Kaihui and she had been a shy seventeen year old, the daughter of his teacher, when Mao is said to have fallen in love with her in 1918. Her creamy skin, round face set off by small deep-set eyes and her physical daintiness marked her a classic Hunan beauty, while her artistic nature and education were ideal qualifications for her to become a wife and mother. Her father had not encouraged her to continue her education, accepting the traditional view that 'A woman who lacks talent is virtuous'. After moving to Beijing University Yang Kaihui's father found the 25-year-old Mao a position in the university library and welcomed the young man into his home. When her father died the following year Yang Kaihui returned to Changsha and by 1921 had become Mao's wife. While legend has it that Yang Kaihui was an active revolutionary, just what her tasks were is difficult to discover.[8] When Mao's involvement moved him from Shanghai to Canton and, from time to time, back to Hunan, Yang Kaihui stayed in Changsha with their sons, who were born in 1922, 1923 and 1927.

The early communist intellectuals challenged traditional family and marriage practices by entering into free-choice marriages, or what have been called consensual unions.[9] Young women also saw sexual experimentation as a symbol of independence and of their equality with men, and the romantic notion of idealistic young lovers fighting together for their country became a reality for many. In the midst of violent revolution other couples saw little point in fidelity when they became separated. Whether or not she knew about Yang Kaihui, He Zizhen considered herself to be Mao's wife.

While many women undertook work that was unrelated to their husbands', it was common practice for wives of leading communists to fill official positions with impressive titles. Without belittling the quality of the work these women did, it is fair to say that their real status was office wife. This was because no man could be safer in a volatile political environment than having a full-time secretary whose loyalty and discretion were above reproach, not least because the woman's own life would be in jeopardy should her husband's career be threatened. Mao put He Zizhen to work straightaway in his headquarters at Maoping. There she spent long (and, she later admitted, boring) days gathering information from newspapers that were weeks old, analysing reports and sorting through the written messages that made their way to Jinggangshan. She acted as Mao's confidential secretary, writing out reports and essays from his corrections of early drafts.

Her local knowledge also won her the dangerous job of running the KMT blockade of Jinggangshan on a surveillance mission to Yongxin in the spring of 1928. She owed her life to a peasant family who bundled her under the covers of their sick child's bed during a KMT raid. On her way back to Jinggangshan she stumbled upon the burnt bodies of two of her companions, bound hand and foot.

Although Mao had been dismissed from the party's Politburo for insubordination over the Autumn Harvest Uprising, his success in evading capture by the KMT had won him other supporters. In May 1928 Commander Zhu De led a ragged troop of ex-KMT soldiers into the valley of five villages on Jinggangshan. While he himself remained in good standing with the party, as a practical military man Zhu De recognised the strategic value of the base Mao had established in the inaccessible mountains. He and Mao reorganised their 2000 troops into the 4th Red Army, built barracks, set up a training school and a hospital. The army planted vegetables and confiscated rice from plains-dwelling landlords. Political instructors held meetings with the villagers to explain what the communists' goals were, while Mao and Zhu De hammered out a plan: they would ignore party directives and instead continue to place their faith in the agrarian movement; they would divide the land among the peasants and establish soviets (councils elected by those who lived within the area the councils governed); they would consolidate the soviets in the border regions between the provinces and gradually expand from there.[10]

One hundred or so women made their way into the soviet base on Jinggangshan, all of them from either Jiangxi or Hunan province. They came in the hope that the communists would fulfil their promises to eradicate the grinding poverty of their lives and save them from soul-destroying arranged marriages. Some assumed the traditionally female tasks of food preparation and washing clothes. Others joined the growing ranks of villagers and farmers who banded together as partisans to defend their homes and engage in guerrilla activities. The Red Army on Jinggangshan had no uniform, unless the rags most soldiers wore when they joined up counted as a uniform. Partisans looked much the same as the soldiers, the main differences between them being that most partisans remained in their native place when the army moved out, and that women could be partisans but not soldiers. He Zizhen worked from time to time as a partisan, taking part in raids to confiscate money and grain from local landlords, and mingling with the peasants on reconnaissance missions.

As the community grew from 2000 to 5000 and the KMT strengthened its blockade, garrisoning troops in all the main towns surrounding Jinggangshan, so the mountain's ability to provide for them diminished. For months they ate little but squash until lack of food finally drove them off Jinggangshan. He Zizhen was pregnant when they crept out of the mountains in early January 1929. Years later, Zhu De told Agnes Smedley how they managed to escape detection. At first light they began walking south in single file along the jagged crest of the mountains. Snow lay on the ground and:

> an icy wind lashed the bodies of the column that inched forward, crawling over huge boulders and hanging on to one another to avoid slipping into the black chasms below. By nightfall they reached a small, sloping plateau of solid volcanic rock where they ate half of the cold cooked rice which each had brought along. Huddling together and linking arms they sat down on the slope and spent the night, shivering and coughing. At daybreak they were again creeping southward, and by late afternoon reached an overgrown trail that led down a wooded mountain slope towards the village of Tafen, where a battalion of enemy troops was stationed. Here they halted to eat the last half of their cold rice. When darkness fell they began moving stealthily down the trail, under strict orders not to make a sound, forbidden even to cough.[11]

They surrounded and took the village, capturing many enemy rifles, stocking up on ammunition and eating their fill before marching quickly southward. They moved swiftly, making lightning strikes on landlords and enemy-held towns to arm, feed and clothe themselves.

Over a period of months they established soviets further south in Jiangxi; they won territory and followers in the neighbouring province of Fujian; they commandeered sewing machines, allowing them to standardise the Red Army uniform—grey-blue with leggings, and a cap with a five-pointed red star on it.[12]

He Zizhen endured with Mao the gruelling spring and summer of guerrilla warfare after they left Jinggangshan, and she cared for him when he went down with malaria in the autumn. In Fujian Province she gave birth to her first child, a girl, possibly at a place called Longyan. When the communists decided to leave Fujian early in 1930, He Zizhen was faced with a heartbreaking choice: she could either keep her baby and remain in Fujian, alone, or she could go with her husband and her comrades and leave her baby behind. The communists were still at that stage a roving band of guerrillas living solely on their wits. Not only did they face a continual struggle to feed themselves, their lives were in constant danger from enemy soldiers and betrayal by informers. There was no place in their ranks for babies or children. He Zizhen chose to leave her baby daughter in the comparative safety of a peasant family and go with Mao. For many days as they trekked back across the mountains into Jiangxi she lagged behind, refusing to walk, sitting down and crying. The others would call Mao to come and reason with her—his Little Red Pepper he called her, on account of her Jiangxi temper. Eventually she would pick up her pack and trudge on.

By the time winter gave way to spring the spark of life had rekindled in He Zizhen and Mao had recovered from his malaria. More lives were lost in the endless battles; areas already won were consolidated and expanded, and the Mao–Zhu agrarian movement began to fall into place. In the summer, the party leaders in Shanghai ordered the Red Army to capture several major inland cities, including Changsha, where Mao's wife Yang Kaihui was living with their sons. Mao and Zhu De failed in their attempt to take Changsha, and were forced to withdraw in September after weeks of fighting. In the meantime, Yang Kaihui and several female members of Mao's extended family were arrested by He Jian, the warlord who occupied the city. All were released, except for Yang Kaihui and Mao's younger sister or cousin, both of whom were tortured then killed.[13] Their crime was not that they were revolutionaries but that they belonged to the clan of the Red leader Mao Zedong.

By the end of the following year, the military successes of the Red Army of Mao and Zhu De had enabled them to establish a soviet base with a population of three million people, its capital in the town of Ruijin, about 200 kilometres south-east of Jinggangshan. In late 1931 they proclaimed themselves the Soviet Republic of China, commonly referred to as 'the Jiangxi soviet' to distinguish it from four or five other soviet bases in central, western and northern China. Like a giant fan 600 kilometres across with Ruijin as its hub, the Jiangxi soviet spread out to the three capital cities of the provinces of Hunan, Jiangxi and Fujian.

Mao was recuperating in Ruijin from another severe bout of malaria when He Zizhen gave birth to her second child, a boy. Since conditions within the soviet were relatively settled and there was no hospital in Ruijin, they decided she should be escorted to a well-equipped missionary hospital within communist-held territory where the Western-trained 'Christian doctor' Nelson Fu could attend to her. In the spring or summer of 1932 she travelled up into the mountains and across the border to Changting in Fujian for the birth. They named the boy Mao Mao, but everyone was soon calling him Xiao Mao (Little Mao).

Despite his obvious success in establishing the Jiangxi soviet, Mao was considered by the party leaders to be too wayward to be trusted. His unorthodox style of guerrilla warfare, while successful, was disapproved of, as was his reluctance to follow the Russian Marxist line and his conviction that the future of the revolution lay with the peasantry rather than the urban proletariat. The younger men who opposed Mao had studied in Moscow and were known as the '28 Bolsheviks'. When pressure from the KMT became so great that they could no longer operate as Communist Party headquarters in Shanghai, the young party leaders removed themselves to Ruijin towards the end of 1932, immediately shunting Mao aside and stripping him of his military posts.

He Zizhen moved with Mao and their son to Yunshishan in the cool heights north of Ruijin where they made their home in a small temple. Since Mao retained his position as Chairman of the Soviet Republic of China (that is to say, the Jiangxi soviet),

He Zizhen became Secretary of the Central General Office; in other words, she was still Mao's confidential secretary. Her job involved scanning the newspapers, telegrams, reports and letters that flowed into the Chairman's office. She admitted later that she felt inadequate, knowing she made mistakes and was not as reliable as she should have been; the only part she really enjoyed was reading the newspapers. Her confidence suffered further when she became aware of the general feeling in the community—quite possibly justified—that hers was not a real job and that she was taking advantage of her privileged position as Mao's wife to avoid work. She nursed Mao through his recurrent bouts of malaria, but was helpless in the face of his depression at being sidelined by the '28 Bolsheviks'. She hadn't lost her Jiangxi fire and tempers would sometimes flare, a situation not unfamiliar to Mao, who had grown up arguing violently with his strict father and suffering beatings as a boy.

He Zizhen took on additional recruiting and propaganda work among the local women and was even persuaded to perform in one of the 'living newspapers' written by singer–songwriter Li Bozhao. Since the illiterate peasants of China could read neither newspapers nor books, the communists used 'living newspapers' to get their message across. These performances were based on the tradition of travelling operas and wandering storytellers, and Edgar Snow and Agnes Smedley both commented on how effective was this Red Theatre. Snow wrote:

> There is no more powerful weapon of propaganda in the
> Communist movement than the Reds' dramatic troupes, and
> none more subtly manipulated. By constant shifts of
> programme, by almost daily changes of the 'Living Newspaper'
> scenes, new military, political, economic and social problems
> become the material of drama, and doubts and questionings are
> answered in a humorous, understandable way for the sceptical
> peasantry. When the Reds occupy new areas, too, it is the Red
> Theatre which calms the fears of the people, gives them
> rudimentary ideas of the Red programme, dispenses great
> quantities of revolutionary ideas, and counter-propaganda, to
> win the people's confidence.[14]

The three characters in the topical skit in which He Zizhen played, called 'Who are we sacrificing ourselves for?', were

Imperialism (wearing a large moustache and a Western hat), Generalissimo Chiang Kai-shek, and his beautiful American-educated wife Song Meiling (played by He Zizhen). In real life Song Meiling was a stylish and worldly young woman from a powerful and wealthy family—her oldest sister was the widow of Dr Sun Yat-sen—so He Zizhen's incongruously shy and tentative portrayal of her brought hoots of laughter from her unsophisticated peasant audience. 'Living newspapers' never pretended to be high art and He Zizhen took it all in good part, but she counted it the lesser sacrifice to step down from the stage forever when the skit's short season drew to a close.

The Jiangxi soviet was an island of communist territory surrounded by KMT and warlord armies. Bent on its annihilation, Generalissimo Chiang Kai-shek initiated an 'encirclement and extermination' campaign against it in 1931. He staged two more in 1932 and another in 1933 but all failed. In late 1933 the Generalissimo's German military adviser hit upon the plan of encircling the soviet with massive concrete pillboxes or blockhouses. As soon as the first ring of fortifications was completed they started building a second ring closer in, then a third and then a fourth, until there was in theory not a pathway leading in or out of the mountains around Ruijin that did not have a rifle trained on it. After six months of this siege the soviet had run out of salt, rice was in short supply, and the Red Army had suffered crippling losses in the continual fighting.

He Zizhen had become pregnant when Little Mao was about a year old. In the early spring of 1934 she went into premature labour and gave birth to a boy. Although she was again attended by Dr Fu, now Head of the Red Army Medical Corps, the baby died soon after birth. It is clear that neither she nor Mao attempted to practise any form of birth control, whether it be the rhythm method, coitus interruptus or abstinence, and she was soon pregnant again. It is hard to imagine a worse time for this to have happened.

During the hot wet summer of 1934 the communists started a recruiting campaign; orders were given to dismantle and pack certain large pieces of machinery such as printing presses and X-ray machines; women attached to the Red Army were set to work alongside local women to hand weave 200 000 pairs of straw sandals and hand sew thousands of rice pouches. The Red Army's treasury reserves—gold hairpins and gold buckles, silver ingots and silver dollars, jewellery and valuables confiscated from landlords—that had been buried in 1932 in a secret cave high in the mountains near Ruijin, had already been dug up in the spring and carried back down to the township.[15]

Little Mao was just over two years old when He Zizhen received a message one morning in October asking her to send Mao a clean change of clothes and telling her to prepare to evacuate Ruijin by three o'clock that afternoon. The Red Army and party headquarters were moving out, no-one could say exactly where or how long it would take, and she was going with them. This decision had not been made by Mao, who had been excluded from all high-level discussions on the means of ensuring the survival of the party leaders and the Red Army, but by three other men: Bo Gu; the German Otto Braun whom Moscow had sent to the Jiangxi soviet to represent the Comintern; and Zhou Enlai. Mao was told only after the decision was made.

He Zizhen knew she could not take her child, she had been through that before. She did not have to be reminded that there was no place on a forced march for those who could not look after themselves; she understood how the cry of a hungry or tired baby might jeopardise the lives of hundreds of fighting men. She was aware that even without her son she was already a double burden in the eyes of the men, who did not believe women could match their pace and who would resent limited resources and time wasted on non-combatants, especially pregnant women.

Hardly daring to think, she bundled up Little Mao's winter clothes and his bedding and summoned her sister He Yi, married now to Mao's youngest brother Mao Zetan. When they came on horseback to fetch their nephew He Zizhen passed the bundle up to her sister without a word then bent down to pick up her son. She sat him on her hip: 'You're going with Auntie and Uncle for a while, Little Mao. Be good! I'll be back as soon as I can.' She hoisted him on to his uncle's saddle and quickly turned away. Later that afternoon she grasped the red-tasselled spear that was issued to her, shouldered her pack and walked resolutely out of Ruijin with most of the other women and several older men whom it was considered dangerous to leave behind.

She was not the only pregnant woman in this small Red Star Brigade. The Cantonese textile worker Chen Huiqing, who was two or three months pregnant and married to the head of the Red secret police, was marching, too. She could not be left behind to be captured and interrogated. Irrepressible Liao Siguang, four or five months pregnant, was married to the officer in charge of youth activities and had herself done valuable underground work for several years in Shanghai. Zeng Yu had been a partisan on Jinggangshan and had attached herself to the Brigade against orders: she was seven months pregnant to one of the divisional commanders and had decided to run the gauntlet of communist disapproval rather than risk the sword of KMT vengeance.

One woman who did obey the order to stay behind was the prominent union activist Huang Changjiao, whose pregnancy had been discovered during the recent medical many women had undergone. Left by the evacuating army to fend for herself, Huang Changjiao set out with three other women and the new-born baby of one of the women on a nightmare trek across the mountains to the Jiangxi–Fujian border. She was near to collapse by the time she stumbled upon a small group of partisans. After her baby was born she kept him with her all through the harsh years of her lonely guerrilla activity in Jiangxi.[16]

Huang Changjiao and He Zizhen were friends. Both were pregnant but one had *guanxi* (connections) while the other didn't. *Guanxi* pervades every aspect of life in China, whether it be the bureaucrat who recommends the appointment of an old school friend; the businessman who employs a clan member, no matter how distantly related; students from the same village or province who band together while studying overseas. What Westerners see as Chinese inscrutability is often the circumspect behaviour of those who are conscious of the intricate web of interrelationships they are a part of. Who you know and who you're related to can make or break you. In traditional China familial *guanxi* could even be the death of you, entire clans sometimes being wiped out in revenge killings by rulers seeking to consolidate their power. As late as 1930 Mao's former wife, Yang Kaihui, had been arrested and executed solely because she was his wife, an instance of this negative *guanxi*. The positive spin on *guanxi* for He Zizhen in 1934 was that, as the wife of the chairman of the party, she was evacuated from immediate danger in Jiangxi. The widow Huang Changjiao wasn't so lucky: truly alone and without *guanxi* in a man's world, she was left behind.

The question that comes to mind is not simply why these pregnant women were allowed to go on the Long March, but why *any* women were allowed to go. Not only do Chinese sources offer no explanation for the women's presence, they appear to have not even formulated the question. This probably has more to do with politics than historiography.

The 1st Front Red Army that abandoned the Jiangxi soviet was a fast-moving military machine made up of about 85 000 men, mostly peasants in their late teens or early twenties. They left behind over 20 000 wounded comrades in makeshift hospitals in the mountains and in the care of local villagers, a nominal rearguard of about 6000 soldiers, the partisans, the children, the elderly, and all but thirty of the women. Three years later Zhu De told Agnes Smedley what had happened to those who were left behind:

> The enemy used twenty full divisions to occupy the main Soviet cities and towns. They never succeeded in completely conquering the countryside where the people had arms, but they did succeed in slaughtering hundreds of thousands of people. Large numbers of women and girls were captured and sold at five dollars a head to [KMT] soldiers, officers, landlords, and brothel keepers.[17]

For party headquarters (the political face of communism) to accompany the Red Army (its military face) on this massive retreat was in itself unusual. It seems clear, therefore, that the wives of the party leaders who were being evacuated with the army were taken along because their husbands requested it, to prevent their inevitable capture, interrogation, torture and eventual execution. These fifteen wives included He Zizhen, Kang Keqing (the wife of Zhu De), 30-year-old Deng Yingchao (the wife of Zhou Enlai; she was ill with tuberculosis), and 34-year-old Cai Chang (a 'professional revolutionary', one of Mao's oldest friends and the wife of his old army colleague Li Fuchun).[18]

Realising that this would leave them open to criticism as elitist, the party–army leaders could well have decided to take a few other women, not too many, just enough to cover their tracks and to support the wives. Four young women who may have been party officials of some sort but who were simply described as 'students', and eleven young peasants were selected as these token women. They were assigned the duties of propaganda workers, political instructors, fund raisers, and scouts for food and labourers.[19]

Over a ten-day period[20] starting in the late afternoon of 10 October 1934, the 85 000 fit young male soldiers of the 1st Front Red Army,[21] all wearing new straw sandals, began to walk out of Ruijin. It was rumoured that they were going to try to join other Red Army units and together march north to fight the Japanese. Relatives gathered to see them off, the men calling, 'Don't worry, we'll be back soon!' They first headed south-west, then due west once they reached the Jiangxi–Guangdong border. Apart from his own rifle, each man carried ammunition, a quilt, warm clothing, an extra pair of straw sandals, a mug, chopsticks, ten days' supply of rice in his long rice pouch slung across his chest and, for running repairs, a needle and cotton threaded into the peak of his cap. Moving under cover of night the soldiers padded along narrow mountain paths. On moonless nights they carried flaming torches of pine boughs and split bamboo to light their way along the unfamiliar foot tracks.

The sheer audacity and speed of their evacuation carried the Red Army the first 300 kilometres, out of Jiangxi and past three of the KMT's rings of concrete pillboxes. Also crucial was the tacit truce Zhou Enlai managed to negotiate with the warlord of Guangdong, which allowed the communists to continue their westward march unmolested across the top of Guangdong Province and into Hunan. It was almost three weeks before Generalissimo Chiang Kai-shek realised the extent of the communist withdrawal and ordered his troops to pursue them.

The army marched in a U-formation that stretched for 100 kilometres from first out to last out: the two leading regiments marched quickly at night more than a kilometre apart, two more regiments guarded the two flanks, and a fifth curved around as a rearguard. Cocooned in the very belly of the U-formation, protected from all but air attacks, was the Central Column, which was made up of party officials and army headquarters; the Red Army University; the communications units (carrying radios and telegraph cable); civilian bearers (carrying heavy machinery parts, the sewing machines of the Red Army Uniform Factory, lathes, trunks of silver, gold and valuables, theatrical costumes and scenery, and countless reams of documents); the General Medical Unit with its wounded and stretcher-bearers; and the women.

The Red Star Brigade, which set out as part of the General Medical Unit, was made up of the women, the wounded, some KMT prisoners and several elderly men. They, too, carried a quilt, rice, a change of clothing, a notebook, an enamel mug and a toothbrush. They had been formed into a special unit because of their special needs; He Zizhen, for instance, was excused from official duties because she was pregnant.

This status immediately caused problems for the women. Many of the young soldiers resented the women being provided with horses, and complained about their resting after a day's march and spending time heating water for washing and for bathing their feet. There is no question that the women had more privileges than any of the soldiers, but it was a quarrel about food that finally brought these feelings to a head. Everyone was supposed to carry their own rations of rice or cold cooked food, which were pooled at the end of the day in a common meal. When the women realised they were going hungry because some of the men were scrounging meals without carrying their fair share of the food they complained loudly. From the powers that be (many of whom were their husbands) the women won the right to inspect the soldiers' packs each morning to ensure that anyone not carrying rations was not permitted to eat from the common wok.

They also won the right to travel as an independent women's unit under the captaincy of 26-year-old Liu Qunxian, whose husband Bo Gu headed the party leadership clique. Liu Qunxian, who had gained respect over the years for her work as a labour activist, was an excitable young woman 'given to sudden indignations and enthusiasms';[22] she was perfect for the job. The women had grown unhappy about walking at the rear with the wounded because the soldiers who marched ahead stripped the countryside of food: the *smell* of roast pork was not enough to live on, the women complained. One night they discovered that they had been assigned sleeping quarters in a village another three or four kilometres' trudge from where bodyguards had begun to prepare camp for the leaders, who were yet to arrive. Liu Qunxian stormed into the camp and yelled at the bodyguards:

> OK Headquarters, you're moving on up the road. The waterfront pavilion gets the moonlight first and this time *we're* going to be the ones who occupy the fine house and get to kill the pig and eat pork. We've been trailing behind you for weeks. You don't really expect us to walk for another eight *li* at this time of night, do you? Get moving! You are relieved as of now![23]

The women's unit worked well for several weeks but was disbanded once they were across the Xiang River and into Guizhou Province where four months of non-stop warfare made it too dangerous for the women to travel as a group. From Guizhou on, all of the women except Cai Chang, Kang Keqing and four others were formed into a Convalescent Company attached to the General Medical Unit.[24]

The weak, the sick and the wounded, be they men or women, knew that if they fell behind on this forced march they would be captured, tortured to extract any strategic information and then executed. It was not only the wounded and the women who found it difficult to keep up, as a Red Army general wrote of a similar experience:

> I was not used to walking at night. The further I walked, the worse my feet became. I walked quickly in the dark night—one step high, one step low. Sometimes I stepped on stones, and this was painful. Sometimes I fell down. Although I tried my hardest, I could not avoid lagging behind the team. A member of the team who walked behind me urged me to keep up. He even quietly sang a song about lagging behind the team. I remember that one part was: 'The man who lags behind has no sense of shame. Ai-yao-yao! no sense of shame.' I didn't want to lag behind, and I made up my mind to train myself to be as strong as they were. Although I was sweating all over and panted when I climbed up a slope, I ground my teeth and tried my best to keep up.[25]

While the army assigned searchers to round up stragglers at the end of each day's march, those who were too exhausted or weak to go on were taken to the nearest human habitation, given some food, a rifle and ammunition and eight silver dollars. Everybody was clear-eyed about this: the army simply could not afford to be slowed down. It may have seemed harsh, but at least they were not abandoned by the roadside to die a lingering death. Ever pragmatic, the party expected that if those who were left behind in this way recovered then they were to carry on the revolution and spread the gospel about communism. The prospect, however, for a lone young woman left with poor peasants far from home where the people also spoke foreign dialects was unthinkable. So the women plunged gamely on, their marching song reflecting their determination: 'Don't fall behind, don't get wounded, don't get captured, don't get the eight silver dollars.'

The maverick Zeng Yu was not issued with clothing, bedding or rations because she was not supposed to be there, so the other women harboured her, sharing their food and their body warmth at night. She was at least eight months' pregnant when her husband's division was massacred by KMT troops at the Xiang River in early December; he was one of the few survivors but came close to summary execution for the loss of his men. Only Mao's intervention saved him from a court martial.[26] The ordeal following the Xiang River was crossing Laoshan, a steep and rugged mountain about 1500 metres high that was inhabited by an ethnic minority people called the Miao. It was on Laoshan that Zeng Yu had her baby.

Laoshan's treacherous paths were cold and wet by day, freezing by night, and offered no place to rest. At one point the track led to a vertical cliff face called Thunder God Crag. One by one the women clambered up narrow steps carved into the rock and crawled through a cleft in the rock barely half a metre wide, as if negotiating the gates of hell. They hauled rifles, knapsacks and the wounded through after them, and men pull–shoved horses and mules up the cliff. Terrified animals baulked and plunged into the depths, along with their handlers. Softly in the darkness the men chanted to the tune of the well-loved 'Flower-drum' folk song of Fengyang:

We're Red Army strong, Red Army strong,
we overcome every trial.
Marching to smash Old Man Chiang,
heading north to kick out the Japs.[27]

Zeng Yu went into labour on a cold, wet December afternoon. She was bundled onto a stretcher, then dropped as the bearers bolted under fire. The other women heaved her onto a horse. Her water broke so they prised her off the horse and, walking, she staggered on. As the baby started to come down she collapsed. One of the women supported the baby's protruding head while two others carried Zeng Yu to the night camp where she gave birth to a fat little baby. In the pre-dawn dark of the next morning He Zizhen watched as the sleeping baby, gender unrecorded, was placed gently on a pile of rice straw while someone wrote a note in large clear characters and Zeng Yu was steered from the hut. She saw Zeng Yu turn back instinctively at her baby's sudden waking cry, then let herself be led away, tears streaming down her face.

For several days the women took turns helping Zeng Yu walk. When she finally collapsed from exhaustion they carried her on a wooden plank, but they couldn't find food for her. Some precious powdered milk appeared from headquarters courtesy of Cai Chang, who, in Paris in 1923, had placed her own baby girl in her mother's hands at birth; the baby's grandmother had taken her straight back to China for safekeeping. Cai Chang had not seen either of them for over four years.

The second birthing on the Long March was Liao Siguang's, her baby born premature at seven months during an exchange of rifle fire with the enemy in the bitter January or February of 1935, just after crossing Ma'an Mountain in Guizhou. The baby was wrapped up in a towel and someone scribbled a note explaining that he was a child of the Red Army and giving his date of birth. Just twelve months earlier Liao Siguang had given her baby daughter to the International Red Cross hospital when she left Shanghai for Ruijin. This time, however, she left her baby son knowing he would not survive; she held her tears but she couldn't bear to look back.

The pregnant women who left Jiangxi with the 1st Front Red Army did so because it was the only way they could survive: to stay behind was to face almost certain execution. No-one really knew where the army was going when it left, and certainly no-one knew how long they would be on the march. In their revolutionary optimism many of the marchers must have believed they would soon reach a safe place and establish a new soviet base, possibly in Guizhou or Yunnan in south-western China. The women undoubtedly hoped they would reach this safe place before the birth of their babies.

The Chinese readily acknowledge the suffering of these Long March women who sacrificed their babies for the revolution, thereby making possible the happiness of generations of children yet unborn, to paraphrase the official line. The women themselves did not speak of their pain at leaving their new-born babies for strangers to find, knowing all the while there was little likelihood of them surviving. Yet, forty-five years later, He Zizhen still remembered with distress the baby 'whose face she could not even recall' whom she left in Guizhou.

No-one forced these women to abandon their babies, they had the same choice He Zizhen had faced in Fujian in 1929: to stay behind alone with their baby, or go on with the group to safety. It was clearly not much of a choice, however. Had they not been part of a military retreat and under constant attack by the enemy, most of the women would have kept their babies at least until they could place them with a Han Chinese family they knew would care for them. The choice these women made was one of survival. It must not be seen as callous and self-serving, because their commitment to communism as the saviour of China was genuine—most of them had already looked death in the face at least once for their cause.

While personal survival was a significant factor in the choice these women made, many had, like Cai Chang, passed their children into the care of others to leave themselves free to continue with their revolutionary work. They did not do this for the sake of propaganda nor were they indulging in heroics. They believed the poverty in which the Chinese people lived and the corruption of landlords and the government to be so extreme that no sacrifice was too great.

The Chinese tradition of children belonging to the extended family rather than just to individual parents must also be borne in mind. Orphaned children were taken under the wing of some family member, often a distant one, as a matter of course, but tales also abound of impoverished widows asking a brother or sister or cousin to raise their children so as to give them a better chance in life. The communists expanded this clan relationship, claiming that all Chinese people belonged to one family, a concept often invoked to justify the abandonment of babies in favour of revolutionary work. One hopes these women found some consolation in it.

In general, husbands and wives led separate lives on this forced march and there was little opportunity for sexual relations. However, quite early on, nineteen-year-old Li Jianhua, a student and assistant telegraphist, did become pregnant. She had married the army's telegraphist just two months before leaving Ruijin. She had heard that a folk remedy for an unwanted pregnancy was to tie musk to the waistband of your trousers, but when this inevitably failed she had no option but to let nature take its course.

One young woman who was not required to live separately from her husband was Xiao Yuehua (Moonlight Xiao), also nineteen years old, whose height and strength were necessary attributes for the job she had been given, which was to satisfy the sexual needs of the Comintern's representative Otto Braun (a small irony: his Chinese name Li De meant 'Virtuous Li'). While the words 'it is every person's right to choose their own marriage partner' were still warm on their lips, the communists willingly acted as Otto Braun's marriage broker. This was not a free union of two equals but an arranged marriage between a powerful foreigner and an illiterate peasant girl. It was arranged in order to keep Otto Braun happy.

He Zizhen saw little of Mao once they left Ruijin. On their rare extended rest breaks she would seek him out and try to do things for him, much to the disgust of Zhu De's wife, Kang Keqing, who happily let her husband's bodyguards do his cooking and washing. Mao paid scant attention to his wife's ministrations and hardly seemed to be aware of her presence.

At the city of Zunyi, in the middle of Guizhou Province, Mao staged a coup that was not only the turning point of the Long March, but the real beginning of his grasp on the Chinese Revolution and the eventual success of the Chinese Communist Party. Here, during a three-day-long party meeting in mid January 1935, Mao succeeded in removing Moscow, in the human form of Otto Braun and his Chinese ally Bo Gu, from leadership of the party. At this Zunyi Conference Mao was restored to full participation in political and military decisions, from which he had been excluded in 1932, and elected to the newly created position of Chairman of the Politburo. This effectively placed him in full control of the party, a stance he never relinquished. Zhu De and Zhou Enlai were placed in joint control of the military.

Mao immediately called a halt to the communists' headlong flight to the west. Even though they had long since lost radio contact with Moscow and all other Chinese communist enclaves, Mao announced that they were to march north. They were to seek to meet up with the 4th Front Red Army, which had left Hunan Province two years earlier and settled in northern Sichuan. Official sources claim that Mao's intention in marching to northern China was to fight the Japanese, but realistically his sole aim at that stage must have been to avoid extermination at the hands of the KMT.

He Zizhen did not stay with Mao during this extended break in Zunyi. Zhou Enlai shared his rooms with his wife Deng Yingchao; Zhu De shared his with Kang Keqing. Mao, however, settled into private rooms in a two-storey brick mansion, leaving He Zizhen to doss down with most of the other women in a local schoolhouse. If this upset He Zizhen—and there is every reason to believe it would have—there was little she could do about it. Mao had long ago ceased to treat her as his lover, and even though she had acted as his secretary for several years and had access to his political life this, too, was a thing of the past. It is clear that he no longer considered her a fellow revolutionary, if he ever had. To him, she was simply a wife who produced children from time to time, in much the same way as his previous wife Yang Kaihui had.

Guizhou was bitterly cold the night He Zizhen had her baby, and she had walked more than forty kilometres in drizzling rain to stay just ahead of the enemy. Precisely where and in which month in 1935 the baby was born is not clear; childbirth was peripheral to the main events of an army on the march, and the births of babies were not recorded, even though in this case the father was the leader. It seems, however, that the birth took place in a mountainous area inhabited by the Miao people. He Zizhen went into labour as soon as she lay down in an earthen-floored hut at nine that night. Nearly two hours later she pushed forth a baby girl.

'I can't take her with us, they won't let me.' He Zizhen knew the rules. Her eyes bleary with exhaustion she watched the next morning as her baby was wrapped in several layers of clean towelling against the bitter cold. She held back the tears as she let herself be led to a stretcher. Later she nodded stoically when she was told her baby had been given to an old woman they found alone in a hut on the mountainside. 'She said she had no milk for a baby,' someone told her. 'But we left silver dollars and some bowls of opium and she took the baby.'[28]

He Zizhen slept fitfully in the swaying stretcher. Her fourth baby gone to an opium-drenched hag living in inconceivable poverty who was probably only half as old as she looked. Mao did not make time to come to see her.

Two months after He Zizhen had her baby, the 1st Front Red Army was still trapped in Guizhou under constant air and ground attack trying to fight its way north across the Yangtze River. Late one fine spring afternoon the Convalescent Company stopped for a rest break near Zhuchang in Pan County, close to the Yunnan border. They were only five kilometres from the night camp and in the fading light did not bother to place the wounded and the lame in the cover of the nearby trees. A lone KMT airplane suddenly appeared and killed several men on its strafing first run. Yang Houzhen, short and plump and severely handi-capped by her tiny feet, now 'liberated', was wounded. Although no longer tightly bound to restrict their growth, her deformed feet could not regain their normal size or shape; she nevertheless walked the entire Long March unaided, using a stick at times and riding a horse only when she thought there was no option.[29] Many of the women and the wounded were able to scramble into the shelter of the trees but He Zizhen went to help one of the wounded men, and when the plane swooped down on its second run she was caught in the open. She threw herself across the man's body in an instinctive act of protection and self-pres-ervation, and the explosion of the single bomb the pilot let fly caught her full force. One piece of shrapnel ripped a long gaping hole in her right shoulder and at least another sixteen pieces splattered into her chest, head, arms and legs.

It hardly mattered that there was no anaesthetic for the doctor to administer while he popped out the shallowest pieces of shrapnel and dug out as much of the rest as he could, because He Zizhen was unconscious for several days. He poured iodine into her wounds, covered them with gauze and bandaged her up, knowing shards of shrapnel still lay buried in her body. In her conscious moments over the following days she was in such dreadful pain that she is said to have begged the stretcher-bearers to leave her behind so she could die in peace. When told of this, Mao rode back to see her: 'We're not going to leave you,' he told her. 'You're coming with us even if we have to carry you all the way.' From then on Mao's personal stretcher-bearers carried her in the litter he sent back with them.

This special treatment that He Zizhen received was official party policy: army personnel above a certain rank, and 'big shots and their wives',[30] were to be carried by stretcher if they were ill or wounded. When there were insufficient stretcher-bearers, soldiers would even be withdrawn from combat for stretcher duty to carry these privileged wounded while ordinary soldiers were invariably left behind with eight silver dollars and some provisions. Part of the reason for this was that these people's years of party experience and their knowledge of the placement of troops and current military strategics made them both too valuable and too dangerous to lose to the enemy, which was so close on their heels.

He Zizhen remained unconscious and delirious for a considerable time, according to later accounts, so she must have been stretchered up through the mountains and into Yunnan Province. There the fourth communist baby was born when Chen Huiqing gave birth in late April amid the smoke of a mid-morning battle near Kunming, the city of eternal spring. She had disobeyed an elliptic order from her husband (head of the secret police) to detach herself from the communists, take the eight silver dollars and stay with a local Han Chinese family to have her baby.[31] Chen Huiqing's was a panicky two-hour labour during which she summoned her husband to her side, and men stood guard outside the hut waiting to fight off the approaching enemy should they arrive during the birth. The moment she gave birth stretcher-bearers lifted her onto a litter, leaving the tightly wrapped baby girl to whomever might find her.

The historical record does not say just when He Zizhen came round, only that she 'insisted on walking as soon as she was able', a turn of phrase calculated to leave no doubt that she was a courageous communist heroine. She was probably carried all the way through Yunnan's wild and beautiful mountains to the Jiaopingdu ferry crossing of the Golden Sands River at the end of April. She may well have been piggybacked across the thirteen-chain suspension bridge at Luding at the end of May. Even if she was on her feet by the time they reached the high Snowy Mountains on the Tibetan border, she would have been too weak to withstand the thin air, and would have been permitted to ride a baggage mule over the silent white peaks, past the frozen bodies of young soldiers hunched like ghostly milestones along the way.

The 10 000 survivors of the 1st Front Red Army came down off the highest peaks of the Snowy Mountains in the second ten-day period of June. They limped into what seemed to them like Shangri-la—a wide green valley full of food and people—and rested there among the Tibetan people for a week over midsummer, feasting on meat, barley, wheat, millet and peas before attempting the lower peaks of the Snowy Mountains to the north. When they emerged from the Snowy Mountains towards the end of June, a ragged and straggling band, they heard some news that made their hearts turn over. The 4th Front Red Army from Sichuan under the leadership of Zhang Guotao was marching to meet them. Thin and exhausted, they almost shouted for joy at the thought that they were no longer alone. Forty-five thousand communist soldiers were about to rendezvous with them.

Zhang Guotao had been, along with Mao, one of the twelve founders of the Chinese Communist Party in Shanghai in 1921. He was also an old colleague of Zhu De and Zhou Enlai, having fought alongside them in the battle for Nanchang in 1927. While Zhu De then went onto Jinggangshan to join forces with Mao, Zhou Enlai and Zhang Guotao went to the Soviet Union. In 1931 Zhang Guotao was ordered to set up a soviet base in central China. Through negotiations with warlords and battles against the KMT, he gained considerable territory in the north-western province of Sichuan, where he established a soviet base.

The army Zhang Guotao brought with him in June 1935, which included a regiment of women soldiers, had not had far to travel and was fit and well fed, in stark contrast to the thin and tattered remnants of Mao's 1st Front Army. After a joyful coming together in the township of Lianghekou (which means, appropriately, 'Meeting of Two Rivers'), the soldiers of Mao and Zhang, nearly 60 000 all told, marched north at an easy pace. They did not mingle easily, however, the southerners of the 1st Front Army and the Sichuan soldiers of the 4th Front Army having some difficulty understanding each other's dialects. They walked into an empty landscape in this border land in the high far west of Sichuan. It was Tibetan territory with a long history of anti-Chinese feeling, and from old habit the people hid their grain from the approaching soldiers by burying it or concealing it within the walls of their dwellings. Then, driving their animals ahead of them, they disappeared into the scenery until these latest intruders had gone. The communists' new nightmare now that there were 60 000 of them was to find enough food. With nobody to buy it from they left signed IOUs for the ripening grain they harvested from deserted fields—an empty gesture that was never honoured but that nevertheless eased consciences. Mao later joked to Edgar Snow that these IOUs were the communists' only foreign debt.

Mao, Zhu De and the other party leaders waited for several days after the arrival of his soldiers for Zhang Guotao to reach them in the last ten-day period of June. Zhang wrote of this meeting that it took place in the small market town of Fubian, about 45 kilometres north of Maogong. Mao and He Zizhen, he said, had been occupying a house at the southern end of the town where they rested for several days before his arrival.[32]

Mao and Zhang Guotao had never been friends and the political rivalry between them quickly came to a head. Zhang perceived Mao as using the 1st Front Army as the Central Committee's private army and claimed that Mao was discriminating against the 4th Front Army because he did not consider it to be 'a unit of the Committee's own flesh and blood'. At their first formal meeting, Zhang stated that he wanted either to return to northern Sichuan and establish a presence there or to march to the extreme north-west to make contact with and receive support from the Soviet Union, while Mao insisted on going north-east to join communist partisans in Shaanxi Province. Since no agreement was possible the leaders marched slowly north, calling a halt three weeks later at the small Tibetan village of Shawo near Mao'ergai, where they attempted to thrash out their differences. Mao was at a military disadvantage, his troops worn down from their long march and outnumbered three to one by Zhang's better equipped soldiers. It took him another three weeks to convince the military council and the party leaders to accept his plan and for Zhang to agree, reluctantly, to march to the north-east. The matter did not rest there, however. It was decided to integrate Mao's much weaker 1st Front Army with Zhang's 4th Front Army. According to official sources, this was done in anticipation of fierce military opposition from the KMT, whose massed armies to the east had already cut off the communists' easterly path around the Grass Lands. According to Zhang Guotao, however, it was to unify the military command and 'promote mutual understanding and thorough cooperation be-tween the First and Fourth Front Armies'. Whatever the real reason, the merger turned out to be a catastrophe for Zhang Guotao.

The soldiers spread out over hundreds of kilometres awaiting orders were re-assigned into two columns, each of which was a mixture of 1st and 4th Front Army units. The leadership was reorganised. Mao was made political commissar of the Right Column; General Chen Changhao, Zhang's right-hand man, was appointed Mao's military commander. Zhang was made political commissar of the Left Column; Mao's right-hand man, Zhu De, was assigned to be Zhang's military commander.[33] In the last ten-day period of August, both columns headed north.

He Zizhen and twenty other of the Long March women were assigned to Mao's Right Column. Although still physically weak from her shrapnel wounds, He Zizhen was fully mobile and had rejoined the Convalescent Company. They headed towards the Grass Lands (*Caodi*), a treacherous swamp on the high plateau that separates the headwaters of the Yangtze and the Yellow rivers. This was the path the enemy pressing in from the east least expected them to take, and for good reason. Once into the Grass Lands tall grasses stretched to the horizon on all sides. There were no defined paths and no-one to ask the way.

> No tree or shrub grew here, no bird ventured near, no insect sounded. There was not even a stone. There was nothing, nothing but endless stretches of wild grass swept by torrential rains in summer and fierce winds and snows in winter. Heavy black and gray clouds drifted forever above, turning the earth into a dull, somber netherworld.[34]

It took about seven days to cross the Grass Lands, and although each of the women carried a few days' supply of grain there was no way to cook it. Any kindling they found was wet, their matches were wet, and it rained almost constantly, except for brief interludes when it hailed, or turned misty, or cloudy, or sunny and warm. At rest breaks the women would huddle together, sitting back to back, two to an upturned enamel washbasin and sheltering under a second basin held over their heads. At night they sat or stood back to back on any mound of earth they could find; there was not enough room to lie down on the sodden grasses. Hundreds of men died while crossing the Grass Lands, sucked down into the bottomless icy mud as soon as they strayed from firm ground. Zhou Enlai's wife Deng Yingchao almost died when she sank into the mud up to her chest before somebody managed to pull her out. One 1st Front Red Army man wrote this about his crossing of the Grass Lands:

> Today I discovered a comrade struggling in the muddy water. His body was crunched together and he was covered with muck. He gripped his rifle fiercely, which looked like a muddy stick. Thinking he had merely fallen down and was trying to get up, I tried to help him stand. After I pulled him up he took two steps, but the entire weight of his body was on me, and he was so heavy that I could neither hold him up nor take a step. Urging him to try and walk alone, I released him. He fell on the path and shrunk together, but he still clung fiercely to his rifle and tried to rise. I tried again to lift him but he was so heavy and I so weak that it was impossible. Then I saw that he was dying. I still had some parched wheat with me and I gave him some but he could not chew, and it was clear that no food could save him. I carefully put the parched wheat back

in my pocket, and when he died I arose and passed on and left
him lying there. Later, when we reached a resting place I took
the wheat from my pocket but I could not chew it. I kept
thinking of our dying comrades. I had had no choice but to
leave him where he fell, and had I not done this I would have
fallen behind and lost contact with our army and died. Yet I
could not eat that parched wheat.[35]

Once out of the Grass Lands, the Right Column had set up
camp to prepare for the next stage of their march when, according
to official sources, a wireless message from the Left Column threw
the party leaders into confusion. Zhang Guotao told them he
was camped almost 100 kilometres to the west unable to cross
a swollen river. It is claimed that for six days telegrams went
back and forth between the two columns, Zhang refusing to move
unless to return to Sichuan, Mao urging him to continue north.
It is also claimed that Zhang finally sent a coded wireless message
to General Chen Changhao ordering the Right Column to turn
back and that this message was leaked to Mao. This mysterious
wireless message has not been made available to historians and
Zhang Guotao did not, of course, mention it in his autobiography.
While there appears to be some doubt about the truth of this
story, it remains Mao's justification for his subsequent actions,
which he based on the suspicion that Zhang was orchestrating
an armed coup.

Word reached He Zizhen just after midnight on 10 September
1935 to pack quietly and get ready to move out. She and
nineteen of the twenty-one women assigned to the Right Column
slipped away into the night. Li Bozhao had to be left behind
because she was visiting the Left Column that day to organise a
theatrical performance and it was impossible for her husband to
get a message to her in time. Yang Houzhen, on the other hand,
had to leave her husband behind with the Left Column and she
never saw him again; Luo Binghui was later killed in action. Four
thousand soldiers of the old 1st Front Army struck camp at 2 am,
telling their 4th Front comrades they were going to harvest grain.
It was not long before Chen Changhao realised the 1st Front
Army had fled.

The small force hurried north-east, down out of the border-
lands and towards the southernmost point of the Great Wall,

entering the vast north-west region which covers the provinces of Shaanxi, Gansu and Qinghai (plus, after 1949, the Xinjiang Autonomous Region).[36] They were returning to the place whence historically the Han Chinese people originated. By the last ten-day period of September they had emerged from the minorities territory of Tibet and were safely back among Chinese-speaking people, skirting the starting point of the ancient Silk Road. Agnes Smedley recalled one man telling of his joy at coming home: 'I remember when we came out of the Grass Lands and broke through enemy lines into Kansu and saw Chinese peasants. They thought we were crazy. We touched their houses and the earth, we embraced them, and we danced and sang and cried.'[37]

It was autumn, cold and dry, in an area where summers are short and winters descend early. For over a month, while they crossed the province of Gansu, they had scarcely enough water to drink, let alone to wash in. The women's faces grew increasingly dirty until finally only their eyes showed white through the caked-on grime.

They were heading towards the cradle of Chinese civilisation in the great sheltering curve of the Yellow River. Here in Shaanxi Province 6000-year-old stone age villages lay buried under the dry yellow loess soil and the entombed warriors of Qin Shihuangdi stood silently on guard, as yet undiscovered. By the third ten-day period of October 1935 the 4000-strong remnants of the Jiangxi soviet had reached the security of a small soviet in north Shaanxi. It had taken them a year, almost to the day, to make their journey of 25 000 li (about 13 000 kilometres) to this haven. They had walked the distance from London across northern Europe and Russia to the Bering Sea.

The Thirty Women who left Jiangxi had shrunk to The Nineteen by the time they reached Shaanxi. At least six of them had given birth along the way, each, for reasons of survival, abandoning her child: He Zizhen was one of these, and hers was the fourth baby she had lost. Two of the women had been wounded, He Zizhen seriously, and shards of shrapnel were still buried in her body. Her special status as the wife of Chairman Mao Zedong had brought her little privilege beyond that of the other wives of the leaders: it appears that only once had Mao ushered her to his side to soften her isolation and share with her even a few moments of comfort and privacy. Throughout their journey, which under his guidance had been transformed from a retreat into an inspiring odyssey, she had been nothing more than an occasional shadowy presence. While he became a demigod, she suffered physical and emotional devastation.

It would be reasonable to assume, for it is not recorded, that 25-year-old He Zizhen was not there to share Mao's grand gesture towards history when he sat down at his rickety desk in Wayaobu to write a poem of celebration:

> The Red Army fears not the trials of the Long March,
> one thousand mountains and ten thousand rivers.
> The Five Ridges are but gentle ripples . . .
> Laughter in the thousand *li* of Minshan's snows
> and smiling faces when the last pass is crossed.[38]

2

NOT QUITE EQUAL

In the hierarchy of The Thirty Women, cheerful Wang Quanyuan was one of the eleven young peasant women who lacked
guanxi (connections) and had to earn their berth on what became
the Long March.

The early years of her life were so ordinary that hardly
anything is recorded about them. She was born in 1913 in central
Jiangxi Province, the youngest of four children of a family of
poor peasants surnamed Ouyang. Her native village was in a
densely populated area of Ji'an County where the peasants grew
rice and sweet potato and the landlords profited from silkworms
and camphor trees, bamboo, pine and China fir. Apart from
growing up illiterate and undernourished, she seems to have been
luckier than most peasant girls in that she was not sent away as
a child bride but was allowed to stay at home until she was
seventeen. Then, in March 1930, she left her native village to
go to the home of her new husband, a day labourer named Wang
Zhaodou, in the nearby village of Chayuan. He was thirty-three
years old and theirs was an arranged marriage. In accordance
with local custom, Ouyang Quanyuan took her husband's name
and became Wang Quanyuan.[1]

Moving to Chayuan, Wang Quanyuan found herself among
revolutionaries. With its large population of impoverished peasants, Jiangxi was fertile ground for roving communist propaganda
teams. While Zhu De may well have exaggerated the depth and
spread of peasant poverty in Jiangxi when he talked to Agnes
Smedley in 1937, his description breathes life into the appeal

the early communists held for the mass of China's peasants. Zhu
De said that the peasants of Jiangxi (old spelling: Kiangsi)

> were as heavily oppressed as those of my native province [of
> Sichuan], but even more destitute, hopeless and fatalistic. Most
> of Kiangsi is mountainous, and the crops are poor. The
> landlords took as much as seventy percent of the crop as rent,
> and most peasants had to borrow from them at high rates of
> interest each year, so that they and their sons and sons' sons
> were bound by debt in perpetual servitude to the landlords . . .
> They were gaunt, half-naked, and illiterate, and lived in dark,
> insanitary hovels in villages surrounded by high mud walls
> which had only one gate.

Wealthy families often owned entire districts, he said, and several
big houses 'in which they stored their grain, money, and other
wealth. Serf tenants cultivated their land, and they also had
hundreds of land laborers who were virtual slaves working for
nothing but poor food and shelter and such old clothing as the
[families] discarded.'

Zhu De said that the communists attempted to eradicate
entrenched injustice such as this by rousing the people, through
propaganda and example, to *fanshen*, to stand up and free themselves. In every town or city they captured, they confiscated the
food and property of the officials and the wealthy, keeping what
they needed for themselves and distributing the rest to the poor.
They opened the prison gates and released all prisoners, then
called meetings to explain to the people who they were and what
they were doing. They drove a landlord from his home, confiscated his money and valuables then distributed his lands among
his tenants. If Zhu De's version of events is even half-true, it is
easy to understand why, as Agnes Smedley wrote, 'the agrarian
revolution swept Kiangsi like a flame' in 1930.[2]

Two of Wang Quanyuan's new neighbours were a married
couple, also named Wang (as many people in Chayuan seem to
have been), who were prominent local communist activists. The
woman visited Wang Quanyuan and talked to her about the
misery of their lives as peasants. She told her that their suffering
was not inevitable but was visited upon them by an unjust
system, perpetuated now by the gentry-based KMT, which
allowed landlords and officials to grow wealthy by exploiting

ignorant peasants. Their lives, she said, could be changed only if the peasants rose up and demanded justice and equality. This was possible, she believed, under the leadership of the Communist Party. Becoming a communist often happened, however, without even this basic theoretical preparation, as one of the Long March women's amusing recollection of her introduction to the party in 1931 shows:

'Are you joining the Communist Party?'
'What's the Communist Party?'
'The party of the poor, there are advantages in joining.'
'What advantages?'
'Many advantages, later. First, though, you have to bear hardships. If you want to join I'll sponsor you.'
'OK, I'll join!'[3]

The two Wangs formed a Young Pioneers group, which they encouraged Wang Quanyuan to join. She was elected deputy leader. She was accepted into the Communist Youth League in April 1930, the year she turned seventeen, and in autumn was made responsible for women's affairs of the League's local branch. She became so involved in her work that her husband began to complain she was neglecting her wifely duties. While the agrarian revolution may have been 'sweeping Jiangxi like a flame', this was also a time when there was much talk of less popular ideas, such as the liberation of women and the freedom to choose one's own marriage partner. Wang Quanyuan's husband was not a communist—in this he was in the majority—and, with some justification as it turned out, he began to fear he would lose his young wife.

When Wang Quanyuan realised that her husband was trying to prevent her carrying on her work, with the party's support she moved to another district. She continued to spread propaganda to young people, and to visit women in their homes, which was difficult for males to do in rural communities, to discuss what communism could do for them. As a local peasant woman travelling alone she was also able to move about the countryside without attracting the attention of KMT soldiers or troops of militiamen made up of peasants conscripted into service by landlords. Nevertheless, she learnt to use a spear and a sword and carried a pistol.

Reading behind the hyperbole of her biographies, it seems that Wang Quanyuan thrived on her new responsibilities as a roving propaganda worker. The few photographs taken of her later show her to have not been particularly good-looking (despite her lovely name; it means 'Bubbling-up Beauty'), but she was by nature lively and optimistic. One tale, whose details have no doubt been embroidered, that is told of her growing confidence and youthful panache is the following encounter that took place when she was not yet twenty. While travelling as head of the Youth League's women's bureau in Ji'an County, she had just contacted the underground in one district when enemy soldiers approached. With the help of the locals she managed to slip away, and was just stepping into a boat to make good her escape as her pursuers appeared on the riverbank brandishing loaded rifles. She quickly pushed the boat off and, emboldened by the short stretch of water between them, began to lecture the men, reminding them that they were all poor peasants just like her, who must band together to *fanshen* and overthrow the oppression of landlords and officials. The men had no heart for this; they shot a few volleys into the air then turned and trudged away.

The year she turned twenty, Wang Quanyuan attended her first Women's Congress, which was held in Yongxin, He Zizhen's birthplace. She represented Ji'an County at this conference and was promoted to the provincial level as a member of the joint Hunan–Jiangxi women's bureau. The following year she represented Hunan–Jiangxi at a national congress held in Ruijin, and this qualified her to enrol in the Communist Marxist University in the soviet capital. Even though she was illiterate, she was placed in the senior of its two classes, probably in recognition of her boundless enthusiasm and her three or four years of hard recruiting and propaganda work. She was admitted to the party in April or May 1934 and a month or so later was assigned to work on a massive youth recruiting drive with a young man from Hunan named Wang Shoudao.

In the first days of October 1934, Wang Quanyuan was suddenly ordered to report back to Ruijin. There she found herself lining up for a physical check-up with about one hundred other excited young women, most of them still in their late teens, wondering whether they were, as the rumour mongers had it, to be sent to work closer to the front where the KMT was tightening its 'encirclement and extermination' cordon. They were all party or Youth League members who had proven devoted, willing and capable of undertaking a variety of duties. The young women watched the medical workers cull any women with bound feet and any who were patently pregnant. They saw all those who were ill rejected. Finally, anyone who was underweight, by even half a kilo, was told to go home. Wang Quanyuan was quite tall and, in spite of growing up undernourished in an impoverished household, she had grown sturdy and strong enough to pass the medical. She was declared as fit as any man and found herself assigned with eleven other women to the Women Workers' Group of the General Medical Unit of the Red Army that marched out of Ruijin in early October.

One of the early communists' articles of faith was that their illiterate soldiers and workers must be politicised—they termed it education. Besides igniting in the peasants a spark of hope at being offered the chance to take their fate into their own hands, this process of politicisation inspired in them such belief in the cause of their own liberation that they were willing to sacrifice everything for it. The mass of the people had no access to newspapers, and all information was passed on by word of mouth through local networks. The main means the communists used to politicise their recruits was meetings: propaganda workers called meetings to address the people wherever they went, commanders held meetings after every battle to discuss why they had won or lost. The Women Workers' Group was therefore assembled one afternoon in early October 1934 alongside the members of the Red Star Brigade and addressed by Deng Fa, head of the Red secret police and husband of pregnant Chen Huiqing: 'This is a great Women Workers' Group. Some of you are musicians, some are theatrical people and some are writers. You could put on any sort of performance without seeking help from any other units. On top of that some of you are experienced in working with the masses, so altogether you are complete in yourselves.' He concluded his talk with an uncharacteristic giggle.[4]

This brief pep-talk to the fifteen women who were not wives of the leaders gave no hint about why they had been chosen—how could he have explained the inclusion of Liu Caixiang, a peasant who reported into Ruijin on the afternoon of the day they set out and was assigned a place without even a medical examination?[5] All his talk did was guide the women in what was expected of them. It was generally accepted that only women could recruit women, and that women were better than men at propaganda because women were good at acting and dancing, were often talented singers, as speakers they could hold a peasant audience, and they didn't seem to mind the drudgery of pasting up thousands of posters advertising meetings or carrying inflammatory slogans. Also, every woman who did her share of propaganda work freed another man for fighting. Deng Fa's speech caused no ripples.

As to Wang Quanyuan's reaction at being selected to evacuate Ruijin, the official version would doubtless be that she felt pride at being able to serve the party. While she may well have felt proud—she does, after all, appear to have been devoted to the communist cause—the reality is probably more mundane. One can only speculate, but she surely must have felt tremendous relief at the opportunity to escape the KMT's crippling encirclement and extermination campaign.

About five o'clock that autumn afternoon 21-year-old Wang Quanyuan followed the Red Star signs out of Ruijin in her dark blue Lenin jacket, short hair covered by her eight-cornered army cap, enamel washbasin clanking against the buckles of her pack and Mauser pistol tucked firmly in her belt. The women sang, low and soft, as they walked into the deepening night:

> Ai, ya, lei!
> October, autumn blows cool;
> swift Red Army, swiftly goes.
> By night across Yudu's flow;
> old land, young blood—victory![6]

In her capacity as a political fighter, Wang Quanyuan was one of seven strong young women whose duties included organising food supplies for the unit, and hiring bearers to carry the luggage, the medicine chests and the litters on which the wounded were carried. Each of the women were responsible for three or four litters and the wounded in them.[7] Every morning she set off long before the men and followed the crosses and arrows scrawled on white strips of paper that were placed at crossroads as markers by those who had passed that way in the days before her; sometimes a '10', '20' or '30' was written on them to indicate how many *li* it was to the night camp. When she reached the campsite she arranged food supplies for the cooks who were still on their way; other women were assigned the job of buying food from peasants or, where possible, confiscating it from landlords. Then she set out to hire local bearers, replacing them every two or three days, or sooner if men's backs gave out or they disappeared during the night, afraid to walk any further from their native home.

This apparently straightforward work grew increasingly difficult as each day took her further from Jiangxi. The communists maintained their old guerrilla habit of following foot tracks in the mountainous border areas between provinces, which provided cover from KMT aircraft and large troops of enemy soldiers. These areas, out of the reach of officialdom, were largely inhabited by non-Chinese ethnic minorities who demonstrated a healthy fear of any soldiers by slipping away with their food and animals until the danger had passed. More often than not Wang Quanyuan stumbled along dangerous mountain paths for several hours at night before she was able to find anybody. Usually at least one person in minorities communities understood Chinese, but if she could not find an interpreter she would speak slowly and mime her way to a deal with a few locals to work as bearers for a day or two at one silver dollar a day. By the time she found her way back to her unit it was time to break camp and set off again.

During the day she sometimes carried rifles and luggage for the wounded as well as her own eight-kilogram pack. She walked almost half as much again as the men, leaving before them in the morning and returning after them at night, and averaging 50 kilometres a day. Nevertheless, as one of the privileged women on the march, Wang Quanyuan was never without sandals, no matter how many soldiers had to go barefoot over sharp stones and through snow and mud. By the end of each day's hard slog she longed to plunge her swollen feet into a healing basin of hot water. Yet although she heated water ready for the bearers when they made camp, she rarely had time to look after herself. For one woman, however, bathing her feet became an obsession.

Without fail, the first thing Wei Xiuying (nicknamed 'Shortie') did on pitching camp was gather kindling, heat up some water in her basin and soak her feet. So committed was she to caring for her only means of transport that she managed to capture an enamel washbasin during a skirmish with the enemy. She threaded cord through the three holes she punched in the rim and slung it across her back, swearing to defend it with her life. Another woman took a more proactive approach to her feet. Liu Caixiang was said to have been such a formidable walker that few men could stay abreast of her. At the end of each day's walk her relaxation was to run one or two circuits of the campsite to stretch her cramped muscles.

Even in the first weeks the women were sometimes so tired and pressed they had no choice but to make light of their plight. At one stage the Convalescent Company was lagging so far behind as they walked beside a river that enemy snipers came within firing distance and some of the women had to run for their lives. Deng Liujin, aged twenty-three, was tall, good-looking and talkative; she was nicknamed 'The Cannon' because of the loud and boisterous way she spoke. That day as she galloped into the river, long legs lifting high and pack held close above her head like a helmet, bullets hit the water behind her. She waded strongly through the deeper water with a young male nurse close on her heels. 'You're bleeding!' he called as they scrambled up the far bank. 'Where are you wounded? I saw blood in the water behind you?'

Deng Liujin had felt no blow and it took her a little time to realise that the blood he had seen in the water was not from a wound. Her ready tongue failed her for once, and she could not find the words to tell the innocent boy the blood must have been from the cloth she wore to soak up her menstrual flow. All she could offer was a mumbled word and a reassuring wave before turning red-faced to Wei Xiuying: 'It's all right, I'm not wounded, I've got my—you know, my bad luck time—my monthlies!'[8]

By the time the swift Red Army vanguard had reached the fourth, and last, ring of KMT fortifications, those at the end were four full days and 100 kilometres behind them. Marching only at night so as not to be spotted by enemy aircraft, they were falling further behind each day. The bearers carried heavy equipment lashed to carrying-poles, some of which took up to eight men to carry but the narrow paths through the hills were barely wide enough for two people. Each time the bearers stopped to change shoulders the line of soldiers behind them shuffled to a mystified halt, often having to wait hours in the darkness before they could move on again. During these delays, 90 000 heavily armed KMT and warlord troops converged on the Xiang River crossing where the Red Army vanguard stationed themselves to shepherd the tail-enders across.

The Red Army had been holding off enemy troops for over a week by the time Wang Quanyuan reached the eastern bank of the Xiang River. The once-clear waters ran with blood, and artillery explosions and the spit of rifle fire splattered the night sky as she crowded on to a ferry laden with the wounded and equipment. Wang Quanyuan was called upon to double as nurse, able to do little more without training or medical supplies than comfort the shockingly injured young soldiers. Throughout the night men, horses and pack animals waded the icy 100 metres to the other side, shielded by the darkness. The battle was ten days old by the time the last of the Red Army had ferried, forded and swum its way across the Xiang in the first cold, clear days of December. Its trail was marked on the eastern approach by a litter of abandoned lathes, machinery parts, theatrical costumes and scenery, documents, clothing and maps. The human cost of crossing the Xiang River was appalling: an entire communist regiment was wiped out and in just ten days at least 15 000 young men and boys died while helping their comrades cross the river.

As home and family fell below the eastern horizon and exhaustion became their constant companion, to keep up their own spirits as much as the men's the women sang beloved folk tunes to which they put their own ever-changing words. Wang Quanyuan's true voice and natural liveliness won her a place as one of the four most popular singers, along with Li Guiying from Jiangxi; tall Li Jianzhen from Guangdong; and Deng Liujin, 'The Cannon', from Fujian. Agnes Smedley described one of the Jiangxi folk songs she heard as 'the strangest song I have ever heard . . . It was harsh, sharp, clear, militant, jerky. It stirred the blood'.[9]

Ai, ya, lei!
Sharing out land, most urgent;
revolution, for us all!
Revenge, we must, old hatreds;
Japs out! Northward we march. March!

The marchers reached the safety of the forests beyond the
Xiang River then began the steep climb up perilously narrow and
slippery paths onto Laoshan. When days later they emerged from
the mountains they waited in vain for the order to change
direction, to turn to the north and march to join He Long and
Xiao Ke in their soviet base at the junction of Hunan, Hubei,
Sichuan and Guizhou provinces. Instead they continued west.
Their pursuers fell back and left them, unharassed, to march
quickly across Guizhou Province in the mid-December snow.

By mid-January Wang Quanyuan was bivouacked in the town
of Zunyi in central Guizhou. She spent eight days there in the
snow and bitter cold, most of her time taken up with the work
that was expected of her, described as 'mobilising the masses'.
This was an extremely effective exercise in showing the people
the benefits of putting their weight behind the communists.

Before they started in Zunyi, however, the communists called
a small meeting in the Zunyi Catholic church to discuss with the
local party faithful the establishment of a Zunyi Revolutionary
Committee and the election of office-bearers. Later Mao and Zhu
De both spoke at a large meeting held in one of Zunyi's senior
high schools to formally establish the committee. The work of
mobilising the masses then began, putting into practice according
to a well-oiled plan 'the agrarian revolution', summarised in the
slogan *Da tuhao, fen tiandi* (Destroy feudal bullies, share fields
and land). Guided by local informants, work teams confiscated
the land of wealthy landowners who had fled before the Red
Army took Zunyi. The teams searched their empty homes, burnt
the deeds to these lands, and divided the land among the
peasants. In each field they attached a notice to a bamboo pole
stating the size of the plot and the name of the peasant it was
assigned to. It is little wonder that, as communist jargon has it,
'the people responded very positively to the agrarian revolution'.
Young men also flocked to join the Red Army, attracted as much
by its politics as by the offer of a daily wage and keep.

Once the land had been shared out, the work teams stripped the landlords' homes of grain, clothing and cash. They distributed some of this to the poor and packed the rest in trunks and boxes which they dumped by the side of the road for their logistics people to collect when they came through. Their parting act was to leave a note claiming responsibility so that returning landlords would not blame the local people for the damage done.

In Zunyi, in opium-drenched Guizhou Province (where some said even the horses were addicts), the work teams called mass meetings at which they displayed the booty they had confiscated, and talked at length about the aims and purposes of communism and the Red Army so as to encourage young men to enlist. Then, without missing a beat, they offered opium as payment to men who volunteered as bearers. The cynicism of this behaviour is disturbing, but to the communists of the 1st Front Red Army their fight for survival overrode temporal morality and any stance they might take on opium addiction would wait till later.

It was in Zunyi that Wang Quanyuan added character acting to her performance skills. She helped the theatrical group organise propaganda meetings and agreed to take a turn on the stage. Dressing herself as a man, she donned sunglasses and a fierce scowl and played a feudal bully, to the crowd's delight, parodying the provincial governor as an ineffectual walking-stick-waving fool.[10]

It was also in Zunyi that Wang Quanyuan got married, on the seventh night of her eight-day stay. There is every reason to believe that for her husband it was a marriage of convenience; certainly it was not a lasting union. Apart from treading the boards, Wang Quanyuan was assigned to a propaganda team that mobilised the people in a less dramatic way than the work teams. She went about pasting up posters, talking to the local people and holding mass meetings to explain how and why the communists were rising up to destroy rapacious landlords and fat bureaucrats, who were targeted as the personification of the KMT. The leader of this team was Wang Shoudao, with whom Wang Quanyuan had worked on the recruitment drive of autumn 1934 and whom she had known for at least a year before leaving Ruijin. Perhaps an attraction had developed between them then, but it was not until Zunyi that several women in the propaganda team teased the pair into marrying. Wang Shoudao was twenty-eight then, six years older than Wang Quanyuan, and he, too, had been married before. When Helen Foster Snow interviewed him in Yan'an two years later he told her that his first wife had been executed in 1930 in Changsha by the warlord He Jian; this was the man who the same year also executed Mao's wife, Yang Kaihui, and sister in Changsha.[11]

Wang Quanyuan spent only that one night with Wang Shoudao, however, because the Red Army set out the following day. As she squelched through the mud and dust of Guizhou Province over the next three months she caught not so much as a glimpse of her new husband.

This was a perilous time for the communists as they twisted and turned through Guizhou, outnumbered and outflanked by enemy armies which had gathered while they rested in Zunyi. The women mustered their courage and somehow kept up as the Red Army battled to find a way across the Yangtze River following Mao's new directive to go north. Sometimes, in urging on tired stretcher-bearers, the women fell well behind the Convalescent Company. Once, Liu Caixiang was separated by almost 20 kilometres from her unit when an enemy detachment spotted her small band of litters. A tale of tremendous cool-headedness on her part has been told: when the enemy sprayed her group with machine-gun fire, drawing her pistol she ordered the stretcher-bearers to try to catch up with their unit while she successfully scared the enemy off, wounding (or killing) two of them. Another time Liu Caixiang is said to have squatted at the bottom of an embankment and one by one supported a dozen or so wounded men on her shoulders so they could be pulled up by others on the top. Then she scrabbled up and over the embankment as the enemy rounded the bend. Bullets singed her hair and she had bullet-holes in her clothes when she hit the ground on the other side and ran off. Whether or not these tales are exaggerated, there is little doubt that the women did experience terrifying episodes such as this on the battlefield of Guizhou.

In mid-April Wang Quanyuan crossed through the mountains into Yunnan Province, leaving the enemy behind for a time. The women recall that spring in Yunnan was glorious—bees and butterflies busy with the flowers beside the path, vast forests shimmering to the horizon far below, clear skies. They pulled on their round bamboo hats or shaded themselves from the fiercely hot sun with the paper umbrellas of all colours which many of them had carried from Jiangxi.

They continued to live off the countryside, wherever possible ransacking the storehouses and homes of the *tuhao*. Wang Quanyuan was not the only one to pilfer expensive clothing from abandoned mansions but few could match her in exuberance. To replace the spare uniform that fell out of her pack during one of the countless river crossings in Guizhou or Yunnan, Wang Quanyuan appropriated the most colourful silk garments she could find; perhaps she was thinking ahead to her next theatrical role. On the rare occasions she had time to wash her tattered and patched uniform, using for soap a soft thick pulp made from boiling up the ashes from the cooking fires, while it dried cries of, 'Ah, here comes Miss Floral Frock!' would mark her progress as much as the brilliance of her clothing.

Their most pressing problem in this land of spring plenty from which the Yi minorities people had withdrawn at the approach of a Chinese army was a shortage of grain. With no-one to buy food from in those deserted mountains, the Red Army's Three Main Rules of Discipline—'Obey orders in all your actions; Don't take a single needle or piece of thread from the masses; Turn in everything captured'—forbad them taking food from peasants without reimbursement.

A well-known tale illustrates how seriously they took the second rule. When Wu Fulian, one of the eleven young peasant women, collapsed from exhaustion Xie Fei and two others bedded her down in a recently deserted hut. There in the hut Xie Fei uncovered a basket full of ripe pears, and with it a moral dilemma. A single juicy pear might save Wu Fulian's life but, according to the communist code, if the women took even that one pear without its absent owner's permission they would be breaking faith with the people. The women wanted to buy the pear but there was no-one to ask the price. They finally decided to leave twelve coppers (the daily food allowance for one soldier) with a note explaining why they had been forced to take just one of the pears without consulting its owner.

Several weeks later, when barley crops were still green in the deserted fields and the women were made responsible for finding their own seven days' supply of grain to cross the Snowy Mountains, they were faced with a situation that excused them from these moral qualms. Peering into a deserted cattle pen, which was the ground floor of a typical three-storeyed Tibetan house (people lived on the first floor, and the top floor was reserved for statues of the Buddha and sacred scrolls), ever vigilant Xie Fei spotted wheat growing from a heap of manure. Holding their noses against the stench, a trio of hungry women picked through the manure for grain after filthy grain of the cattle's leftover feed, managing to gather several kilograms of wheat between them. They washed the grains in the river, dry roasted them, then wrapped them in little cloth packets which they stuffed in their pockets: seven days' supply of grain![12]

While the episode of the Yunnan pear has passed into communist lore as symbolic of the good faith of the Long Marchers, as with similar tales it is impossible to tease out the truth from the hagiography. This particular story does, however, bring to mind the widespread, almost fanatical, honesty which foreigners visiting China in the 1970s never ceased to comment on. The Red Army was already imposing the Three Main Rules of Discipline on its fighters on Jinggangshan in 1928, Mao told Edgar Snow in 1936, and it was because of the exemplary behaviour of communist soldiers that peasants 'everywhere began to volunteer to help the revolution'.[13] Red Army soldiers 'confiscated' the property of the wealthy because they were the enemy; soldiers were forbidden to steal from peasants because it was on the peasants' behalf that they were fighting. It is widely acknowledged that the Communist Party, the party of the poor, was able to win the support of the masses largely because Red Army soldiers treated peasants, male and female, with a respect unheard of in traditional armies.

From all accounts, some soldiers were guilty of rape in the early days of the Red Army, but this crime was harshly dealt with by the leaders. Zhang Guotao, for instance, wrote of the code of discipline he helped establish in a Sichuan soviet in the early 1930s:

> First of all, it was stipulated that those found guilty of raping a woman would be punished according to the law of the Soviet; in serious cases, the criminal might be sentenced to death.

Those who committed other unlawful acts against the fair sex would be given a legal sanction according to the nature of each individual case. Apart from legal sanction, it was also stipulated that education should be conducted on an extensive scale to encourage legal marriages between men and women.[14]

Edgar Snow called the communists 'the only *politically* iron-clad army in China'. Helen Foster Snow wrote of how even she became infected with the remarkable elan of the Red Army: 'Then, wonder of wonders, I myself became part of this *esprit de corps*; during the ten-day trip when I left Yenan for Sian with the young Red soldiers, though every night I was so exhausted I could hardly crawl into my camp cot, still, every day I actually forgot how sick I was.' She quoted the female writer Ding Ling as saying: 'The Red Army is a new type . . . They are all very young and when I came here I began to feel as young as they are. Before I came, I couldn't sleep, but now I sleep soundly and am becoming fat. The simple life is good.'[15]

During the three months the communists spent lurching through Guizhou—snow and mud in the winter, sunshine and dust in the early spring—several women were left behind with orders to spread communist propaganda in key areas. Xie Xiaomei and her seriously wounded husband, Luo Ming, were given the dreaded eight silver dollars and told to stay behind in Guizhou to attempt to form new communist cells. Thus abandoned in a dangerous and hostile environment the pair were soon arrested and thrown into prison.[16] Li Guiying and Han Shiying were ordered to stay behind in Yunnan and join up with the guerrillas operating in Guizhou–Yunnan–Sichuan. These two women were also eventually captured by the KMT and imprisoned.[17]

When the communists walked out of the Jiangxi soviet, to all intents and purposes they walked out of the consciousness of the Chinese people, who had little idea where they were or what they were doing. For the better part of a year they trekked along the southern and western perimeter of their country through areas inhabited by various ethnic minorities, as isolated from their fellow Han Chinese as if they had migrated to another land. The stories of the Long March women do not figure in official histories, which were concerned with telling the victor's version of the truth through descriptions of spectacular military escapades and momentous political events, but were pieced together over the years from often flawed reminiscences. Wang Quanyuan was a young peasant woman who by the sheerest chance became caught up in the Long March, and what little biographical material there is on her is often sketchy and contradictory.

According to two biographers,[18] at the beginning of May, Wang Quanyuan was ordered to stay behind as part of a 'Special Committee' to work among certain ethnic minorities people in the Jinshajiang area; she was unable to recall later which minorities these people belonged to. Her title was Secretary of the Youth League of the Special Committee (she was still only twenty-one), and again she was assigned to work with Wang Shoudao, who was Secretary of the Special Committee. Wang Quanyuan and her husband spent about a month together—one biographer described it as their honeymoon—'helping politicise the local people and launching national autonomy activities'; in other words, they called the usual meetings and, speaking through interpreters, spread communist propaganda. It was during this time that the Long Marchers covered 400 or 500 kilometres of the most difficult terrain of their journey, travelling at a cruel pace to reach the only possible crossing of the Yangtze River before the KMT cut them off.

Wang Quanyuan and her Special Committee may have stayed in one place for that month and then, travelling as a small group, caught up with the march by following a less perilous route than the Red Army had been able to. Or they may have simply remained in various localities for a few days at a time as they followed the marchers. The details are not clear. All that is certain is that she caught up with her comrades by the time they had reached the foothills of the Snowy Mountains in early June. As soon as they rejoined the army Wang Shoudao returned to his unit. He was attached to the political department of the powerful Military Commission and was soon to become secretary-general of the Central Committee, in which capacity he worked very closely with Mao. Two months later, in August, he took minutes at the Shawo meeting near Mao'ergai at which Mao established his political supremacy over Zhang Guotao.[19] Wang Quanyuan returned to her unit, unaware that her brief marriage was all but over.

Wang Quanyuan was pleased to be back among the women with whom she had forged out of their shared hardships a cheerful camaraderie. She smiled at her friends, no longer aware of their unwashed faces, their unbrushed teeth and wild, uncombed hair. She hardly noticed their filthy, patched, hand-me-down clothes and she was oblivious to their ceaseless scratching for she, too, had lice. When Deng Liujin offered to shave their heads to rid them of one lice breeding ground (her step-father had been a travelling barber), Wang Quanyuan lined up happily with everybody else, and grinned when the men jokingly addressed her as *Nigu* (Buddhist nun).

One day during the trek across the Snowy Mountains, Wang Quanyuan's menstruation began just before she set out. Cramps knotted her abdomen and she felt the awful heaviness in her stomach dragging down till she could barely lift her legs. The icy north wind sliced straight through her cotton shirt and whipped snow into her pallid face with a hiss. When one of the women asked, 'Wang Quanyuan, are you all right? Why don't you stop for a bit and have a rest?' she just shook her lowered head, drew her hands a little more tightly to her belly and kept moving. She had taken that day's instructions to heart and nothing on earth would make her stop: 'You must get right over the mountain before midday because the afternoons often bring snowstorms; wear sandals but don't tie them too loosely or too tight; don't talk unnecessarily, it wastes your breath; take it steady and don't rush; *don't sit down to rest or you won't get up again.*'

From this time on, for the rest of her life Wang Quanyuan was plagued by gynaecological problems; the harsh physical conditions of the Long March were said to be the cause of her infertility.

Dong Biwu, one of the founders the Chinese Communist Party, was just on fifty when he crossed the Snowy Mountains on the Long March. He later described the experience to Agnes Smedley:

We started out at early dawn. There was no path at all, but peasants said that tribesmen came over the mountains on raids, and we could cross if they could. So we started straight up the mountain, heading for a pass near the summit. Heavy fogs swirled about us, there was a high wind, and halfway up it

began to rain. As we climbed higher and higher we were caught
in a terrible hailstorm and the air became so thin that we
could hardly breathe at all. Speech was completely impossible
and the cold so dreadful that our breath froze and our hands
and lips turned blue. Men and animals staggered and fell into
chasms and disappeared forever. Those who sat down to rest or
to relieve themselves froze to death on the spot. Exhausted
political workers encouraged men by sign and touch to
continue moving, indicating that the pass was just ahead.[20]

Wang Quanyuan resumed litter duty once down off the worst
of the mountains, skirmishes with hostile bands of minorities
people giving her more wounded to find stretcher-bearers to carry,
but the women turned the relief they felt at hearing of the coming
reunion with Zhang Guotao's 4th Front Army into a song to lift
their feet:

On Qionglai mountains we'll see a martial meeting,
a warm welcome to our valiant 4th Front boys!
United and strong China's soviets grow—hey!
Turn Sichuan Red!

Tramping ten thousand li o'er mountains and rivers,
iron-willed we join, mourning fore'er our bloodied dead!
At heart our one goal to turn the nation Red—hey!
Red flag! Advance![21]

North of the Snowy Mountains week-long festivities were held
to celebrate the union of the 1st and 4th Front armies. And
there, in Lianghekou some time in late June or early July, Wang
Quanyuan met her husband once more. She let herself be pushed
into Wang Shoudao's arms when several of her shaven sisters
teased him into inviting them all for a meal of duck and then
teased her into not going back to barracks with them. Wang
Quanyuan blushed and laughed and stayed the night with him.
The next morning she was assigned to work in a stockaded
Tibetan village about 30 kilometres west of Lianghekou. That
was the last time she saw her husband.

Wang Quanyuan went to the village with her comrades, as
ordered, to do the same 'local work' she had undertaken a month
or so earlier; in this case, however, the ethnic minority people
were Tibetans. She found someone who spoke Chinese and learnt

a few words of Tibetan herself. Her biographers say she 'familiarised herself with local attitudes and customs', but what this undoubtedly means is that she asked her interpreter to call the villagers to meetings at which she lectured on the evils of landlordism and the virtues of communism. She was there for a month or two before she realised the 1st Front Red Army had moved on without her; she and her group had been left behind.

Wang Quanyuan may have caught up with the Red Army at a place called Zhuokeji, since that is where a sizable part of Zhang Guotao's 4th Front Army were stationed in mid-August. She ended up as one of six Long March women among the hundred or so 1st Front Army soldiers assigned to the Left Column of the reorganised Red Army under the joint command of Zhang Guotao and Zhu De.

The five other Long March women were Wu Fulian, Wu Zhonglian, Zhou Yuehua, Kang Keqing and Li Jianhua. Wu Fulian was transferred with Wang Quanyuan to a new group formed within the General Medical Unit. This was called the Cadres Convalescent Company, 'cadre' (*ganbu*) being a general term for 'various types of government and Communist Party administrative and political workers—officials, civil servants and staff at all levels'.[22] One woman was attached directly to the General Medical Unit of the Left Column because she was pregnant and in hospital when the order was given to commence the crossing of the Grass Lands. This was Wu Zhonglian, a student whose husband was on the staff of the General Political Department. Wu Zhonglian was a veteran of Jinggangshan, where she had become friendly with Kang Keqing, with whom she had also taught at the Red Military Academy in Ruijin in 1932. The other three women became part of the Left Column presumably because they elected to stay with their husbands: Zhou Yuehua's husband was in charge of the General Medical Unit; Kang Keqing's husband, Zhu De, was military commander of the column; and Li Jianhua's husband was Zhu De's telegraphist.[23]

Official Chinese sources provide little information about the movements of the Left Column once the leaders left Mao'ergai in late August, intent only on demonstrating Zhang Guotao's insubordination and blaming him for splitting the Red Army. Zhang Guotao, however, claims that Mao acted in his usual 'dictatorial manner' by taking control of all military decisions and that he jeopardised the safety of the entire army when he took matters into his own hands and ran off in the middle of the night.[24] Wang Quanyuan knew nothing of this power struggle as she walked west with the other women in the Left Column and then headed north to a place called Aba in preparation for crossing the Grass Lands.

Those in the Left Column did not experience the worst of the Grass Lands, because they swung out to the west to avoid its treacherous heart. All of the women survived the crossing, but for Wang Quanyuan the ordeal exacerbated her gynaecological problems and the harsh northern grains she tried to eat left her ill for several days and caused irreparable damage to her stomach. Three days into the Grass Lands, Zhang Guotao halted the Left Column, claiming to be unable to cross a swollen tributary of the Maju River. He turned back and upon returning three days later to his starting point received a message telling him that Mao had secretly broken camp and marched north. The six women, including Wang Quanyuan, assigned to the Left Column had thus effectively been abandoned through Mao's precipitous action. A seventh woman, Li Bozhao, was stranded with them because she was in the process of organising a theatrical performance; unable to contact her, her husband marched north with Mao.

Wang Quanyuan was twenty-two years old, a young peasant woman who knew little of party politics. No-one was aware at that time how significant would become the split between Mao and Zhang Guotao, that Mao would become history's victor and that Zhang would be branded a traitor. Wang Quanyuan had no idea where her fellow Long Marchers were, and even if she had, she could not have reached them by walking alone across or around the Grass Lands. Her only means of survival lay in remaining with her group and staying as close as possible to the General Medical Unit and the Left Column, which now reverted to its status as the 4th Front Red Army.

So she obeyed her orders and headed south, skirting the western fringe of the Grass Lands again and retracing her steps towards the Snowy Mountains. She was led away from Tibet towards Sichuan proper, towards the city of Chengdu. Famous for its brocade, it has been known as 'the brocade city' for 1800 years, since the Han dynasty; its other name, 'the hibiscus city', derives from the masses of hibiscus trees planted there by an emperor of the Five Dynasties period in the tenth century.

By mid-September 1935, autumn was almost over and the northern winter was already closing in. For about a month Zhang Guotao's soldiers lost battle after bloody battle on the western edge of Sichuan and tens of thousands of communist and KMT soldiers died. Zhang decided to retreat to Tibet where the enemy would not follow in the face of the approaching winter. At the end of October Wang Quanyuan and her companions crossed the Snowy Mountains for the second time, travelling west towards the Tibetan settlements of Daofu, Luohe and Ganzi. This time, however, they were better clothed and were led by their guides through a shortcut which avoided the most difficult and dangerous paths. Better planning and preparations than the Long Marchers had been able to manage in the summer made the crossing comparatively smooth. They bivouacked at the snowline on the first day and the following day moved out at first light to cross the mountain, thus conserving their energy and making the best use of daylight.

Wang Quanyuan spent more than six peaceful months in Tibet, from November 1935 to June 1936. It was probably the longest period completely without battles or fighting of any kind that she had experienced for many years. The soldiers continued their training, but also turned their hands to spinning wool and knitting garments to keep out the bitter cold, as Zhang Guotao later recalled:

> During the months of November and December, 1935, our
> army almost turned into woolen textile factories, and not much
> later all our uniforms were made of woolen textiles of various
> colors, with white predominating. We encouraged the soldiers
> by sponsoring competitions and exhibitions to show off their
> efforts. This solved our winter clothing problem beautifully.[25]

So peaceful and settled was this period that when Wu Zhonglian gave birth to a baby boy in the spring of 1936 there was no question about her keeping him. Without the pressure of endless marching and armies attacking from every side, she was not faced with the dreadful choice the Long March women had to make of either staying behind or abandoning their babies.

In February 1936 Wang Quanyuan was appointed head of the Sichuan women's bureau. She continued to work enthusiastically with the local people, sometimes with Kang Keqing but more often with Wu Fulian, who was head of a women's bureau which Zhang Guotao had set up to represent the entire north-west of China. Wang Quanyuan was also sent out from Ganzi to the settlements of Daofu and Luhuo to work by herself. Zhang Guotao described this as an area where the status of women was particularly low. Polyandry was common there, he said, and a woman would be held responsible for any jealousy among her several husbands, who were usually brothers.

> The women must stay away from the lamas when walking along the street, otherwise they are considered immoral. It is considered a sin when a young and beautiful woman dares to attract the attention of the lamas. Wives who cause jealousy among their husbands and women who arouse the sexual desire of the lamas are usually sent to a convent, as nuns. On a small hill on the outskirts of the city of Tao-fu [Daofu] there is a well-organized convent which is full of nuns of this type.[26]

Wang Quanyuan did not mention these nuns, but she learnt through her young interpreter that the Tibetan authorities were killing any of their people found cooperating with the communists. She saw the mutilated corpses of communist stragglers left as a warning and heard the rumours about her: 'The Chinese have sent a sorceress among us. She must be killed to prevent disaster befalling us.' This was not far-fetched, for sorcery and magic have always been integral to Chinese and Tibetan culture.

Despite a long history of dealings between the two nations, Tibet did not become a tributary of Ming China until the sixteenth century. It was made a Chinese protectorate during Qing in the early eighteenth century, with the fifth Dalai Lama installed as its temporal ruler. Relations between the two countries soured after the 1911 Revolution when Tibet broke away and the British stepped in, declaring the ideal political solution for Tibet to be 'Chinese suzerainty and Tibetan autonomy' with a permanent British interest. To individual Chinese such as Wang Quanyuan, to walk into the Tibetan foothills was to cross the

Chinese frontier into unknown territory that had always been inhabited by hostile ethnic minorities.

Wang Quanyuan was no modern-day sorceress, even though she had learnt in Jiangxi how to defend herself with spear and sword, so she gripped her Mauser pistol a little tighter and went about her business among the Tibetan people. The far north-west of Sichuan where it bordered Tibet was a green and beautiful place of rushing streams that summer of 1936.

Zhang Guotao eventually accepted the party's decision that he should leave Sichuan and Tibet and march north. He had not, however, changed his policy of advancing westward and seizing the Gansu Corridor west of the Yellow River in order to shore up the Red Army's military presence in northern Shaanxi. He was determined to station his army in the far north-west as a contact point with the Soviet Union, a plan that gained the approval of Stalin in Moscow. Zhang Guotao delayed his march north, awaiting the arrival from central China of the 2nd Front Red Army commanded by He Long and Xiao Ke. This 2nd Front Army had travelled from the border region at the junction of Hunan, Hubei, Sichuan and Guizhou provinces, along a slightly more western route than the Long Marchers had taken. However, since they were not relentlessly pursued by KMT or warlord armies as Mao's party headquarters contingent had been the previous year, they were able to use more accessible roads—they swung west and avoided the worst of the Snowy Mountains, for example—thus encountering far fewer trials and tribulations, and suffering hardly any loss of life.

Wang Quanyuan was entrusted with preparing a welcome for this fresh army, which reached Luohe, near Ganzi, in late summer. As soon as Commander He Long, the flamboyant co-leader of the army, arrived in June or July 1936, he invited Wang Quanyuan to share a celebratory meal with his staff, a generous gesture which he explained was a reward for her efforts at conciliation with the local people and for 'risking her life to help organise food supplies for his 18 000 soldiers'.[27]

Wang Quanyuan had worked hard among largely hostile people for the better part of a year, and she looked forward to rejoining the friends she had shared so much with on the long journey from their home in the south. She shouldered her pack with its seven days' supply of grain and, with Kang Keqing by her side, once more trudged over the Snowy Mountains, following local guides along less arduous paths than they had walked the previous year. She walked north towards the Grass Lands, but time and circumstance transformed her third crossing of that desolate region almost beyond recognition. The Right Column of the Red Army that had floundered through the dead heart of the Grass Lands in 1935 had been an army of half starved and exhausted peasant farmers on the run. They knew how to grow and harvest food, but they were unable to recognise edible wild plants and apparently never thought of hunting food. When Wang Quanyuan crossed the Grass Lands in 1936, however, the hunters among the Sichuan soldiers of the 4th Front and 2nd Front armies found the icy black waters alive with fish and their Tibetan guides found nutritious herbs among its bitter grasses.[28] The weather was fine and, with no KMT armies prowling to the east, they were able to choose well-trodden paths on the outskirts of the Grass Lands.

North of the Grass Lands they entered the region of China that borders on the Gobi Desert, at the eastern entry point to the Silk Road. In this harsh land, where the people 'wear a fur coat in the morning but a cotton shirt at noon, and in the evening eat melons around a fire', the population was largely Moslems of Turkish descent. Mohammedans descended from Uighur Turks had lived in this area since the ninth century, intermarrying with ethnic Chinese and adopting Chinese culture and language. They had nevertheless retained their Islamic faith and dreamed of winning their independence from China by becoming an autonomous Moslem republic. Numbering over ten million in the 1930s,[29] they were even less welcoming to the Chinese communists than the Tibetans had initially been. Sympathetic to the KMT, the Ma clan of Moslems in particular were an aggressive and terrifying enemy, with their long curved swords, and swift on their short-legged ponies. The Red Army had no experience in fighting cavalry, especially one such as this which would descend out of nowhere in whirlwind raids, night or day.

Zhu De ordered his soldiers to form into groups in daylight raids so they could rake the horsemen with rifle fire instead of trying to pick off individuals; at night, he told them, aim for the glint of the horsemen's slashing sabres. Wang Quanyuan sang up their courage:

> Mounted horsemen don't frighten us,
> they're a big and easy target.
> Shouting 'Kill!' as we fire each shot—
> we draw a bead on them, wipe them out, rout them![30]

Zhu De's wife, Kang Keqing, encouraged Wang Quanyuan to take to the stage at every stopping place, where they held meetings and put on performances. Wang Quanyuan would preface her ludicrous pantomime lampooning the fierce Moslem leader Ma Bufang with a crudely fashioned song of her own, to the delight, it is reported, of the Chinese people living in Gansu:

> A curse on Ma Bufang, north of the Yangtze
> he hinders the anti-Japanese push,
> oppresses the army and the people—ya! Destroy him.
> Red Army units, vanguard of the poor,
> flock to the north against the Japanese,
> striving for the independence and liberation of the Chinese
> nation.

As they walked steadily north towards the Yellow River, in October 1936 Wang Quanyuan was placed in command of the Women's Anti-Japanese Vanguard Regiment.

An independent unit of women had been part of the 4th Front Army in Sichuan Province since 1933, when about 400 women were formed into the Women's Independent Battalion. These women undertook guard and transport duties, were responsible for communications and liaison as well as taking and keeping prisoners, and were involved in day to day fighting with the army. This was unusual in that women in communist organisations were generally trained to do propaganda and organisational work; if they fought as partisans, they remained behind when the army moved on. Official sources give no reason why these particular women were formed into a military unit. The original impetus may have come from an order issued by the Central Committee in Shanghai in 1930, which Mao and Zhu De ignored, that all Red Army commanders make peasant partisans a regular part of their armies and take them with them, as they did soldiers, when they left soviet areas.[31]

According to Zhang Guotao, however, the independent women's detachment was formed 'to satisfy the demands of the women', who were especially active in the Sichuan soviet base. The women's 'stamina was no less than that of the men. They were in the vanguard in prohibiting the use of opium, and they took an active part in the work of the various departments of the Soviet government . . . The women swarmed to apply for membership when the regiment was set up. After some careful selection, more than one thousand were accepted.'[32] It certainly appears that Zhang Guotao found it much easier than Mao to put communist theory on gender equality into practice. He promoted women's participation in military affairs, acknowledged their activism in breaking the hold opium had on the population of Sichuan, and worked on an equal footing with Zhang Qinqiu, who was in charge of the 4th Front Army's Political Department. On a personal level he also appears to have genuinely respected women. His wife, Yang Zilie, was a distinguished revolutionary from whom he was separated for almost seven years, yet he apparently did not take another wife during that period, as so many men of the 1st Front Army did. He Zizhen is reported to have commented to Yang Zilie, with evident envy, on Zhang Guotao's faithfulness as a husband.[33]

About a year after its formation the Women's Independent Battalion was expanded to a regiment of about 2000 women when some hundreds of female workers were added to their ranks. Many of these recruits were the wives and children of the men soldiers of Zhang Guotao's 4th Front Army. In early 1935 a further reorganisation turned them into the Women's Independent Division of nearly 4000 directly under 4th Front Army headquarters. This was a disaster: about half the women in the new division died in battle within a short time, doubtless because they had not been trained and were insufficiently armed. The remaining women then formed the Women's Anti-Japanese Vanguard Regiment attached to General Headquarters. It consisted at that time of about 1300 women and girls, some of them said to be only twelve years old.

Wang Quanyuan was made regimental commander, with Wu Fulian (she who had been revived by that disturbing juicy pear in Yunnan) her political commissar. Each woman in the regiment, hair cropped and calves wrapped in puttees, was issued with just ten bullets and two hand grenades—the entire regiment had only two light machine-guns. As regimental commander, Wang Quanyuan was issued with a handgun and allowed to keep her faithful old Mauser pistol. Since most of the women were cotton mill workers from Sichuan who had never faced combat, Wang Quanyuan's first responsibility was to give them elementary military training. During a short rest break near Lanzhou, the capital of the province of Gansu, she taught them the basics of how to shoot a gun and throw a hand grenade.

A few days after leaving Lanzhou, the armies of Zhang Guotao and He Long halted just south of the Yellow River. Opinions differ as to what happened next and in what order, depending on the political stance of the commentator. Communist sources say that Zhang Guotao ordered troops, including the Women's Vanguard Regiment, to head west across the Yellow River. In the meantime he and the rest of the armies, which included three of the Long March women—Kang Keqing, Li Bozhao and Zhou Yuehua—turned right and marched north-east towards a reunion with Mao. Zhang Guotao, however, claimed that his plan had been to lead his entire 4th Front Army across the Yellow River and march with them to the north-west. Transportation difficulties delayed them and it took three weeks for just over half of the army (20 000 men and the Women's Vanguard Regiment) to cross the river, by which time KMT soldiers seized the crossing, leaving Zhang stranded on the eastern bank. He referred to the soldiers who had succeeded in crossing the river as the West Wing, but they are generally called the Western Route Army.[34] Zhang Guotao is considered to be a traitor for having tried to usurp Mao in August 1935, for insisting on sending this expedition to the north-west, even though it was approved by Moscow, and for later changing sides to join the KMT. Therefore, his explanation has never been accepted by the communists.[35]

Four of the Long March women crossed the Yellow River in October 1936 and marched off the north-western edge of China. They were Wang Quanyuan, Wu Fulian, Wu Zhonglian (carrying her six-month-old baby boy), and Li Jianhua. Wang Quanyuan and Wu Fulian led the barely armed and barely trained Women's Vanguard Regiment into the Gansu Corridor, the slender neck of land between the Gobi Desert and the Qilian Mountains, which led to the Silk Road to Europe. A railway line ran along it to Russia, and it was Moslem territory, the place where the Great Wall finally peters out. From the moment the communists crossed the Yellow River, Ma Bufang's horsemen harassed them, slaughtering them by the thousands. With the Moslems closing in behind the communists could not turn back, even though they must have known they were doomed. In the end it took the Moslem Ma clan's cavalry just over two months to annihilate the Western Route Army.

Wang Quanyuan's 1986 recollection of events differs only in minor details from written accounts and this is what she said happened.[36] During the first skirmishes with the Moslems the women captured thirty camels, which they used to carry the wounded. Then, sometime early in November, near Tumen, a company of nearly 150 women was cut off and massacred. Li Jianhua may have died then; nobody ever found out just what happened to her, only that she was never heard of again after the Yellow River crossing. The Women's Vanguard Regiment was attached to command headquarters, and in mid-November they found sanctuary in a small Chinese settlement near Yongchang where they rested for forty-five days. Wang Quanyuan said they did military training and held the usual meetings, and the locals sewed clothes and shoes for them, showing them how to wrap their feet in felt.

Headquarters decided to start out again for the north-west at the end of December, apparently hoping that blind courage and political conviction would overcome the icy winter and the attacking Moslems, who harassed them continually after they left Yongchang. They reached a settlement called Shandan, where the women dug trenches and fetched the wounded when the Moslems attacked. The Women's Vanguard Regiment was disbanded about this time, however, because it was thought to be too easy a target, and the women were seeded throughout what remained of the Western Route Army. Wang Quanyuan remained with headquarters as they plunged on. They were besieged for three days in the walled town of Linze, women and men without weapons or bullets pelting the enemy with rocks as the death toll rose. Cannons pounded the city wall and Moslems clambered up ladders and ropes shouting: 'Charge! A wife for every man who makes it over the wall!' By the time the communists broke out on the fourth night, at least 400 women had been killed.

The 10 000 survivors of the Western Route Army gathered at a small settlement from which they made repeated efforts to break out to the west. The Women's Vanguard Regiment was re-formed, with Wang Quanyuan in command and Wu Fulian her deputy, as before. By day the women supplied what ammunition and food they could to the fighting men and fetched the wounded from the battlefield; by night they stood sentry and ventured out to dig ice for drinking water from the river's edge. Their casualties mounted.

One woman among them did not belong to the Women's Vanguard Regiment, but such distinctions hardly mattered now. Zhang Qinqiu was head of the Western Route Army's political organisation section and she had been six months pregnant when she crossed the Yellow River in October. Some time in January during a break in the fighting she gave birth to a son, who died. She was later captured by the Moslems. Her husband, General Chen Changhao, the political commissar in charge of the Western Route Army, managed to avoid capture, eventually making his way to the communist base in Yan'an.

In March 1937 the remnants of the Western Route Army withdrew into the wild Qilian Mountains to the south. Trapped, exhausted and without food or ammunition they telegraphed details of their predicament to Red Army headquarters in Shaanxi Province. This unhelpful reply came back within twenty-four hours: 'Can only suggest you attempt to retain what remains of your strength either by trying to break out or by re-forming into guerrilla units. Whichever option you choose you must billet the wounded, make your own decisions from now on, travel light, and adopt unpredictable strategies.'[37]

Now officially abandoned, the few hundred women survivors split up into small groups and scattered, travelling by night to avoid capture.

Having already placed her baby safely with a local family in January, Wu Zhonglian turned once more into a partisan but had little opportunity to practise her accurate grenade skills for she was soon captured. She escaped and somehow rejoined the

Western Route Army but she and Zhang Qinqiu were captured again in early April by Ma Bufang's cavalry and sent to work in a factory.[38]

Wu Fulian, co-leader of the Women's Vanguard Regiment, took off with a group of about one hundred. They wandered through the mountains and foothills living off bark and leaves but many died. Wu Fulian was among the few who survived but she was finally detected, was wounded while being captured and, thin and weak, was placed in an old prison compound in the town of Wuwei in early summer.

Wang Quanyuan headed east with four other women, five boys under the age of sixteen and several pack horses. They stumbled through the arctic nights trying to find a way out of the mountains for nearly a month before they came across a shepherd who told them the Ma clan cavalry were prowling the eastern foothills. The women therefore decided to head for the northern slopes and that night walked about 30 kilometres, bedding down just before dawn in an abandoned cave dwelling.

Moslem bayonets pressing into their chests prodded them into horrible wakefulness. Their captors were soldiers under the command of Ma Bufang's brother Ma Buqing. They bound the women and took them back to Wuwei, where they imprisoned Wang Quanyuan with about one hundred other women captured since late March. Three months later Ma Buqing tramped into the temple at the head of forty tall, dark-skinned bodyguards. 'Starting tomorrow,' he told the women, 'all female prisoners will be allocated as concubines to my officers. Anyone who doesn't toe the line will be despatched to the Western Paradise in three days' time.'

Wang Quanyuan's nightmare had just begun.

3

THE GIRL COMMANDER

'I don't know whether I killed anyone or not—I couldn't see the results of my shooting—but I am a very good marksman. I must say this was a happy day for me.' Kang Keqing was aged twenty-three when she thus earned her nickname 'the Girl Commander', she told Helen Foster Snow in her low throaty voice three years later.

> Once while I was working at the rear in 1934 I led the troops in battle . . . I went out to inspect the work of the Party, and by chance we met the enemy and had to grab our guns and fight. I was temporarily elected commander by the three hundred men there. I was the only woman. We fought for two hours; then the enemy retreated . . . The enemy learned that I was in command and I heard they were afraid of me because they said: 'Zhu De's wife has come and she is very fierce.'[1]

A photograph of Kang Keqing taken at Yan'an when she was twenty-five or twenty-six shows her dressed in the belted cotton jacket of a Red Army soldier, cropped hair under her blue-grey cap with the five-pointed star at the front. With well-shaped eyebrows and high cheekbones, she looks like a handsome boy. Helen Foster Snow described her as:

> pretty, with unusual light brown almond eyes and a round face with clear-cut features and beautiful strong teeth. When she came to see me, she shook hands with the only rough, sizable woman's hand I have felt since I came to China and was very cordial to me. She is taller than the average, weighs 120 pounds and is very strongly but symmetrically and smoothly

built, and has a quiet, dignified manner. She did not remind
me of any peasant that I had ever seen, but I thought what a
wonderful study in simple strength and character she would be
for a Millet or Daumier. The picture of health, her bronzed
face and red cheeks shone with honest scrubbing. I am sure she
has never had a dress, and probably never will.[2]

Kang (Healthy) was her family name, but she had chosen her
own personal name in 1930—Keqing (Vanquish and Unequivocal). Her name suited her: Kang Keqing (Healthy Unequivocal
Vanquisher). More than anything else in the world, she wanted
to be a soldier.

The story of Kang Keqing's early years is the story of millions
of Chinese peasants. Many details of her childhood that appear
in biographies and her reminiscences were very possibly added
much later, when she was well known, as a way of proving that
she was a true child of the masses. Since her story as told to
Helen Foster Snow in 1937 is the earliest biographical material
available, that is what has in the main been used here, even
though it does project at times an image of a naive, stoic
revolutionary lass reciting a pat propaganda line—which indeed
she was.[3]

Like He Zizhen and Wang Quanyuan, Kang Keqing was born
in Jiangxi Province, a rain-drenched and fertile land of rice fields
and fish ponds. Jiangxi's northern border is the splendid Yangtze
River that rises in Tibet and flows more than 6000 kilometres
across central China to Shanghai on the East China Sea, dividing
China into north and south. The mountains on three sides have
shaped Jiangxi into a shallow scoop tilted to drain north. Rivulets
and waterfalls spawned by summer rains cascade into the Gan
River until, calmed by Lake Poyang, the country's largest fresh-
water lake, they swirl into the Yangtze.

To the south, Jiangxi turns its back on outward-looking
Guangdong. China's southernmost mainland province,
Guangdong became the West's entry point to China last century
and is the native place of most of the world's male Chinese
emigrants, who poured out through Canton to make their fortunes in the fabled goldfields of San Francisco and Australia. To
the east, Jiangxi is separated from the island of Taiwan by the
mountainous coastal province of Fujian and the Taiwan Strait.

To the west, it snuggles up to its geographical twin Hunan, the province south of Lake Dongting.

Kang Keqing was born under an oil-cloth shelter on a flat-ended fishing boat in 1911 or 1912. In the way of peasants her parents were oblivious to contraception and abortion, bringing forth babies which they culled according to the timeless dictum that boys are valuable and girls are worthless. 'My mother had a girl-child every year,' she told Helen Foster Snow. 'Six of the seven of us were given away at birth to other families because my father was a poor fisherman and could hardly provide rice enough for his three sons, much less for unwanted daughters. We were not even sold—we were given away to become servants, farmhands, and kitchen slaves.'

She was given to a local farmer's family so she knew her biological father, Kang Niangou, and her biological mother, Huang Niangu. She understood it was the way of things for the poor to give their children away and that, as the saying goes, it is more profitable to raise geese than daughters, but she deeply resented her parents not considering her worth feeding. Nevertheless, it was Kang Keqing's first good fortune in life that her parents did give her away instead of drowning her or leaving her in some conspicuous place in the vain hope that somebody would take her in before she died of exposure.

Her foster parents lived in Wan'an, a small county of ten townships, where their native village of Luotangwan nestled by the river at the foot of a mountain. The village children played among the grazing buffaloes on the flat between Luotangwan's two streets—Above Street and Below Street. Sets of worn stone steps led from Below Street to the river, acting as landing platform, laundry, meeting place and front door for the people of Luotangwan. Their houses were of mud brick, two or three small rooms with low ceilings and a steep roof thatched with local grasses. Narrow ventilation slits in the walls did for windows and in every kitchen there was a vat to store water carried from the river, and a stone mortar for grinding rice.

Kang Keqing's foster parents had no children, so she was spared the fate of most peasant girls of being sold or given away as a child bride, often to a boy not yet born. They named her Guixiu and expected her to earn her keep from an early age, giving the care of the family's water buffalo into her five-year-old hands. The water buffalo towered over her, but they are gentle creatures and each day they went together up the mountain, the animal to graze, the child to collect firewood and mushrooms along the way.

Later biographies tell of her good fortune in being delivered from the awful burden and disfigurement of bound feet, relating a screaming match between her grandmother, who wanted to bind her feet, and her mother, who wanted to retain her natural feet. They quote Kang Keqing as saying: 'It's thanks to these big feet that I am a revolutionary soldier and have travelled all over the place!' This tale is probably not true because, although peasant girls sometimes were subjected to footbinding by mothers who saw it as a means of marrying them up in class, as a rule they were far too valuable as workers to cripple. It was little girls of the wealthy gentry whose tender young feet were cruelly bound when they were about six years old in long strips of cloth that forced their toes down underneath the foot and restricted their growth, leaving them to hobble painfully for the rest of their lives on broken feet.

The Gan River flooded the year Kang Keqing turned fourteen or fifteen, forcing her family off their fields. Crops throughout the province failed and tens of thousands of people went hungry. Kang Keqing told Helen Foster Snow that in 1926 a communist organiser visited her district and 'explained the peasant problem to the farmers. My foster father was immediately influenced and became chairman of the village Peasant Union which was formed at that time.' She said that the poverty she lived in was the direct reason she herself became a revolutionary, and it was this universal poverty that the communists stressed in their successful appeal to the peasants. Kang Keqing also claimed to have been influenced by 'the Communist party and the idea of the emancipation of oppressed humankind' but, while many intellectuals did indeed join the communists for idealistic reasons, this is clearly something she learnt to say after she had become a communist.

She became actively involved with the communists as a result of frequent visits to her village by roving propaganda teams of men and women who told her that the only way to break the endless cycle of crippling rent and taxes she had been born into was to unite with her fellow peasants to wrest back the land that rightfully belonged to them. It didn't take much to convince her that the rapacious landlords and gentry of the KMT were her enemy, as she explained to Helen Foster Snow.

> Though I was only fifteen and could neither read nor write, in 1927 I was made Communist Youth Inspector of the work of the union in our district of ten townships. I joined the Communist Youth League and was Captain of the Young Pioneers. At this time the Great Revolution failed and the Kuomintang began expelling the Communist elements. In order to escape arrest, I ran away and hid in the mountains about fifty or sixty *li* [about 30 kilometres] from the house. The Kuomintang had a list of suspected Communists for arrest, and told the people of the village that their houses would all be burned to the ground if they did not find us.

KMT soldiers and landlord militiamen committed atrocious acts of intimidation during this time: in the month of February 1927, for example, the KMT executed one thousand peasants in Kang Keqing's district alone, most of them not even communists.

> Some Communists were killed openly in the fields without even benefit of arrest. Some were caught and beaten in order to get them to betray the hiding places of their comrades and were afterward killed. Some were stripped naked and burned slowly at the stake. Many women and pregnant mothers were executed. The wives and children of Communists were killed with them. Many Communist Youth boys and girls were executed also. Even many revolutionary sons of landlords were executed, and the landlords were arrested . . . Some Communists betrayed to the Kuomintang at this time, but I wanted to continue the revolution.

She told Helen Foster Snow, 'The killing of my comrades made me furiously angry and more revolutionary than before. I plotted with some other comrades to revive the movement, but we had no organization left. Though the Communist chief in the district had not been killed, seven or eight leaders had run away.'

With no specific place or group to go to, Kang Keqing did not run away to join the communists for another year, soon after she had come face to face with the threat of an arranged marriage.

Helen Foster Snow reports her as saying that her father locked her in a small room when she tried to escape this marriage. Chinese biographers put in Kang Keqing's mouth words that convey the spirit, if not the facts, of this encounter:

> One day I came home and found someone had left gifts on the table. I realised my parents had arranged a marriage for me. I simply refused. I told them I wasn't going anywhere. 'I won't belong to anybody,' I said, 'and as soon as that go-between shows his face I'll tell him he can get lost.' Things began to get out of hand and when Father wanted to tie me up to keep me quiet, I threatened to report him to the women's bureau for domestic violence! We left it at that for a while. All I really wanted from life was to not get married, and to be a soldier.[4]

Kang Keqing had grown up with tales of heroes and ghosts and entrancing women warriors. These were the often fantastical versions of history passed down in traditional folk tales, and performed as local opera by touring groups of actors, singers and acrobats during annual week-long visits.

The legend of resourceful Hua Mulan (known in some dialects as Fa Mulan), was told in several versions. When her father fell ill while on leave, Hua Mulan resolved to fulfil his soldierly duty herself. Disguised as a man she went in his stead to the front in the bleak north of China, fought bravely and for twelve years was accepted by her fellow soldiers as one of the men. Returning home on leave one year with one of her comrades, she revealed that she was a woman and declared her love for him. They married and lived happily ever after. Another version of the legend, less sanguine and perhaps older, has her soldiering on towards death or the pension until she receives a serious wound to the body and her fellow soldiers, seeing her naked, realise she is a woman. Her valiant spirit and years of faithful service count for nothing in the face of her being a mere girl and she is sent home in disgrace to try to piece together a more normal life. The story of Hua Mulan, woman warrior of the Northern and Southern dynasties period (about AD 500), seized the imagination of the people and was embroidered to a rich texture of myth and fantasy over the next 1400 years.

On autumn nights even the children were allowed to stay up late when peasant and gentry families alike flocked to watch the glittering spectacle of spellbinding operas. A favourite was the story about the Yangmen nüjiang (female generals of the Yang family). Set in the Northern Song dynasty (about AD 1074), it centres on two women who have married into the Yang family: Mu Guiying, aged fifty, and She Taijun, who is one hundred years old. The tale is set in motion when She Taijun's eight sons and a grandson are slaughtered in battle. Enraged, the old woman takes command of the remnants of their army and leads the family's widows into battle to avenge the killing of their men. Courageous Mu Guiying, still a fine rider and accomplished swordswoman, plunges into the field in full armour, sword flashing and brilliantly coloured pheasant plumes streaming from her helmet. She succeeds in driving the enemy off. Over the centuries Mu Guiying has become a storybook heroine revered for her brave deeds and fighting skill.

Chinese heroines were not all safely tucked away in legend, however. An undeniably flesh and blood woman warrior well known in the south was Qiu Jin, proud martyr to the anti-Manchu cause in the long run-up to the 1911 Revolution. Qiu Jin was born in Fujian Province into the privileged ruling class. She could ride a horse and handle a sword, she dressed in men's clothing, carried a dagger and was fascinated by gallants, heroes and female warriors, adopting for herself the name Gallant Woman of Mirror Lake (Jinghu nüxia). At the age of twenty-six, Qiu Jin left her husband and two young children to travel to Japan as a student in 1905. She became active in radical student organisations, learning while she was there how to make explosives. On her return to China she devoted herself to spreading revolutionary propaganda, and planning assassinations and armed uprisings against the Manchu Government. Her wish was to become the first woman to die for the anti-Manchu cause. She was captured in the summer of 1907 after a botched assassination-cum-uprising, and her beheading the following morning caused a public outcry, her exploits quickly passing into folklore.

From the mid 1920s the KMT, which was the party of wealthy gentry and landlords, had no place for peasants or women in either their political or military organisations; warlord armies and landlord militia, also all-male units, lacked any political commitment except preventing peasant uprisings. The only way Kang

Keqing could become a soldier was by joining the communists, and this she did when some units of Zhu De's 4th Red Army passed through Luotangwan on a recruiting drive. The army did not stay long, she explained to Helen Foster Snow, and it was fear of KMT reprisals against the village that prompted about one hundred people to go with them. 'I joined, together with six other girls about nineteen years old or so, some of whom were in the Communist Youth and some not Communists at all. Therefore, I joined the Red Army in 1928 at the age of sixteen.' Kang Keqing and her fellow villagers 'were not regularly enlisted in the Red Army but were partisan organizers. We organized partisan movements and distributed guns to them from the Red Army. Many returned to my native *hsien* [county] to fight there. I was a partisan leader but did not carry a gun, as I did organizing and propaganda work.'

The Red Army which Kang Keqing joined was comprised of groups of ill-equipped and largely untrained peasants under military commanders who gave them grand names such as the 20th Army, the 1st Division of the 1st Peasants' and Workers' Army, the 1st, 4th or 5th Red Army. In the eyes of the KMT they were simply bandits. Lacking guns and ammunition, lacking even a supplier to buy them from in the unlikely event they had the money, the communists got all their guns and ammunition from KMT soldiers they killed or captured through ambush and guerrilla warfare.

The Zhu–Mao Red Army was based on Jinggangshan, about 80 kilometres due west of Kang Keqing's village, and she eventually spent five months as a partisan organiser in those wild mountains to which Mao had retreated in September 1927 and which Zhu De had entered with his troops in May 1928. When she first left home, however, she went to Suichuan, 20 or 30 kilometres west on the foothills of Jinggangshan and there, in August 1928, she first saw Commander Zhu De:

> Zhu–Mao had acquired an air of magic in people's eyes and I
> was filled with awe and reverence as I waited by the roadside
> for my first glimpse of Commander Zhu. I gazed down the
> road in the direction of the pointing fingers and saw a man of
> medium height and robust build walking towards us; he looked
> a little like a kindly elder. As he approached I saw that he was

wearing a faded grey uniform and straw sandals. He looked travel weary but he was smiling and his strength was permeated by a certain gentleness. My initial impression of Commander Zhu was that he was extremely amiable, for all the world like a real peasant.[5]

Agnes Smedley described Zhu De in similar terms when she met him some nine years later in Yan'an:

In height he was perhaps five feet eight inches. He was neither ugly nor handsome, and there was nothing whatever heroic or fire-eating about him. His head was round and was covered with a short stubble of black hair touched with gray, his forehead was broad and rather high, his cheekbones prominent. A strong, stubborn jaw and chin supported a wide mouth and a perfect set of white teeth which gleamed when he smiled his welcome. His nose was broad and short and his skin rather dark. He was such a commonplace man in appearance that, had it not been for his uniform, he could have passed for almost any peasant in any village in China.

. . . His eyes, gazing at me, were very watchful and appraising. Unlike the eyes of most Chinese, which are black, his were a deep and soft brown, large, and gleaming with intelligence and awareness . . .

One thing I sensed at once: every inch of him was masculine, from his voice and movements to the flat-footed way in which he stood. As my eyes became accustomed to the murkiness of the room I saw that his uniform was worn and faded from long wear and much washing, and I noted that his face was not immobile, but exceedingly expressive of every emotion that passed through him.[6]

Zhu De was a native of Sichuan Province in western China. Just what his antecedents were is unclear, principally because class has always been of such importance to the communists that wherever possible they will ascribe lowly origins, preferably of the peasantry, to their leaders and heroes. Born in 1886,[7] he attended school then went on to military college and became an officer in the army of a Yunnan warlord. He had already begun to see the futility of seeking a military solution to China's political problems when, during the 1919 May Fourth Movement, he became aware of socialism and communism. He studied for four years in Germany, where he secretly joined the Chinese

Communist Party. Upon his return to China in 1927 he was placed in command of KMT troops, whom he brought with him when he declared himself for communism after the shaky KMT–Communist alliance broke down that same year.

He told Agnes Smedley that he had last seen his second wife and his only son in 1922 and that he had taken a young Hunanese revolutionary named Wu Ruolan as his new wife in early 1928.[8] This young woman became a martyr to the Communist Revolution when she was captured during a reconnaissance mission off Jinggangshan: someone recognised her as the wife of Zhu De, she was tortured and then publicly executed. Kang Keqing told Helen Foster Snow that Wu Ruolan, whom she met only once, on Jinggangshan, had been executed by the KMT at the end of 1928, and that Zhu De made her his fourth wife in January 1929.

The marriages of the early communists would be considered by many Westerners more common-law relationships than the legal contracts Western marriages have become. The communists were not usually sexually promiscuous, however, and while their marriages were 'consensual unions' they tended not to be transient liaisons. In theory each couple had to gain the permission of the party or the specific organisation to which they were attached to marry or divorce; even Mao Zedong had to gain party approval for his divorce and remarriage in Yan'an. Towards the end of her life, Kang Keqing reminisced about how her relationship with Zhu De began. Zhu De had been in the habit of chatting with the young partisan women in the soviet base on Jinggangshan whenever he had a few spare minutes, she said, but one afternoon he sought her out when she was alone and asked her to marry him. She was taken aback and asked for a little time to think it over; he had her brought to his quarters the next day to hear her answer. She said Zhu De responded to her awkward silence with the words: 'It looks like you're too shy to say. How about this: you don't have to say anything unless you're opposed to the idea. I mean, can I take your silence as a yes?' When Kang Keqing didn't move a muscle, Zhu De said, 'So, I'll say it again. Will you marry me?' Kang Keqing was glued to the bench, speechless. After several minutes Zhu De concluded the one-sided negotiations with: 'So it looks like that's a yes, then.'[9]

Wu Ruolan had been captured some time before this and while no-one knew whether she was alive or dead, messages had no doubt filtered through that she was being tortured, leaving little hope that she would come out alive. One of the other young women put it to Kang Keqing that the loss of Wu Ruolan had been a blow to Zhu De and that Kang Keqing could comfort him and help him get on with his work by becoming his wife. This would not have shocked Kang Keqing. While women of the gentry were expected to guard their widowhood, peasant women had greater freedom to remarry, and widowed men traditionally remarried, frequently after what Westerners would consider an indecently short period of mourning. Also, the needs, sexual or otherwise, of leaders such as Zhu De and Mao were automatically placed above those of their followers. Still, Kang Keqing said that her first reaction was outright rejection of the idea. She was not quite seventeen, Zhu De was forty-three; she was an illiterate peasant, he was her commanding officer, admired and respected by everybody, including herself, and she was anxious about the vast discrepancy in age, experience and education between them. Finally, however, unable to raise a valid objection, she bowed to the inevitable and became Zhu De's bedmate. Compared with He Zizhen's story of how she and Mao became lovers, this account is probably close to the truth.

The enduring marriage of Zhu De and Kang Keqing has always been considered a comradely and loving union of exemplary revolutionaries, in much the same way as was the marriage of Zhou Enlai and Deng Yingchao. It did not start off as a love match, however, as Kang Keqing revealed to Helen Foster Snow: 'I didn't fall in love with Chu Tê in the romantic manner when I first met him, though I liked him very much because he lived as a common soldier and did the same work. Of course, everybody loved Chu Tê as a revolutionary leader. We have always been the best of comrades—and I must admit that, after a transition period, I probably did fall in love with him.' Helen Foster Snow noted with obvious delight the comradeship Kang Keqing and Zhu De shared, recording this description of them at lunch one day:

She socked the Commander-in-Chief playfully on the arm, and he seemed to like it enormously as he beamed at his young prodigy. She never refers to him as her husband, but as 'Comrade' in a sort of third-person tone of voice. I beamed at them both and thought what a marvelous pair they were, and what attractive personalities they both happened to have. They were so honest and straightforward, so completely natural and unspoiled.[10]

In the same month as Kang Keqing married Zhu De, the Red Army moved off Jinggangshan to escape the KMT blockade. As a partisan organiser, and Zhu De's wife, she went with them, crawling along icy ridges and down ravines, and scrambling onto the lower slopes of Jinggangshan to slip through the cordon.

Over the next two years Kang Keqing followed the Red Army through Jiangxi, Fujian and Hunan as they fought running battles with the KMT, building their numbers from 2000 to 20 000 and their armaments to 10 000 rifles and various cannon and mortars—her only regret was that they had been unable to capture an aeroplane. She carried a gun, she told Helen Foster Snow several times, but did not fight: 'When we came down from Jinggangshan, I was one of the partisans. Sometimes I carried a gun but I did not fight in battle. I was doing propaganda work'; 'I always carried a gun and several times was ordered to prepare to fight with the Guard Regiment but I never actually engaged in battle. Nearly every day since I left Suich'uan in 1928 I had been in the middle of fighting, and had no fear of it whatever, although I had not myself participated in battle.'

After the Jiangxi soviet was established towards the end of 1931, Kang Keqing spent little time in the capital of Ruijin, 200 kilometres south-east of Jinggangshan. Her response was characteristically simple when Helen Foster Snow asked her about what was then described as the Women's Problem: 'I don't care much about the women's problem; I always work with men, not women. And I'm afraid I can't tell you about women's life in the Soviets, because I was never a part of it.'[11] Without realising it, Kang Keqing had noticed that women were not equal among the communists. Relegated as they were to the women's bureau, women were excluded from the main business of the party— making decisions and making war. Intent on learning to become a soldier, she must have used her *guanxi* as Zhu De's wife to be excused from working in the women's bureau, concentrating instead on propaganda work and partisan organising in the field. She also worked in the statistics department of the arms and munitions stores, and held what she described mysteriously as 'a very important and confidential job in the radio code department of the Revolutionary Military Council'. She was given impressive titles, including Director of the Headquarters Guard Regiment, Inspector of Communications, and Director of the Youth School, and she was accepted into the Communist Party in 1931.

As Director of the Youth School she was responsible for educating young soldiers in the theory upon which the communists based their bold claim for justice. Her remark to Helen Foster Snow on her grasp of communist theory shows considerable naivety, yet her obvious pride in her accomplishment is touching: 'I have read the *ABC of Leninism*, the *Principles of Leninism* and reports by Stalin and Dimitrov. I understand Marxism as far as I have yet studied it, and I am now working hard on theory.'

She said she taught herself to read and write from slogans, although it is more likely that other young women such as He Zizhen and Wu Zhonglian coached their illiterate comrades. Wu Zhonglian was a tall athletic young woman from southern Hunan who had followed Zhu De onto Jinggangshan as a partisan. She had attended a local girls' school and become politically active in her teens, joining the party in 1927. She was three years older than Kang Keqing, an enthusiastic propaganda worker, singer of revolutionary songs, and deadly accurate with a hand grenade. They became fast friends.[12] The two of them were transferred in 1932 to the Red Military Academy in Ruijin to provide six months' training for about 180 local peasant women of the Women Volunteers. As regimental commander Kang Keqing was responsible for teaching military skills and drill; as political instructor Wu Zhonglian taught politics and literacy (or 'culture'). At no other time did the Zhu–Mao Red Army attempt to form women into military units, and it would appear that this exercise was Zhu De's feeble attempt to follow the letter but not the spirit of the Central Committee's 1930 directive that partisans be incorporated into the Red Army.

Kang Keqing had not relinquished her dream to be a soldier, however, and in between training the Women Volunteers she audited the men's classes in military science. Again, it can only have been her *guanxi* with Zhu De that then resulted in her being allowed to enter the Red Military Academy as a full student, where she 'turned out to be an excellent student and made a great advance in military as well as political knowledge. I was second in my class.' Kang Keqing mentions that she and a middle-school student were the first girl-cadets to study there but that the girl was expelled for taking the wrong political stance. Yet, despite her good work and her military aptitude, Kang Keqing did not come out of the academy a soldier; she was ordered to the rear on inspection work before she graduated. It was during one of these inspection tours of fortifications and communication trenches built by local guerrillas and partisans that she experienced her 'happy day', when she led troops in battle and earned her nickname 'the Girl Commander'. No good reason was given for her untimely withdrawal from the academy, Kang Keqing did not link it to the fact that she was a woman, and one can only surmise that allowing her to enrol in the first place was simple appeasement.

It was glorious autumn weather with moonlight to show the way the night Kang Keqing walked with Zhu De out of Yudu, just west of Ruijin. The first units were already three days ahead by the time they clattered over a wooden pontoon, which the light from hundreds of red paper lanterns along the banks transformed into a rippling bridge of gold in the shallow waters of the Yu River. Marshalls halted the long line of soldiers still waiting on the eastern bank to let Zhu De and Kang Keqing pass.

The Long March 'was as easy for me as taking a stroll every day', Kang Keqing told Helen Foster Snow in 1937. She had not been surprised at the order to move out, aware for some time that the Jiangxi soviet could no longer withstand Generalissimo Chiang Kai-shek's encirclement and extermination campaigns. She set out as part of the 10 000-strong field operations column and was in constant touch with Zhu De, whom she saw every day. She was twenty-three years old, sturdy, strong and in her element, a soldier in everything but name. 'Usually I walked with the others and carried my own belongings, sometimes helping those who were weaker. I usually carried three or four rifles. I did this in order to encourage the others, because the wife of the commander in chief should always be a model for others to follow in these matters.'

The leading regiments travelled at great speed, breaking through the first three rings of fortifications with little opposition, and within a month Kang Keqing had walked 300 kilometres from the Jiangxi soviet. One night she came upon a railroad, her first. In the darkness she crouched low to the ground, reaching out to stroke the icy-cold metal of the track. She ran her hand over the rough wooden sleepers and wondered how a train would move along those two slim iron rails. Cushioned as she was on all sides by the Red Army, only the constant crack of rifle fire ahead and behind gave her any indication of distant danger.

She realised five weeks out that they were in trouble when she heard that the vanguard had broken through the last ring of fortifications at the Xiang River while the baggage train was falling further behind each day and would need another four days to reach the river. Without the baggage train, the Red Army could have marched swiftly on and escaped the tens of thousands of enemy troops belatedly massing at the river. But the army stayed and defended the river crossing for ten days, until the field operations column and the Central Committee and the Convalescent Company got across.

She calculated that of the 86 000 Red Army men who set out from Jiangxi, just over 30 000 crossed the Xiang alive. Of this massive loss of life at the Xiang River Kang Keqing had little to say in her later years except to blame it on the bungling of the current leaders, Bo Gu and the German Otto Braun. While it is difficult to understand such apparent callousness at losing a good half of your army, the magnitude of the casualties the communists suffered over the years must have demanded some such psychological adjustment. Helen Foster Snow remarked on this: 'I have heard it said that Chinese women make the best revolutionaries of all because they do not go to pieces under the strain as Western women do. It often seemed to me that this was because they had a curious lack of feeling and callousness to the sight of suffering.'[13] However, these women's public utterances must to a considerable degree have been constrained by the dictates of party discipline, which did not tolerate individual dissent from what had been agreed upon as the necessary means for achieving their admirable ends.

With enemy soldiers to the north, the south and behind them, the 1st Front Red Army disappeared into the forests of the Yuecheng Mountains straddling the Hunan–Guangxi border. The Miao and Yao ethnic minorities people who lived in these mountains were suspicious of Chinese intruders and fearful of Chinese soldiers. Many of them understood Chinese, however, and the communists convinced them they were only passing through and needed their help to negotiate the mountains.

Anxious for the Red Army to regain speed, Zhu De ordered all personal possessions be discarded so that the army could travel light. Never one to do anything by half, Kang Keqing bundled up her mosquito net, eiderdown quilt and extra clothing and handed them in a conciliatory gesture to the wary Yuecheng villagers. Head and shoulders protected from the ceaseless rain by her round southerners' hat of oiled paper sandwiched between layers of thin bamboo, she followed the local guides on to the ancient winding goat-paths of Laoshan. Many of the soldiers were barefoot, their two pairs of straw sandals long since worn through, and the rocks were sharp under their feet. They marched at night to gain time but their flaming torches gave out little light after a few hours and were useless on nights so misty the marchers could hardly see a hand in front of their face. Sudden wild storms blew exhausted men off the mountain. Others slipped in the dark and tumbled into black nothingness.

Off Laoshan and two months out from Jiangxi the leaders agreed to abandon their attempt to reach northern Hunan, deciding instead to remain in the far south-west and head due west into Guizhou where, the saying goes, 'not three days are fine; not three *li* are flat; not three coins in anyone's pocket'. Guizhou is part of the region known as China's green jewel, covering the three provinces of Guizhou, Yunnan and Sichuan. It is a place of grey mountains where the people, mostly ethnic minorities, had to sell every last grain of rice from their fields to pay rent and interest to the landlords. Sucked empty, they lived on corn, cabbage and opium and called themselves 'dried people' (*ganren*).[14] At that time Guizhou was opium country, where even the poor were able to sweet-dream away the hell of their lives.

Under cover of snow and sleety rain the Red Army moved quickly across the relatively flat eastern half of Guizhou, covering over 300 kilometres in less than three weeks. Where before they might have slept out in the open, rain and cold drove them to seek shelter in villagers' huts and spare sheds or in commandeered mansions. Often the men would use as beds the long wooden panels that were erected as night-shutters on shopfronts or houses, sliding the panels from their frames at night and carefully replacing them in the morning before setting off again. Considerate acts such as this were an integral part of the Red Army's code of conduct, which the mainly illiterate Red Army soldiers learnt by heart as the 'Eight Points for Attention', and sang as a marching chant:

1. Replace all doors when you leave a house;
2. Return and roll up the straw matting on which you sleep;
3. Be courteous and polite to the people and help them when you can;
4. Return all borrowed articles;
5. Replace all damaged articles;
6. Be honest in all transactions with the peasants;
7. Pay for all articles purchased;
8. Be sanitary, and, especially, establish latrines a safe distance from people's houses.[15]

Marching songs served an important political purpose in the Red Army, reinforcing the basic theory in which all young peasant recruits were indoctrinated by political workers such as Kang Keqing during recruiting and education procedures. Zhu De wrote down many of these songs in notebooks which he later showed to Agnes Smedley. A typical example was 'Three Great Tasks', sung to a well-known folk melody:

Our Red Army has three great tasks:
To destroy imperialism and the feudal forces,
To carry out the agrarian revolution,
To establish the people's sovereignty.
To each according to his needs,
From each according to his ability.
Our speech to the people must be friendly.

Spread Red Army principles among the masses.
Enlarge its political influence.
To be a model Red Army man,
Take not one needle or strand of thread
From a worker or peasant.[16]

By the end of the first week in January 1935 the Red Army had taken the large town of Zunyi where the leaders rested for twelve days. Kang Keqing was assigned to a team recruiting soldiers for the army and to the work of confiscating grain, valuables and cash from landlords. She was given rooms with Zhu De in a splendid two-storey mansion, where Zhou Enlai and his wife Deng Yingchao also stayed, while Mao ensconsed himself in a separate building to concentrate on bending the will of the Central Committee to his purposes.

While the Red Army was catching its breath and Mao was being restored to the leadership of the party, KMT and warlord armies surrounded them. Anticipating Mao's decision to head north, Generalissimo Chiang Kai-shek ordered all Yangtze River ferries withdrawn to the northern bank and despatched troops to guard every crossing of the Yangtze. He then ordered KMT and warlord armies to seal off the province of Guizhou to the north, east, south and west, determined to crush the Red Army once and for all.

For nearly three months Mao tried to fight his way out of Guizhou and across the Yangtze. As winter gave way to spring the communists marched for days and nights at a stretch, lurching about the muddy countryside as if they were clinging to the tail of a bad-tempered dragon. They paid good lives to cross rivers only to be ordered to turn back when they reached the other side. They forged north, split up into separate columns and veered off in several directions then regrouped in a few days' time. Kang Keqing was never involved directly in the almost ceaseless fighting, but during one of the army's attempts to break through the enemy to the Yangtze in late January she was caught in crossfire and had to dive for cover. She does not mention this incident in her reminiscences, apparently because this particular battle was a costly debacle for the Red Army for which only Mao, Zhu De and Zhou Enlai could be blamed, since they were by that stage in full command, and which the official version of the Long March appears to have therefore consigned to oblivion.[17]

Weariness numbed the marchers, empty bellies rumbled but neither the silver dollars the porters carried in solid trunks nor the opium they confiscated could buy what the Guizhou country-side couldn't provide: food. The peasants of the Red Army were farmers, not hunters, and it never occurred to them to hunt for live food in Guizhou, where foxes, squirrels, leopards and wolves roamed the mountains. Kang Keqing walked steadily through the snow and rain, turning back at the end of each day's march to round up stragglers before they were picked off by snipers. One night she stumbled into camp well after dark, supporting a limping soldier and holding high a pine-bough torch which locally hired porters had told her helped scare off stray tigers.

Generalissimo Chiang Kai-shek had taken up residence in the provincial capital of Guiyang in March to oversee the extermination of the main Red Army and, with it, the Central Committee of the Chinese Communist Party. In the second ten-day period of April, shock communist troops under Commander Lin Biao wheeled purposefully towards Guiyang. Alarmed at the speed of this unexpected attack on the capital, the Generalissimo called in for his own protection the warlord army that had been guarding the route west across the majestic Wumeng Mountains into the province of Yunnan. The Red Army's feint worked. With the obstructing troops now removed, the communists marched briskly around Guiyang and slipped across the border into Yunnan.

Tucked away at the foot of the Tibetan mountains in the far south-west, Yunnan was the Siberia of China, the province where disgraced and out-of-favour officials had traditionally been sent. If the communists were to stay there, the warlord controlling Yunnan would quickly wipe them out. Their other options were to keep marching to either Burma or Tibet. It was clear that their only hope of reaching north China and survival lay in Tibet, but first they had to get to the headwaters of the Yangtze River before the Generalissimo had time to swing his troops that far west. The communists turned north and broke into a run.

The wild and trackless north-west they were heading for, only sparsely inhabited and then by ethnic minority tribes, was the

land of the ancient mystical being Xiwangmu (Female Ruler of
the West). In Chinese cosmology and literature Xiwangmu,
having herself attained the Dao (old spelling: Tao, usually translated as 'the Way'), had the power to confer immortality, and
she played a significant role in maintaining the rhythms of the
cosmos. She gave the peaches of immortality to the legendary
Yellow Emperor, and her divine prestige was later invaluable to
countless female Daoist divinities who claimed kinship as her
daughters. The Chinese instinct for neat parallels located
Xiwangmu in the paradise of the west, on the edge of the flowing
sands near the fairyland of Mount Kunlun (northern Tibet), to
balance the paradise of the east, located somewhere off the
north-east coast of China.[18]

Virtually mapless since the Xiang River catastrophe, the Red
Army had relied on old small-scale maps that gave them only a
general idea of where they might be. In a magic turn of events
a vehicle carrying thousands of new and detailed maps fell into
their hands during a skirmish with the enemy in Yunnan. 'Truly
the doings of ghosts and gods!' was Zhou Enlai's stunned reaction. 'Chiang Kai-shek must have known we needed these—he's
sent us charcoal in snowy weather.'

Food would have been infinitely more welcome to the rank
and file marchers than either charcoal or maps as they pushed
through the deep forests of this alien land. On one occasion they
were able to gorge on ham confiscated from wealthy packers, but
spring in Yunnan was little different from winter in Guizhou:
grain was simply not to be found for 25 000 visitors. They walked
on empty stomachs for days at a time, driven by the desperate
need to reach the Yangtze before their way was blocked yet again.

Kang Keqing's attachment to field operations meant that she
often walked in close proximity to Cai Chang. The most senior
of the women politically and in age (she was born in 1900), Cai
Chang was a fellow provincial of Mao and one of his oldest
friends. She had joined the Chinese Communist Party in Paris in
1923 at the age of twenty-three and Helen Foster Snow accurately dubbed her the 'Dean of Communist Women', calling her
'the leading woman Communist of China'. Cai Chang's beloved
brother and his wife Xiang Jingyu, the first head of the women's
bureau, had been executed by the KMT and others of her family

had been imprisoned. Given her high profile, Cai Chang's work as an underground agent in Shanghai and Hong Kong after the 1927 Communist–KMT split demanded enormous cool and courage. Her husband Li Fuchun was deputy director of the Red Army Political Dept, and she was one of the few women privy to high-level party discussions. This is Helen Foster Snow's description of Cai Chang, whose name she transcribed as Tsai Ch'ang, and whom she met in Yan'an in 1937:

> Tsai Ch'ang came to call on me as soon as I arrived in Yen-an. I was considerably surprised at the appearance of such a veteran revolutionary of thirty-seven. She is petite, dainty and delicate in appearance . . . extremely feminine, but perhaps this impression was much enhanced by the fact that she spoke French in a soft lisping accent. Her face is very unusual and must have been beautiful when she was younger, though now it carried lines of sad experience. It was triangular, with high cheekbones and a firm pointed chin. She has a charming smile, with strong, healthy teeth. In spite of her gentle, almost spiritually quiet manner, it was easy to perceive that Tsai Ch'ang was a woman of individual character and great determination. I liked her immediately.[19]

Cai Chang became a communist, she claimed, under the influence of her mother Ge Jianhao, who suffered throughout her life the handicap of bound feet. Ge Jianhao enrolled herself in school along with her three children when she was fifty years old, divorced her bully husband and on Christmas Day 1919 in her late fifties sailed with her daughter to France. Cai Chang worshipped her mother, Helen Foster Snow said, and 'brought a worn picture of her mother to show me, a picture carried as tenderly as a fetish all through the Long March. It showed a strong face full of resolution like Tsai Ch'ang's own.'

Cai Chang's resolve became a by-word among the communists. As with many tales about the early communists, the stories of her exploits may well be apocryphal but they serve to show the esteem in which she was widely held. In Jiangxi there was a saying: 'A woman who ploughs will be struck by lightning; even out of a clear blue sky she will be struck by lightning.' With all the young men joining the army it was counterproductive to have able-bodied women in the Jiangxi soviet thus avoiding the work of ploughing, so Cai Chang slipped off her shoes, rolled up her trousers and asked the old folk to teach her how to plough. Once seen to have survived ploughing unstruck by lightning, she was then able to wave the women into the fields to plough for the next plantings. She was said to have next turned her attention to logging, leading the women into the hills on timber-cutting and re-afforestation expeditions with similar success.

Now, pushing north through Yunnan Province, stomachs rumbling and weak with hunger, the women concluded that since they couldn't have real food they'd have to make other arrangements. It was probably Cai Chang who first suggested that they form a company: a manufacturer of spirit food. The sole function of this company, to be registered under the name of Braggarts Inc, was to organise mass meetings very much like the mass meetings the communists themselves habitually organised in the towns and villages they passed through, except that the meetings of this company were known as 'spiritual mass eatings'. Braggarts Inc was open for business during rest breaks and at night-camps. A typical agenda for a spiritual mass eating might begin with a comrade who had been abroad lecturing on the wonderful taste of French bread. Here Cai Chang would enthral the audience with exotic names of pastries pronounced enticingly in her lisping French. Next, a country cousin from Jiangxi would advertise the wonders of Jiangxi dishes, followed by a comrade from Sichuan eulogising the flavour of Sichuan food. The mass eating might be brought to a close with several Hunanese singing the praises of peerless Hunan food. Overall, the person who made everyone drool—the most accomplished braggart—was acknowledged as having made the greatest contribution on that particular day to Braggarts Inc.

Kang Keqing attended these mass eatings but she didn't seem to be up to bragging. She hadn't been abroad so she couldn't discuss foreign food, and coming from a poor household she knew very little of Jiangxi's famous dishes. Still, she appreciated the work of the others.[20]

In their race to get to the Golden Sands River (Jinshajiang) tributary of the Yangtze River before the Generalissimo's forces, the Red Army vanguard had only one thing to rely on: the almost superhuman speed at which they could travel through wild and unfamiliar territory. They tramped 300 kilometres in ten days, at one stage covering 140 kilometres in a phenomenal 24-hour sprint. The Generalissimo's order that all ferries be withdrawn to the north bank of the Yangtze River remained in force, but when the vanguard reached the Jiaopingdu crossing of the Golden Sands River at the end of April they found a single small boat flouting that order. The gods, it seemed, were again on their side, and with this one boat they conjured six more from the north bank. Kang Keqing crossed the Golden Sands River in the first days of May, the voices of the men waiting their turn floating over the water:

> Golden Sands waters fast and deep.
> Hand in hand, heart to heart,
> brothers and sisters united by class.
> A million enemies will never stop us.[21]

For nine days and nights without a break those seven small boats plied the Golden Sands River carrying the 20 000 troops that were left of the 1st Front Red Army across to Sichuan, China's westernmost province and Zhu De's native place. But they were not yet across the Yangtze; 500 kilometres north there remained another major tributary at which they could be stopped. Enemy planes were tracking and sometimes bombing them and they knew that KMT troops were moving parallel to them on the east. Scouts sent back messages that crowds of warlord soldiers were gathering up ahead. Pushing themselves almost beyond endurance, the communists clawed their way through dense undergrowth and clambered across gullies and gorges to emerge about fifteen days later on top of the sheer cliffs that formed the western bank of the Dadu River. They followed the river north.

Kang Keqing stayed close behind the vanguard unit as it wound its way along goat-tracks, or sometimes no track at all, above the raging torrent. Rain made the rocks slippery and from time to time she caught sight of enemy soldiers moving along the eastern bank keeping pace with them. Several times she had to wait while the engineers cobbled together footbridges over watercourses and narrow chasms, carving out a path for those coming behind. Still, she covered the 160 kilometres to Luding

Bridge in three days, and by the time she got there the bridge had been won.

Luding Bridge was a 200-year-old bridge of wooden planks suspended across 100 metres of whitewater by thirteen thick iron chains. The communist vanguard had reached the southern end of the bridge to find the planking removed and a KMT machine-gun nest trained on them from the northern end. In a sublime act of bravery, twenty-two of the army's shock troops crawled out along the iron chains under enemy fire, three of them falling to their death in the treacherous current 160 metres below. As the surviving communists swung closer the defenders of the bridge poured kerosene over the remaining planks and set them alight, only to see the young heroes burst through the flames like immortals.

Kang Keqing muttered to herself as she clutched the cold iron chains and stepped carefully across hastily laid planking swaying high above the swirling water: 'Look straight ahead, don't look down . . . and don't look to either side. Look straight ahead, don't look down . . . and don't look to either side. Look straight ahead, don't look down . . .'[22]

For some other women, the 160 kilometres along the cliffs to the Luding Bridge were the most difficult of the entire march, when even the singers among them lacked the energy to sing their spirits up. Li Jianzhen fell well behind when her animal handler, a boy who had been with her all the way from Ruijin, was badly wounded in the legs by sniper fire from the far bank. Unwilling to leave him and with no spare litters, she hoisted him onto her back, carrying him a considerable distance until he had lost so much blood that he began to pass out. She struggled on under his dead weight and finally came to a bridge where there was a shrine and some empty huts. Carefully, she placed him inside one of the huts, leaving a little food and some salt by his side, and putting a few silver dollars in his pocket.

Physically and emotionally exhausted, she plodded on alone and by first light had caught up with the wounded, animals and medicine chests belonging to her unit, stranded at Luding Bridge unable to cross. The planks laid across the iron chains had been adequate for able-bodied soldiers to stride across but they were spaced too far apart for stretcher-bearers and pole carriers to maintain their rhythm. The stretcher-bearers weren't able to keep in step which meant the wounded could bounce right out of the litters and off the bridge; the porters were also in danger of being jounced into the river by the heavy medicine chests swinging out of synch at each end of their poles. Terrified, most of the hired porters had fled.

When asked, bodyguards travelling with Mao carted some of the medicine chests and piggybacked some of the wounded across, but more equipment arrived in the meantime and the women were left to deal with the problem. They finally decided to tie each stretcher to the women's shoulders with their cloth puttees, one woman at each end, which left their hands free to hold on to the chains, and then with another woman in front and one behind they inched their way across the swaying bridge. Returning across the bridge, they strapped the medicine chests onto their backs and step by careful step made their way back across the bridge holding on to the chains. Then, one woman on each side, they helped the walking wounded over. Presumably their handlers managed to coax the pack animals onto and across the suspension bridge. With enormous relief the women immortalised their efforts in song:

> Ai–ya–lei—
> The Red Army took Luding Bridge,
> Gunfire licked the heavens, iron chains rocked.
> Feet planted on iron chains, unfazed,
> The women wrestled the medicine chest poles.[23]

The Red Army was now across the Yangtze River and safely in north China. With midsummer drawing on, their primary goal was to find the 4th Front Red Army and together push north-east before the early northern winter closed in. They sloshed through drenching rain unable to light cooking fires and eating little else but the wild chives that grew out of grey rock. They found it hard to imagine why Sichuan was reputed to be 'the land of abundance'. Rice was a thing of the past, corn and buckwheat the only grains they could buy from the few inhabitants. Unaccustomed to these harsher grains, the entire army suffered from diarrhoea and stomach disorders.

Zhu De led small field expeditions to identify the edible plants of this his native province and explained to the cooks how to prepare them, but the tail-enders were forced to sift in desperation through the harvest leftovers. All they found was the dry core of the seeds. It tasted like chewed wax and was difficult to swallow. Their stomachs growling with hunger the women took to gulping the seeds down whole so they wouldn't have to taste them. Cai Chang hunkered quietly at the edge of the group one day patiently chewing the seeds to a soft mush that was sweet enough to swallow. 'Don't swallow them whole,' she told the women. 'Chew them slowly, chew the sweet from out of the bitterness. They don't taste all that bad really—and they're sustenance, after all.'[24]

The first ten-day period in June found a thin and drawn Kang Keqing almost 6000 metres above sea level, surrounded by snow-capped peaks at the foot of the Snowy Mountains on the Sichuan–Tibet border. She was climbing onto the roof of the world. She set out strongly but once past the tree line had difficulty breathing, felt weak and giddy and couldn't swallow any food: she was suffering from altitude sickness. Her companion that day was singer–songwriter Li Bozhao. As a native of Sichuan Li Bozhao was rather more at home in the extremes of the high country, so she shouldered Kang Keqing's knapsack and guided her steadily up the rocky trail. When Kang Keqing's steps slowed, Li Bozhao urged her on. Still Kang Keqing's eyelids drooped and her step slowed, as even Li Bozhao started to flag. For the first time in her life Kang Keqing's strength was not up to the task. Her lungs were seizing up, her legs were buckling, it was too hard. She could not go on.

She tried to sit down. Li Bozhao grabbed her arm and held her upright while an animal handler clucked his mule close to. Kang Keqing grasped the docile animal's coarse tail and lurched forward as it stolidly resumed the climb. Her entire world view restricted to the mule's round rump and two large ears, she concentrated every ounce of her will into holding on to its tail and lifting one leaden foot after the other. It was late morning by the time the handler halted his mule at the top and stood in the whipping wind while Kang Keqing unfurled her cramped hands. Hardly daring to glance at the silent world of white below she allowed Li Bozhao to guide her. Obediently she sat down and, wind whistling in her ears, slid down the icy trail of those who had gone before. Many of the men were so exhausted from the climb they slid right off the mountain to their death.

When she reached the snowline Kang Keqing finally looked up. Behind her she saw the mules treading their slow safe way down a steep trail. Ahead, between her and Zhang Guotao's 4th Front Red Army, she saw only silent snow-covered peaks.

Kang Keqing crossed the Snowy Mountains twice more during the year she spent with the 4th Front Red Army, after she and Zhu De were assigned to the Left Column in August 1935. Her later account of that year, however, is rather open to question.

Events and relationships within Zhang Guotao's 4th Front Army from the time he disobeyed the party directive and turned back from the Grass Lands are dogged with ambiguity. Although Zhu De refused to discuss that period of his life, Agnes Smedley claimed that Zhang had taken Zhu De prisoner. Edgar Snow mentioned nothing of this, simply saying of the dramatic parting of the ways between Mao and Zhang, when Mao broke camp at 2 am and slipped away to march north, that: 'There was disagreement about the correct course to pursue.'[25] While Kang Keqing did not say Zhu De was taken prisoner, she insisted that he marched south with Zhang under protest and that at various times they were both kept under guard and treated badly. Historians, however, deny that Zhang restrained Zhu De's movements in any way during that year, and have found no hard evidence to support Mao's suspicion that Zhang intended to stage a military coup—although they concede that Zhang may well have been contemplating such a course of action.[26]

Zhang Guotao challenged Mao's power over the party in 1935 when he refused to march north. After he relented and rejoined Mao in Yan'an he was placed on trial for 'violation of Red Army and party principles and policies'.[27] In April 1938 he defected from the communists and joined the KMT. Mao, on the other hand, led the communists to victory over the KMT, from the Long March right through to 1949 and beyond. He also had a good memory for anyone who had crossed him. Little wonder those who had had the misfortune to be associated in any way with Zhang Guotao were anxious to let it be known that they had recognised all along his traitorous tendencies and that they themselves had simply been victims of circumstance. Kang Keqing took this opportunity in her reminiscences, dictated when she was in her mid-seventies, starting her account with Zhu De's dramatic refusal to renounce his allegiance to Mao:

> Everybody knows Zhu–Mao, Zhu–Mao can't be separated. Even if you cut me in two you couldn't break Zhu–Mao apart, and you certainly can't force Zhu to oppose Mao. The party and the military council commissioned me to lead the Left Column north. Since you are ignoring that order and insisting on going south, I must go with you wherever you go; but I wish to follow party orders and lead the Left Column north.[28]

In Zhang Guotao's version of the aftermath of the split, however, Zhu De simply looked 'unhappy' and 'depressed', constantly expressing the hope that 'the comrades would turn a big problem into a small problem and try to patch up the breach' and that 'some room will be left for future negotiations'.[29] Zhang Guotao hardly mentioned Zhu De during this period, indicating by this that he considered Zhu De to be of little consequence and had sidelined him.

Kang Keqing claimed that during that year she was not allowed the unusual privilege she had experienced until then of working continuously by her husband's side, and this may have coloured her perception of how she was treated. To begin with, she said, she acted as a conduit between Zhu De and their comrades from the 1st Front Red Army, asking Wu Zhonglian, her friend from Jinggangshan, to discreetly pass on reassuring messages that everything was under control and there was no need to consider revolt against Zhang. Small indignities were visited on Zhu De: he was excluded from meals and discussions with the other leaders, access to daily despatches was made difficult. His favourite horse was slaughtered for food. Then rumours circulated that Kang Keqing was spying for Zhu De so she was transferred to work in the women's bureau, and a female 'companion' was assigned to keep her under surveillance. She worked in the women's bureau for an unspecified period, probably three or four months, doing local work (meetings, propaganda) and 'studying' (practising and improving her reading and writing skills) as they walked south, back across the Snowy Mountains and into Tibet. Her colleagues included Zhang Qinqiu (wife of

Zhang Guotao's right-hand man), Wang Quanyuan and Wu Fulian, all of whom were later caught up in the ill-fated expedition to the north-west. Soon Kang Keqing was forbidden to have any contact with Zhu De, she said.

At some stage she was diagnosed as having paratyphoid fever, and she was carried on a stretcher to the foot of the Snowy Mountains as they began their retreat to Tibet after several crushing military defeats. She recalled that the crossing of the mountains was even more of a nightmare for her than the first time; she was very weak but couldn't be carried, and several times her hands had to be tied to the tail of a horse to pull her along, with somebody pushing her from behind. By the time they had negotiated the mountains and she was allowed to go back to be with Zhu De, she was thin and weak. She recuperated from her illness over the months they spent in Tibet and by summer felt she was in the same good health and as fit as she had been at the start of the Long March.

Kang Keqing's recollection fifty years on of her illness is in sharp contrast to Helen Foster Snow's description of her as 'the only woman I met in the veteran Communist ranks who was in glowing health'. The difficult time she said she had with the 4th Front Army is also at variance with what she told Helen Foster Snow in 1937 of her Long March experience:

> I think the most difficult spot we found was in Tsok'êchi, in Szechuan, or later at Moerhkai, where we could get no food. We ate barley, grass, and the bark of trees . . .
>
> I crossed the Grasslands twice. The first time was when Mao Tsê-tung's army crossed the Grasslands successfully but we did not. We tried to cross in two routes, but our route was blocked by a flooded river in the middle of the Grasslands called the 'Huang Ho'—this was as much our 'sorrow' as the big Yellow River is 'China's Sorrow.' We had to go back and spend the winter in Tibet, where we lived on horse meat, yak meat, mutton, and beef. It was there that Chu Tê got his big Sikang dog which barks at anybody who does not wear a red-starred cap.[30]

No indication of rifts or difficulties in this simple account of a military bivouac, although on that particular issue the communists no doubt felt it politic to close ranks against the foreigners, whom they wanted to use for their own public relations purposes and not to air internal divisions.

Zhang Guotao did not mention Kang Keqing in his autobiography, but he wrote of his 'fond memories' of a 'Cultural Recreation' project that was set up in Luohe. The singer-songwriter Li Bozhao, who had been stranded with the 4th Front Army at the time of the split with Mao, was in charge of this project, whose performances of short plays, dances and songs Zhang Guotao said he and Zhu De frequently attended.[31]

After the armies of He Long and Xiao Ke joined the 4th Front Army in Tibet, Kang Keqing walked north again with them. She often walked in the company of Wang Quanyuan, but they were separated when the Women's Vanguard Regiment followed part of the 4th Front Red Army across the Yellow River in September 1936. From the Yellow River crossing, Kang Keqing marched north-east and at the end of November, just over two years since she had left Jiangxi, she finally took off her knapsack in the settlement of Bao'an, where the communists had been living in derelict temples, two-roomed caves and makeshift huts for ten months. With a semi-permanent home and plans in place to fight the Japanese, Kang Keqing trusted it would not be long before she became a fully fledged soldier.

PART II
THE BATTLE FOR CHINA
1937–1949

PART II PROLOGUE

The communists' immediate goal in marching out of Jiangxi in 1934 had been to escape destruction at the hands of the KMT. What they achieved through this retreat, however, was not only their survival, but increasing support from the Chinese people. That they had survived the ordeal of the Long March lent an almost sacred aura to the communists' cause. That they had reached north China despite constant harassment from the KMT and regional warlords and were preparing to fight the Japanese transformed them into a symbol of Chinese resistance. No-one benefited more from the Long March than Mao, whose many disastrous errors of judgment in terms of lives lost, during battles as well as because of the sometimes unnecessarily difficult route he chose, faded into oblivion as his control of the party increased. It has been suggested that the later deification, or cult, of Mao had its genesis in the Long March, since he was 'the prophet who had led the survivors through the wilderness'.[1]

And none gained more from Japan's attempt to colonise China than the communists, whose well-publicised stand against the Japanese ensured their 'sudden return to life from the brink of death'.[2] Japan was an unwelcome and increasingly ominous military presence in China from the 1920s, and by the early 1930s Manchuria and large areas of north China were completely under Japanese control. Intent on first resolving his domestic problems by exterminating the Chinese communists, Generalissimo Chiang Kai-shek offered little resistance and effectively abandoned north and east China to the Japanese, a strategy incomprehensible to most Chinese. Frustrated at the Generalissimo's apparent lack of patriotism one of his own officers, the 'Young Marshal' Zhang Xueliang, took the extraordinary step of kidnapping him in the city of Xi'an just before dawn on 12 December 1936. Held captive for thirteen days, the Generalissimo agreed to the Young Marshal's plea to turn the guns of the KMT on the Japanese instead of on their fellow Chinese. This bizarre affair, known as the Xi'an Incident, resulted in a temporary halt in KMT–Communist hostilities. All political prisoners were immediately released and the two sides agreed to form a united front against the Japanese.

Then, one night in July 1937, a lone Japanese soldier visited a brothel in a tiny town near the Lugouqiao, better known to Westerners as the Marco Polo Bridge, on the southern outskirts of Beijing (then called Peiping). Japanese authorities complained that the soldier had been kidnapped, claiming that the normal practice of Japanese soldiers was to visit brothels en masse. In retaliation for this perceived offence, the Japanese Army attacked the town on 7 July then marched on Peiping. This Marco Polo Bridge Incident was a clearly contrived act of war by Japan and marked the beginning of the Sino–Japanese War. It is also considered by many historians to have been the opening gambit of World War II. Having occupied Peiping, the Japanese Army moved on to take the coastal city of Tientsin (now spelt Tianjin). When Japan then attacked Shanghai in August the United States ordered the evacuation from China of all American women and children. By 1938 Japan occupied much of northern and eastern China and had set up a puppet government in Peiping and later in Nanking (now spelt Nanjing). It then announced its plan to create a pan–Asian New Order, which was another way of announcing that Japan was finally preparing to usurp China's traditional position as overlord of Asia.

While the union of the KMT and the communists eventually agreed to by Generalissimo Chiang Kai-shek was more form than substance, both sides gained from it. For the anti-communist Generalissimo it brought immediate financial and military aid from Russia, which wanted to relieve western Russia of the pressure of Japanese attack by strengthening China. 'Trading space for time' the Generalissimo withdrew to the high plateau of Sichuan Province in western China. He established himself in the city of Chungking (now spelt Chongqing) where waters from the Grass Lands and the Great Snowy Mountains of Tibet pour into the Yangtze before it plunges through the Three Gorges. He stationed some of his well-equipped troops in the east to try to stem the Japanese advance but held his best soldiers and aeroplanes in reserve against the day he could unleash them on the Chinese communists once the Japanese were defeated. In the meantime, he quietly ordered a blockade on all supplies to the communists in the north-west.

The communists for their part gained from the united front the freedom to mobilise, arm and train as many peasants as they were able. They concentrated in this period on politicising and activating the masses, initiating agrarian self-sufficiency programs and organising vast border regions into 'liberated areas' directly under their control. Among the party faithful Mao Zedong clearly stated the communists' priorities: 'Our fixed policy should be 70 per cent expansion, 20 per cent dealing with the KMT, and 10 per cent resisting Japan.'[3]

The mass of the Chinese people began to trust in the communists, rather than the KMT, as the communists proved themselves heroes in the war against the Japanese. To a world preoccupied with the prospect of a second European war and wholly dependent on news reports issued by the Generalissimo, however, the communists holed up in the loess caves of Yan'an were no more than Red bandits. In the late 1930s several foreign journalists made their way to north-western China in search of the *real* story, and from the pens of the three American journalists Edgar Snow, Helen Foster Snow and Agnes Smedley flowed first-hand reports and stories that transformed the world's perception of the Chinese communists, putting very human faces to the names of Mao Zedong, Zhu De and Zhou Enlai.[4]

The reports of these journalists may have seemed biased—the KMT were decadent, uncaring and exploitative of the common people, they wrote, while the communists were honest, sturdy and genuine in their concern for China's future. However, the fact remained that the KMT did nothing to rescue the people from the abyss of their daily lives. The Generalissimo's obsession with wiping out the communists before resisting the Japanese was denounced by many intellectuals as traitorous, and it was reported that KMT soldiers were so brutally treated they had to be roped together to be led into battle. His politics were a rehash of nineteenth-century efforts at modernisation, and a thinly disguised return to traditional values: oppose imperialism, revive the Confucian social order that subordinates the individual to the state, and establish industry on a large scale for national self-defence. His administration in Chungking was corrupt and the black market flourished. His economic policy brought on galloping inflation and a plummeting standard of living to the extent that by the time Japan had been defeated in 1945 one American dollar was worth 100 000 *yuan*. When, two years later, a bowl of rice cost 30 000 *yuan* and 'in restaurants if one sat down, one paid first, for often the meal would have gone up ten or twenty per cent in price by the time it was ended',[5] the KMT Government had completely lost the trust of the people.

In stark contrast, the communists showed themselves to be as good as their word. They stood their ground against the Japanese in the north. They set up workable administrative systems, paying fair rewards to the people for labour and just prices for all transactions. They abolished class distinctions, and male and female communist officials worked side by side with the people on an equal footing. The people began to believe the communist rhetoric that the Communist Party and the people were one and the same, their single common aim to free the Chinese people from oppressive tradition. When the United States withdrew from China in 1946 after the defeat of Japan, Generalissimo Chiang Kai-shek found to his dismay that American tanks, trucks and aeroplanes and American-trained troops were no match for an inspired peasant army marching under Mao Zedong's red flag of communism. The Chinese countryside rapidly turned Red and in 1949 one after another the major cities fell to the communists: Peiping and Tientsin in January, Nanking in April, Shanghai in May, Canton in October, Chungking in November. Mao proclaimed the People's Republic of China on 1 October 1949 and Generalissimo Chiang Kai-shek withdrew with his followers to the island of Taiwan across the Taiwan Strait.

The communists remained in Yan'an for ten years after the Long March and lived a spartan life that has passed into legend as joyful and egalitarian—the famous 'Yan'an Spirit'. During this time Mao concentrated on developing a theoretical framework for what came to be known as Maoism, or Mao Zedong Thought. An important aspect of this were the techniques of 'thought reform' and 'ideological remoulding' that became characteristic of Chinese communism.[6] For their first eight years in Yan'an the communists gave lip service to a united front with the KMT against Japan. The four years after the end of World War II were devoted to civil war. He Zizhen cracked under the strain of being Mao Zedong's wife; Wang Quanyuan was left to make her own way home; and Kang Keqing went to war, as she had always wanted.

4

COMMUNICATION
BREAKDOWN

He Zizhen fell pregnant in January 1936 as soon as the communists settled into the abandoned temples and ancient cave dwellings of dusty Bao'an. For the rest of the winter and into spring she and Mao lived a quiet life. He Zizhen revelled in the luxury of simply staying in one place, cooking meals in their cosy two-roomed cave while Mao continued his largely nocturnal life of reading and planning, rarely going to bed before two in the morning. No-one paid much attention to their occasional arguments, putting her short temper down to the aches and pains of the shrapnel still buried in her body. Although it was generally not discussed, many considered these injuries a small price to pay for being alive when tens of thousands of comrades suffering from similar wounds, or from exhaustion and deprivation, had died or been forced to drop out of the Long March.

One hot midsummer afternoon in June 1936 the American journalist Edgar Snow led his emaciated 'languishing nag' through the narrow pass into Bao'an. Snow was intent on breaking the headline story of China in the mid 1930s: to discover who and what were the Chinese communists and be the first foreign journalist to interview Mao Zedong, whose inspired leadership had led the Red Army on 'the historic Long March of 6,000 miles, in which they crossed twelve provinces of China, broke through thousands of Kuomintang troops, and triumphantly emerged at last into a powerful new base in the North-west'.[1] While the West knew little about Mao, the people of China had

110

begun to turn to him to lead the fight against the Japanese invasion of northern China.

The urbane Edgar Snow was flippant about the dangers of his week-long trip from Peiping, during which he had skirted the Japanese war zone and negotiated a hostile KMT blockade of the communist base area. With a tip of his hat to Mark Twain he quipped that 'the reports later published of my death—"killed by bandits"—were exaggerated'.[2] However, about his historic interview with Mao, whom he considered to be the most influential communist in China, he was deadly serious. He described 'the Red leader' thus:

> a gaunt, rather Lincolnesque figure, above average height for a Chinese, somewhat stooped, with a head of thick black hair grown very long, and with large, searching eyes, a high-bridged nose and prominent cheekbones. My fleeting impression was of an intellectual face of great shrewdness, but I had no opportunity to verify this for several days. Next time I saw him, Mao was walking hatless along the street at dusk, talking with two young peasants, and gesticulating earnestly. I did not recognize him until he was pointed out to me.[3]

Edgar Snow found Mao to be 'a very interesting and complex man', and went on to describe his character:

> He appears to be quite free from symptoms of megalomania, but he has a deep sense of personal dignity, and something about him suggests a power of ruthless decision when he deems it necessary. I never saw him angry, but I heard from others that on occasions he has been roused to an intense and withering fury. At such times his command of irony and invective is said to be classic and lethal.

Snow all but ignored He Zizhen, whom he usually referred to as Mrs Mao. To him she was a pregnant presence—'Mrs. Mao was in an adjoining room making compote from wild peaches purchased that day from a fruit merchant'—who listened raptly by candlelight to 'the Chairman' as he sat, long legs crossed, at the little table she had neatly covered with a cloth of red felt, telling the story of his life. Snow described her as a former school teacher, but then he was not always right; he also described Mao as 'a monogamist if nothing else'.[4] Perhaps He Zizhen was antagonistic to foreigners; perhaps as the Chairman's wife she was quietly declared off-limits to journalists; perhaps she was simply invisible in the shadow of the 'military and political strategist of considerable genius' Snow considered her husband to be. Whatever the reason, He Zizhen was silent and apparently unknowable. It seems clear that, by the end of the Long March, He Zizhen the revolutionary no longer existed, having been replaced by Madame Mao Zedong, who fussed over her husband and bore his children. Edgar Snow ignored her in Bao'an; in Yan'an Agnes Smedley also ignored her, but to her peril, while Helen Foster Snow was kindly dismissive of her.

In mid-October 1936 Edgar Snow departed from the 'hills like great castles, like rows of mammoth, nicely rounded scones, like ranges torn by some giant hand, leaving behind the imprint of angry fingers. Fantastic, incredible, and sometimes frightening shapes, a world configurated by a mad god—and sometimes a world also of strange surrealist beauty.'[5] Just before Snow quit Bao'an with his precious biography of Mao, He Zizhen produced a healthy baby girl, whom she called Jiaojiao. He Zizhen had just turned twenty-six and this was her fifth child, her third daughter: there appeared to be no reason she would not be able at last to keep this baby.

In that winter of 1936–37 water shortages and lack of space in Bao'an drove the communists to move house. They walked 50 kilometres to Yan'an in high spirits, the KMT having ceased their air-raids after the Xi'an Incident that saw Generalissimo Chiang Kai-shek kidnapped in December and a KMT–Communist united front declared.

Yan'an was a small walled town of nearly one thousand people that nestled in a hollow in the soft loess hills where three river valleys joined. It was an ancient settlement with one main street lined with small shops. 'At one end of the street was a large abandoned Catholic church and at the other a magnificent gate dating from the Song dynasty (954–1268 AD). Perched high on a mountain overlooking the citadel was an eighth-century Buddhist pagoda.'[6] Outside the city walls were what Otto Braun described as 'hundreds of really decent-looking houses and farms', some quite large and beautiful, which the communists promptly occupied until persistent Japanese bombing raids later in the year forced them to move further away from the city.

He Zizhen was exempted from work because of her shrapnel wounds and new-born baby but there were mutterings about privilege and her willing acceptance of this special treatment.[7] So in January she put three-month-old Jiaojiao in the newly established creche and enrolled at Red University, term one, senior class. She was not up to the ten-hour days at university, however, still thin and weak from the privations of the Long March and obviously under some emotional strain. Finally, she fainted one morning in the toilet block and was carried home. She stopped going to class. She and Mao continued to argue.

In January 1937 the second American journalist arrived in Yan'an from Xi'an, where she had reported to the world on the kidnapping the previous month of Generalissimo Chiang Kai-shek. Agnes Smedley's arrival in the insular community of Yan'an turned He Zizhen's life upside down. She was followed four months later by Helen Foster Snow, Edgar's wife. The two American women did not get on. Agnes Smedley thought that Helen Foster Snow was 'politically naive, intellectually superficial, and vain about her looks. [Helen Foster Snow] considered Smedley a psychotic prima donna of the left, and a shrill one at that.'[8] The following description of Agnes Smedley is taken from Helen Foster Snow's cutting, at times patronising but often amusing, commentary of that period in Yan'an.[9]

Agnes Smedley was an abrasive woman who had a 'special charm, even wit and humour' that escaped most people. In her forties, she looked at times 'like Bette Davis in her queen of England roles', with flashing blue eyes and a temper to match. The depression she was suffering in the summer of 1937 was put down to back pain caused by a fall from a horse in Yan'an, but her 'psychiatric difficulties' were of a more enduring nature. By the time Helen Foster Snow arrived in May, she found Agnes Smedley no longer on speaking terms with the other two foreigners in Yan'an—grumpy Otto Braun and the 'normal, charming' American doctor George Hatem—both of whom said Smedley 'had "told lies" about them'. Her black moods stretched even Helen Foster Snow's goodwill to the limit: 'Miss Smedley made a Christian out of me during the summer,' she wrote in

her ironic fashion, 'there was no other way to get along with her.'
Smedley's only friends in Yan'an seem to have been the contro-
versial female author Ding Ling and Kang Keqing's husband, Zhu
De, with whom some say she became infatuated.

Agnes Smedley's partiality towards Zhu De was in striking
contrast to her dislike of Mao, as Helen Foster Snow later wrote:
'Agnes Smedley told me she thought Mao sinister and feminine,
and hated him on first sight.' Be that as it may, Agnes Smedley
saw a great deal of Mao during her nine months in Yan'an. Soon
after she arrived, she decided to hold Western dance classes at
which she played American phonograph records and taught the
male leaders square dancing and the foxtrot. The wives opposed
these weekly dances because they believed dancing to be 'immoral
and "suggestive"', according to Edgar Snow, while Mao told
Agnes Smedley it was because they themselves couldn't dance.
The opposition of the wives only seemed to encourage Smedley
who, for an avowed feminist, exhibited an alarming lack of
camaraderie towards other women.

The Chinese women's fears that Smedley was indulging in
illicit relations with their husbands was ill-founded. Smedley was
a revolutionary and a journalist, not a femme fatale: 'Never in
her life had Agnes worn makeup—her style was Early Woman
Suffrage', wrote Helen Foster Snow. Her live-in Chinese interpreter, however, was a pretty young actress named Wu Guanghui
(Lily Wu) who had recently arrived from Peiping, and Mao was
apparently having or about to have an affair with her. The affair
was largely conducted in the Agnes Smedley–Lily Wu quarters
on Phoenix Mountain, about a kilometre from where Mao and
He Zizhen lived, with Smedley a gleeful collaborator.

By all accounts it was Agnes Smedley who arranged a rendezvous between Mao and Lily Wu in the farm dwelling which Otto
Braun and George Hatem shared, when neither of the men was
there and without their knowledge. Not much could go on behind
paper-covered lattice windows without word getting round, however, and He Zizhen (who, Otto Braun says, 'was not fooled by
this') quickly uncovered her husband's deceit along with the
American reporter's duplicity. He Zizhen argued with Mao about
this affair, quite violently according to Otto Braun.[10]

He Zizhen quickly grew to hate Agnes Smedley, who later told

Edgar Snow that she 'thought [He] Zizhen led a colorless, cloistered existence and did not have the necessary qualifications to be a revolutionary leader's wife. She made this clear by ignoring [He] Zizhen. As a result, although there had been no specific quarrel between the two women, there was much mutual animosity.'[11] He Zizhen argued more often and more violently with Mao and she began to demand a divorce, whether in earnest or as a threat she herself was probably not clear about at the time. During one of their arguments after they moved into a reasonably spacious cave apartment in Phoenix Mountain Village their next-door neighbour and fellow Long Marcher Liu Ying rushed in to try to mediate. Liu Ying found a cool (and therefore, she presumed, joking) Mao waving a scribbled divorce agreement at He Zizhen and saying: 'Well, you wanted a divorce, didn't you?' When he invited Liu Ying to be a witness to his signing the agreement, He Zizhen snatched the paper out of his hand and ripped it up.[12]

With the new freedom of choice in marriage for both women and men divorce in itself was not big news among the communists, so long as the decision was mutual. After all, since these early communist marriages were consensual unions undertaken without benefit of a marriage ceremony or marriage certificate, divorce was equally consensual and uncertificated, requiring only the consent of the Communist Party. What was, in theory, no longer acceptable was for a husband to divorce his wife simply because he was tired of her and wanted a new one; the reverse situation rarely arose, thereby creating the fiction that wives never wanted to divest themselves of husbands. When Helen Foster Snow arrived in Yan'an, however, she reported that Otto Braun had decided he was tired of his comfort wife, the young peasant Xiao Yuehua and wanted a divorce; the decision was not mutual, which placed communist theory in a parlous situation. Rumours have circulated in China for a number of years that it was Xiao Yuehua who wanted to divorce Otto Braun because he was beating her, but this cannot now be substantiated. Helen Foster Snow treated the incident as an example of the collective strength of The Thirty Women ('the dictatorship of the proletar*iette*'), but it is clear that to her there was in it an element of farce:

A certain insurgent comrade Li [ie, Li De, or Otto Braun] had voted to divorce his wife [Xiao Yuehua] on purely esthetic grounds. But the wife, who had come with him on the Long March and just borne him a bouncing son, voted against the break-up of family life. The phalanx [of The Thirty Women] rallied to her support, and the war against a reaction into marital anarchy was on. Comrade Li was a professional warrior and, having nothing to lose but his chains anyway, determined to carry on the campaign. He discreetly retired into a cave with several bodyguards and a poker companion while sending his case to the highest tribunals in the land.[13]

Given their political sophistication, the attitude of the foreigners in Yan'an towards the Long March women was surprisingly supercilious and patronising—Edgar Snow, for example, summarised the prevailing view thus:

The women cadres controlled their husbands easily by applying the time-honored technique of not sleeping with their spouses. As a result, they gradually ignored personal appearance. They thought it bourgeois to braid one's hair prettily, and so they let their hair grow long and unkempt, casually cutting it short with a knife when it became bothersome.[14]

What this facile conclusion failed to take into consideration was the dilemma in which the Long March women found themselves in Yan'an. Apart from the obvious fact that, lacking a reliable means of birth control, the women had to either remain single or abstain from sex if they did not want to become pregnant, the foreigners were apparently unaware of how crucial marital *guanxi* was to women's survival. As the writer Ding Ling later pointed out, women in Yan'an were under extreme pressure to marry and, once married, were expected to have children, which they were then expected to stay home to look after, thereby sacrificing any chance of carrying on their work outside the home. The men, however, were untouched by this complex web of obligations and when a prettier and younger woman presented herself they had little compunction about seeking a divorce, privately referred to as 'changing horses'.

There was no equality between the sexes in Yan'an and divorce had a far more insidious effect on the Long March women than the foreigners realised. For these women, maintaining their marital *guanxi* was the only means they had of maintaining their political position, that is, their jobs and the social and economic status that went with them. Marriage and divorce was not, for them, a parlour game in which they could afford to flex any feminist muscles they might have possessed. Ding Ling perceived the significance of the attitude of men towards women in Yan'an, but she appears to have been one of the few women to suspect that the commitment of communist males to the liberation of women was less than geniune.

In the case of Otto Braun's request for a divorce, almost all the senior Yan'an women stood on the side of Xiao Yuehua while, in general, the men supported Otto Braun's right to a divorce. Kang Keqing saw no shades of grey in the matter and was one of the few women to cross the floor: 'I think divorce should be easy and free,' she told Helen Foster Snow when pushed for an opinion. 'If the two do not agree politically, they absolutely must divorce. In this particular case, Comrade Li's wife was not a good housewife, and she was also backward politically, so I have no sympathy for her. Either one of them can get another mate whenever they wish, so why shouldn't each be free?'[15]

Otto Braun did in fact soon remarry: he and a young actress named Li Lilian, who had travelled into Yan'an from the east in July or August 1937, entered their names at the Yan'an registry office in 1938. They lived together happily for a year or so until the late summer of 1939 when Braun was tersely advised before dawn one Sunday that a seat was available on a plane leaving immediately, and he was whisked back to Russia. That was the last Braun and Li Lilian saw of each other. As the discarded ex-wife of a foreigner who was well known to be a personal enemy of the Chairman, Xiao Yuehua was not an attractive proposition as a wife to ordinary comrades, however. She did finally remarry, her second husband being a Long March veteran who was head of a military supply department and with whom she sank back to the obscurity whence she came before Otto Braun requisitioned her body.

Helen Foster Snow conducted several long interviews with at least seven of the women in Yan'an who had completed the Long March, one of whom even offered Snow her baby son for adoption because she was 'too busy, and anyway conditions here are bad for children'. This was Liu Qunxian, who had been in charge of the independent women's unit on the Long March. But Helen Foster Snow did not interview He Zizhen, of whom she had only this to say:

> Then there was Mao Tse-tung's wife, Ho Tzu-ch'ün, a small, delicate woman with a pretty face and a shy, modest manner, who devoted most of her time to caring for her husband—whom she worshiped—and bearing children . . . She had suffered more than any other woman in the war, for along with having borne several children, she received sixteen shrapnel wounds from an air bomb during the Long March.[16]

Even though He Zizhen was married to the leading Chinese communist, Helen Foster Snow didn't interview her because, as a wife and mother, He Zizhen obviously could not compete in the interest stakes with women such as Cai Chang, professional revolutionary, or Kang Keqing, Girl Commander, both of whose lives offered scope for interpretation and analysis of the Chinese Revolution. As for He Zizhen, she may have declined to be interviewed because of her antipathy to Agnes Smedley and Smedley's aggressive attitude towards the Chinese women. He Zizhen was certainly not shy and modest, as she was soon to demonstrate. She argued increasingly frequently with Mao, who was not above physical violence when his patience grew thin, and by the summer of 1937 she had reached the end of her tether. What happened next was later documented by Edgar Snow who, while not in Yan'an at the time, reconstructed the story from Agnes Smedley's letters and conversations they had about the incident.

> Late one evening after Agnes had already gone to bed there was the sound of cloth shoes outside her cave and she heard the sound of Mao's soft southern accent. The chairman was in Lily's cave next door and the light was still on. Smedley had heard him knock, then the door opening and closing. She tried to go back to sleep and just when she finally was drifting off, she heard the sound of footsteps rushing excitedly up the hill. Then the door of Lily's cave was pushed open and a woman's shrill voice broke the silence: 'You idiot! How dare you fool me and sneak into the home of this little bourgeois dance hall strumpet.'
> Smedley leapt out of bed, threw on her coat, and ran next

door. There was Mao's wife standing beside the seated Mao beating him with a long-handled flashlight. He was sitting on a stool by the table, still wearing his cotton hat and military coat. He did not try to stop his wife. His guard was standing at attention at the door looking perplexed. Mao's wife, crying in anger, kept hitting him and shouting until she was out of breath. Mao finally stood up. He looked tired and his voice was quietly severe: 'Be quiet, Zizhen. There's nothing shameful in the relationship between comrade Wu and myself. We were just talking. You are ruining yourself as a communist and are doing something to be ashamed of. Hurry home before other party members learn of this.'

Suddenly Mao's wife turned on Lily, who was standing with her back against the wall like a terrified kitten before a tiger. She railed at Lily, saying, 'Dance-hall bitch! You'd probably take up with any man. You've even fooled the Chairman.' Then she drew close to Lily and while brandishing the flashlight she held in one hand, she scratched Lily's face with the other hand and pulled her hair. Blood flowing from her head, Lily ran to Agnes and hid behind her. Mao's wife now directed her anger against Agnes.

'Imperialist!' she shouted. 'You're the cause of all this. Get back to your own cave.' Then she struck the 'foreign devil' with her flashlight. Not one to turn the other cheek, Smedley flattened Mrs. Mao with a single punch. From the floor, Mao's wife, more humiliated than hurt, shrieked: 'What kind of husband are you? Are you any kind of man? Are you really a communist? You remain silent while I'm being struck by this imperialist right before your eyes.'

Mao rebuked his wife, saying 'Didn't you strike her even though she had done nothing to you? She has a right to protect herself. You're the one who has shamed us. You're acting like a rich woman in a bad American movie.' Furious but restraining himself, Mao commanded his guard to help his wife up and take her home. But she made a fuss and refused to cooperate, so Mao had to call two more guards, and they finally led Mao's hysterical wife from the room. As they proceeded down the hill, Mao followed in silence, with many surprised faces watching the procession from their caves.[17]

The antagonistic dynamic between Agnes Smedley, Mao and He Zizhen cannot but have coloured Smedley's version of this event, and it must also be remembered that Smedley was well known for her tendency to dramatise reality: her Chinese was said to have been hardly more than basic, so she must have invented the wording of these exchanges unless Lily Wu told her later exactly what had been said. Would Mao, who had probably seen few if any American films by 1937, really liken the scene to a bad American movie? Was Smedley really the only person capable of coolly stopping He Zizhen in her tracks?

While there can be no doubt that this fight did take place, Smedley's account did not become known to the Chinese until the 1990s. What is curious is that Chinese biographical materials omit Lily Wu entirely from the story of the separation and subequent divorce of He Zizhen and Mao. They have steadfastly overlooked the whole Lily Wu affair, ignoring the earlier claims of some Westerners that Lily Wu was the trigger for the He Zizhen–Mao break-up. The Chinese have maintained the fiction that the divorce was sad, yet unavoidable, and brought about solely by the difficult behaviour of a mentally unstable and argumentative He Zizhen. No mention was ever made of Mao's womanising, which was obviously excused in the male world of Yan'an as a sign of the virile and exceptional manhood of the Chairman.

Even more astonishing, however, is the attempt to conceal Mao's adultery and exonerate him from all opprobrium by not only obliterating Lily Wu but by insinuating Jiang Qing, Mao's future wife and evil empress, into the Mao–He Zizhen break-up. This patently anachronistic and mischievous invention is perpetuated in Chinese writings where Jiang Qing is said to have visited Mao's home to 'consult' him while He Zizhen the perfect hostess graciously peeled her a pear.[18] Mao is thus effectively freed of any charge of random womanising since he eventually married Jiang Qing, while He Zizhen still carries the blame for the breakdown of the marriage and Jiang Qing's scheming ways, of which she was accused after the Cultural Revolution, are confirmed. Jiang Qing did arrive in Yan'an about two months before He Zizhen left, but she told her biographer Roxane Witke that she never met He Zizhen, and most Chinese sources guess at May or August 1938 as the beginning of Mao and Jiang Qing's relationship.[19]

Nevertheless, the Chairman could not ignore the tawdry

midnight brawl with Lily Wu which so many residents of Yan'an overheard, so he duly reported it to the party. The party listened to the various conflicting stories, among them He Zizhen's formal charge against Lily Wu for having alienated her husband's affections. Edgar Snow and Agnes Smedley say that Mao requested a divorce, which was granted in July, while other sources say the divorce was not approved for at least another year. In the best bureaucratic manner the party did nothing and declared the matter closed. For his part the Chairman further bypassed his personal responsibility by labelling Agnes Smedley the troublemaker and ordering her to leave Yan'an. She set out (carried at least part of the way on a stretcher) on 7 September with Helen Foster Snow, Kang Keqing and Liu Qunxian. It is not known what became of Lily Wu for the Chinese say nothing of her. Edgar Snow says it was the wives who arranged for her to be assigned to the Front Service Group; Agnes Smedley says she departed for the front with Ding Ling, outspoken and unpopular advocate of free love, and the Front Service Group on 20 August; Otto Braun says she was sent 'to her native Szechwan'.[20]

He Zizhen was dismayed to find that Mao did not pay more attention to her after the removal of Lily Wu or Agnes Smedley, nor did her physical and emotional pain ease. She therefore decided to seek medical treatment to have the vicious metal shards removed from her body. This, she reasoned, would free her from pain and allow her to get on with her life. Her youthful rebelliousness had solidified into adult stubbornness and once she had made her decision to leave Yan'an she could not be persuaded otherwise. She left in good spirits, having made the decision to leave of her own free will. This is the official version.

Both Edgar Snow and Otto Braun believed, however, that He Zizhen was exiled from Yan'an for her unseemly and inconvenient behaviour.[21] Given that He Zizhen stayed away so long the assessment of these two foreign contemporary observers is far more convincing than the sanitised official account. It was not Mao's way to push people—he preferred to withdraw support and let them jump so that he could not be held responsible for their actions—and he would have had no need to apply direct pressure on He Zizhen. With Japan having officially declared war on China in July, and pretty young students and actresses streaming into Yan'an to join the communists, he doubtless did little to persuade her to change her mind and was relieved to have her off his hands.

By this time He Zizhen was pregnant again, this, her sixth child, conceived in August when the Chairman was arranging for Lily Wu and Agnes Smedley to be dismissed from Yan'an (and, incidentally, after the divorce Agnes Smedley says was granted to Mao). In the first ten-day period of October, He Zizhen consigned her daughter Jiaojiao, now almost one year old, to the care of the Yan'an creche and set out on the muddy twelve-day journey to Xi'an with Deng Yingchao, the wife of Zhou Enlai.[22]

He Zizhen waited in Xi'an for her travel permit to Shanghai to be processed. One day as she wandered the cosmopolitan streets of the city she ran into her sister-in-law, the wife of one of Mao's brothers. Qian Xijun had made the Long March alongside He Zizhen and was married to Mao Zemin. She had just returned from Shanghai and she told He Zizhen to abandon her plan to go there for treatment because the Japanese had just occupied the city. He Zizhen remained in Xi'an trying to decide what to do. The official version of this period, and there is no other, says that Mao sent her a blanket and a letter suggesting she might reconsider returning to Yan'an. He may well have done this, knowing that she would not respond, for it is difficult to believe that Mao would have felt any remorse for what had happened. It is clear that even if He Zizhen had returned to Yan'an at that time she would not have been able to revive her marriage to Mao. Mao was no longer interested in her, and she was not prepared to overlook his philandering and endure the humiliation which so many Long March women suffered as their husbands openly indulged in extramarital relationships. He Zizhen did not reply to Mao's letter, nor did she return to Yan'an. Her mind was made up; it was now just a question of where she could run to.

Liu Ying, the woman who had witnessed Mao taunting He Zizhen with his written agreement to a divorce, arrived in Xi'an. Having succumbed like so many comrades to tuberculosis she was on her way to Russia for medical treatment. He Zizhen seized the chance to go with her. She received immediate permission from the 8th Route Army office and some time in November

1937 boarded the train for Russia that snaked along the Gansu Corridor past Lanzhou and Wuwei, where Wang Quanyuan and several other women soldiers of the doomed Western Route Army were being held captive.

From the beginning, the Chinese communists had a troubled relationship with the Russian Communist Party, which grew even more strained by the late 1920s. For their own purpose of strengthening China to lessen Japan's ability to attack western Russia, the Russians continued to favour the KMT machine over the smaller Chinese Communist Party. From time to time they excommunicated mavericks such as Mao Zedong, who saw no point in agitating for the urban revolution then required by communist dogma but insisted instead on arousing the anger of the miserable and impoverished Chinese peasantry to create an agrarian revolution based in the countryside.

The appeal of Russia's Leninist-flavoured Marxism was nevertheless such that many Chinese intellectuals travelled to Moscow to learn it at first hand. They were an eclectic group, and many of them aligned themselves with Moscow against Mao and his pragmatic focus on the Chinese peasants. One of the earliest students was Generalissimo Chiang Kai-shek, who spent four months studying the Russian military system in Moscow in 1923. The '28 Bolsheviks', who were such a thorn in Mao's side from 1932 until he wrested back leadership in 1935, had all studied at the Sun Yat-sen University (later to become the University of the Toilers of the East) in Moscow between 1926 and 1930.

Among the women who had studied in Russia was the intellectual Wei Gongzhi, one of the few women on the Long March whose feet had been bound in childhood. She was sent to study in Moscow between 1929 and 1931, returning to find herself expelled from the party as a Trotskyite. Another was Liu Qunxian, who had also spent three years in Moscow as a student at the Sun Yat-sen University and married her fellow student, Bo Gu, one of the '28 Bolsheviks'. Liu Ying, with whom He Zizhen was travelling, was herself revisiting Russia; she graduated from Sun Yat-sen University in 1932.

Because the Chinese communists' medical facilities were extremely primitive, Moscow was also a destination for the ill and exhausted, as well as the emotionally and politically troubled.

Liu Ying's journey to Russia was as much for emotional as physical reasons: one after another over the previous year she had gone down with pneumonia and gastric troubles, had been running a chronic high fever and was suffering from nervous exhaustion. She had become friendly with Zhang Wentian (known then as Luo Fu) in Jiangxi and worked with him on the Long March but refused to consider marriage because she did not want children to interfere with her revolutionary work. Liu Ying married Zhang Wentian at the end of the Long March and gave birth to a baby in Yan'an, but the child became ill and died. She was pregnant when she travelled to Moscow with He Zizhen, but her baby died in Russia.[23]

He Zizhen was twenty-seven years old when she arrived in Moscow in January 1938. As the wife of the Chairman of the Chinese Communist Party she was accorded a degree of respect above that of an ordinary visitor. She moved into Dongfang daxue (Oriental University) in the south-west of that great old city, and started medical treatment for the shrapnel wounds. She enrolled in politics with several other Chinese students and attended classes on the history of the Russian Communist Party, political economy, philosophy and the history of world revolutions. But she could make no sense of the Russian language, the soft purr of its cadences grating in her ears; as a rice-eating southern Chinese she had trouble adjusting to the diet of the Russians; she was allowed only a small stipend and had brought little money with her; her student accommodation was of the most basic kind and largely unheated. In addition, her pregnancy wearied her and she grew listless. She began to skip early morning classes. A fellow student covered for her by taking detailed notes but she was not really interested in her studies and soon abandoned them.

In May 1938 she gave birth to her sixth child, a boy. She held to her breast this tiny memento of all she had left behind, mother and baby each comforting the other. But her body had weakened to the point where her milk could not nourish him. He cried and grew weaker, she treated him with herbs she had brought from China. He contracted pneumonia and finally he died in her arms. Almost mad with grief He Zizhen buried him in a secluded corner of a park in the university grounds. She did not have the strength to return to class; she stopped studying and reading altogether; she gave way to depression. Her fellow students resented what they saw as self-indulgence on her part and became irritated with her, unable to accept that she could not simply overcome her depression and get on with her life. They began to avoid her. She grew more isolated. Her depression deepened.

The extraordinarily stressful conditions under which He Zizhen bore all six of her children mask the likelihood that she suffered repeatedly from postnatal depression. Her difficult behaviour in the early days when she was forced to leave her first daughter behind in Fujian; her collapse after giving birth to her fourth child on the Long March; her argumentativeness and reclusiveness in Yan'an after the birth of Jiaojiao; her crushing depression in Moscow after burying her sixth child: all these were linked to birthings that for He Zizhen were shrouded in grief, loss and sometimes sheer physical exhaustion. She was not the only woman to give her children away, not the only woman to abandon her new-born child, not the only woman whose premature baby was stillborn, not the only woman whose baby died. She was not the only woman to suffer from the invisible illness of postnatal depression. She was not even the only one to have a preoccupied and philandering husband (although she *was* the only one to be married to a demigod in the making). She was unlucky enough, however, to have all this sadness descend upon her, and before she turned twenty-eight.

From time to time over the next few years some of He Zizhen's old friends travelled to Moscow. The Chinese who lived there were students and diplomatic staff representing the KMT Government, and they formed a tightly knit community, as ex-patriots often do. He Zizhen, however, was not an active part of the community, this in itself indicating that her depression was linked to her being exiled from Yan'an rather than having gone voluntarily. Even Liu Ying was unable to find lasting common ground with her beyond the devastation of the death of their babies.

When Cai Chang arrived in the autumn of 1938 for medical treatment she may have brought He Zizhen money or letters from Mao, but their lives had begun to move in opposite directions and it is unlikely they had much to do with each other.

Cai Chang remained focused on revolution, while He Zizhen's series of pregnancies and illness, compounded by her exile, had effectively put an end to active revolutionary work. Cai Chang enrolled in Moscow at the Comintern School and kept herself busy with her medical treatment, her studies and her work with children. Her fifteen-year-old daughter was sent to Moscow to keep her company, but Cai Chang alienated her by being too busy working with other young children and orphans to pay her own daughter any attention. Cai Chang stayed in Moscow for about eighteen months and later never mentioned any contact she may have had with He Zizhen.

Two of The Thirty Women who appear to have been exiled to Russia soon after He Zizhen were Jin Weiying and Liu Qunxian. Jin Weiying, aged thirty-four, had been coughing up blood in Yan'an, and she and her husband appear to have just separated when she travelled with Cai Chang to Russia for medical treatment and 'to further her studies'. Small and delicate, she was generally known as Ah Jin, or simply Elder Sister; she had been known in her hometown as the 'Girl General of Dinghai', but that was when she was in her early twenties and just stepping out on the revolutionary path. Since then she had taught school, set up a night school in Shanghai for textile workers, slipped into Shanghai factories to foment strikes, and led the female textile workers out onto the streets. She had married Deng Xiaoping but they divorced in 1933. In 1934, when she was thirty years old and had already been a party member for eight years, she married Li Weihan, who held the quite powerful position of secretary to the party's central organisation unit in Ruijin.

The Long March did not defeat her, and once settled in Yan'an Jin Weiying enrolled along with He Zizhen and Kang Keqing in the university, where she was at one stage elected to head the women students' association. In Moscow, she turned out to be a 'difficult' student: she would not sit quietly in class and frequently challenged her Russian lecturers on matters of principle. The Russians responded by labelling her a lunatic, shaving her head and committing her to an asylum. The Chinese authorities did not interfere, adding weight to the suggestion that she was in exile, and she is said to have died in a German air-raid towards the end of 1941.[24]

Liu Qunxian suffered a similar fate. Liu Qunxian was the outspoken 27-year-old who had captained the independent women's unit in the early days of the Long March. She joked at one stage that her hardworking mule had been much dearer to her than her husband. Helen Foster Snow became quite friendly with Liu Qunxian in Yan'an, describing her as a 'healthy little person— quite pretty—fussy about her appearance' who, although very kind, 'did not spare the tongue-lash when correcting errors'. She dubbed her the women's 'revolutionary attorney' and concluded (no doubt tongue-in-cheek): 'I got the impression that not a few of the ferocious Red warriors were afraid of her.'[25]

Be that as it may, Liu Qunxian soon buckled under the strain. She left Yan'an in late 1937 to travel with her husband to Wuhan, heart of KMT territory, where she was to work with the 8th Route Army. However, highly strung as she was, a sudden illness led to her breakdown and she was sent to the southern port city of Amoy for a little over a year to recuperate. She attempted to return to work but was instead sent to Russia in March 1939 for medical treatment. At a whistle stop in faraway Xinjiang Province in the north-west she ran into Liu Ying, who was on her way back from Moscow, and entrusted to Liu Ying a letter to her husband, whom she hadn't seen for at least two years. Chinese sources say she was committed to a lunatic asylum in Moscow and evacuated, along with Jin Weiying, when the German air-raids began in the summer of 1941. Like Jin Weiying, she was never heard of again.

Liu Qunxian's husband had already set up house with a replacement wife in Yan'an while she was on her way to Moscow so Liu Ying decided not to give him her letter. In 1946 he died in a plane crash.

Other Long Marchers visited Russia on official business: Zhou Enlai and his wife Deng Yingchao escorted Otto Braun to Moscow in late 1939 then flew back to China in March 1940 with Cai Chang; He Zizhen's brother-in-law Mao Zemin was also in Moscow in December 1939 conducting an investigation into Otto Braun.[26]

Why did He Zizhen stay on in Moscow? Why didn't she go

home to China after her baby died? The only answer to these is another question: where could she have gone? It would have been difficult for her to return to Yan'an, even if she had been able to gain permission. Her sister, He Yi, had failed in her attempt to get Mao to change his mind when she travelled to Yan'an with her new husband and accused Mao of abandoning He Zizhen.[27] By the time He Zizhen's last baby was born in Moscow Mao was already involved with his new love, the young Shanghai actress Lan Ping/Jiang Qing. Within a few months this affair had become a live-in relationship that raised enough influential eyebrows in Yan'an to force Mao into demanding that the party consent to his divorcing He Zizhen so that he could marry Jiang Qing, who by the summer or autumn of 1938 was pregnant with his child. Jiang Qing is also understood to have been jealous or fearful enough of He Zizhen's return that she brought pressure to bear to keep her in Russia, or at least out of China.

Even if He Zizhen had wanted or been allowed to return to Yan'an, in 1939 she received notification from the party that her marriage to Mao was officially over. This notification became her passport to a lifetime of loneliness, because no man would dare take up with the ex-wife of the Chairman. Had she asked to be assigned work elsewhere, in all probability the party would have refused her request, preferring not to run the risk of her being captured by the KMT (even as the ex-wife of Mao she would have been a prize catch), or killed by the Japanese. In the eyes of the party, she was safest in Russia, well out of the way.

Whether as compensation or out of compassion, He Zizhen's daughter, Jiaojiao, was sent to Moscow to be with her mother. The confusion in biographical material as to just when Jiaojiao went to Russia is a good indication of how little is known and how much embroidery has been done around the edges of this period of He Zizhen's life in the absence of hard evidence.[28] What follows is a judicious recounting of what appear to be the essential elements of her experience in Russia.

Jiaojiao was four years old when she was sent to Moscow, around the end of 1940. Mao's two teenaged sons by Yang Kaihui, Mao Anying and Mao Anqing, were also consigned to the care of He Zizhen about this time, some say because Jiang Qing was jealous of their blood relationship with Mao. He Zizhen may have been receiving a small stipend from the Russian Government with which to support her little band of Mao children but with the onset of World War II living conditions in Moscow had worsened. The pale light of bleak winter days faded into dusk by two or three in the afternoon, followed by a total blackout. Hot water became a vaguely remembered dream, and as winter took firmer hold and coal became harder to come by, heating was turned on less often. Shops closed as supplies ran out; their windows were boarded up. Museums and libraries were closed down for security as much as economic reasons. Muscovites lived nevertheless in stoic hope and never left home without their little 'perhaps bags': perhaps they might be lucky enough to find something to buy, perhaps not.[29]

When hostilities broke out between Russia and Nazi Germany in the summer of 1941 He Zizhen, Jiaojiao and the Mao boys were among the many foreigners evacuated with the International Nursery to the textile city of Ivanovo nearly 1000 kilometres north-east of Moscow. Ivanovo may have been safer but daily life was more difficult in that provincial city where clothing and other goods were more scarce than in the capital. Even when the temperature in Ivanovo plummeted to −30°C coal could still not be found for heating, at least not by foreigners who did not understand the many ways and means the Russians had constructed over the years for survival.

Food rationing was introduced on the principle of 'from each according to ability, to each according to the work performed'. He Zizhen's 'work performed'—which some sources claim was knitting socks and jumpers for Red Army soldiers, although which Red Army is not specified—relegated her to Group 3 (housewives, people partly or wholly unemployed, the aged, dependants and school children). This entitled her to very close to a starvation diet: her daily ration ran to a tiny portion of meat (14 grams) and fish (16 grams), a palmful of cereal (32 grams), a teaspoonful of sugar (7 grams) and a teaspoonful of butter or oil (7 grams) plus a small loaf (500 grams) of black bread. The bread was not such a boon as it sounds, for a southern Chinese accustomed to a diet of rice and vegetables. The two teenaged Mao boys were entitled to the same food rations. Four-year-old Jiaojiao, however, fell into Group 4 (children under the age of six) and thus received more butter and cereals as well as a milk ration; children in schools or nurseries also had a hot midday meal. He Zizhen placed Jiaojiao in the International Nursery in Ivanovo to ensure that she received the best food and care possible under wartime conditions, although this meant being separated once more from her little girl, who was required to live-in at the creche.

It must have been in the winter of 1941–42 that Jiaojiao contracted pneumonia; she was five years old. Staff at the nursery cared for her for a time but when they saw her start to slip away they gave up. They wheeled her bed to the waiting room outside the mortuary and left her to die. Somehow He Zizhen discovered this and, in a panic fuelled by the horror of the death of her last baby from pneumonia, gathered Jiaojiao up and rushed back to her rooms. She managed to obtain sugar and milk, and spoonful by spoonful she fed this mixture to her little girl. Jiaojiao recovered.

When Jiaojiao was well enough He Zizhen let her go back to the International Nursery but she refused to let her stay over-night. This was against the rules, as the director repeatedly told her, but He Zizhen refused to give in. When the director continued to object to her taking her child home each night, He Zizhen argued, often and violently, with him until finally he declared she was unstable and had her confined.[30] Another, less plausible, version of the arguments that led to her admission to a mental hospital, or sanitorium, is that they were caused by her refusal to return to her work of knitting socks and jumpers for the Red Army after Jiaojiao recovered.[31]

He Zizhen spent the next four years undergoing 'treatment for mental illness', and it is believed that she was heavily sedated for much of that time. Some sources say that Jiaojiao stayed with her, but it is more likely that Jiaojiao became a boarder at the International Nursery. The inmates of the Moscow sanitorium to which He Zizhen was transferred were evacuated to the country-side for a time during further German air-raids on the Russian capital in 1942. The Chinese authorities made no effort to intervene on her behalf and left her entirely to the care of Russian doctors. The communists knew of her predicament for among those who visited Russia were high-ranking personnel who had made the Long March with He Zizhen. One such was the young

Red Army commander Lin Biao whose spectacular manouevres had opened up for the communists an escape route from Guizhou Province. Lin Biao and He Zizhen had been comrades-in-arms for at least fourteen years and had first met on Jinggangshan when Mao took her as his wife.

Of He Zizhen's years in the Russian sanitorium all that Chinese sources say is that she developed a fear of white coats. She would probably have stayed there for the rest of her life had it not been for the persistence of Wang Jiaxiang, an old friend from the days of the Jiangxi soviet and the Long March, during which he had been one of Mao's staunchest political supporters.

The head for many years of the Red Army's General Political Department and a member of the powerful Politburo, Wang Jiaxiang had spent several years in Moscow off and on since his student days there during the 1920s and was at home in the city as well as being fluent in Russian. Wang Jiaxiang asked the students in Moscow where He Zizhen was when he and his wife Dr Zhu Zhongli visited in 1946. Wang Jiaxiang and Dr Zhu Zhongli had to make repeated requests to the Comintern to have He Zizhen released, but one bright autumn day in 1946 He Zizhen shuffled into their apartment with ten-year-old Jiaojiao by her side. She was clad in new hospital-issue skirt and blouse whose stiff folds encased her thin body. When Wang Jiaxiang and Zhu Zhongli rose to greet her she let her old friend take her hand but looked at him dully, without recognition.

'Elder Sister He, how are you feeling?' Zhu Zhongli asked.

He Zizhen nodded her head slowly. 'Good.' The simple syllable was awkward in her mouth.

'Comrade He Zizhen,' Wang Jiaxiang said, 'you've suffered a great deal these last few years. We want you to know your comrades back home send you their warmest greetings.'

'Have you come from China?' He Zizhen responded slowly, the trace of a smile bringing the first sign of life to her dark face.

As Wang Jiaxiang and Zhu Zhongli talked with her they realised how crushed she still was, physically and emotionally. Her hopes of regaining her health in Russia had come to nothing, and the shards of shrapnel were still buried in her body. She was unaware of events in China over the past few years, including Japan's defeat the previous year.

Having gained He Zizhen's release from the sanitorium, Wang Jiaxiang and Zhu Zhongli telegraphed Mao, who agreed to allow He Zizhen to return to China. Nearly nine months later, in the summer of 1947, He Zizhen stepped from a train in the city of Harbin, icy capital of Heilongjiang Province in the far north of Manchuria. She was coming home to China with her daughter and two suitcases that contained all her belongings, but the China she alighted in was so changed she hardly knew it.

When she left Yan'an in 1937 the communists were a rebel minority fighting a holding war on two fronts. To the north they were standing their ground against the aggressive Japanese war machine, hoping only to hold out until the West (essentially the United States of America) defeated Japan and forced the withdrawal of Japanese troops from China. In the rest of the country they had been doing all they could to undermine the KMT while quietly recruiting peasants by the million. Now, ten years later, the Japanese had been gone from the north for nearly two years and the long-anticipated civil war between communist and KMT Chinese had engulfed the country.

Just before He Zizhen reached Harbin in mid 1947, Generalissimo Chiang Kai-shek's KMT aeroplanes bombed Mao out of Yan'an and sent him into hiding in the countryside; a fish in the sea of the Chinese peasantry. Within three months the tide had begun to turn for the communists as they notched up victories over the numerically superior KMT armies. KMT soldiers brought their rifles and ammunition over to the communists in their thousands, each defection weakening the Generalissimo's self-proclaimed mandate to rule China. By the end of 1947 Commander Lin Biao, recovered from his wounds and returned from Russia to lead the battle for north China, had begun to demolish the Generalissimo's confident armies in Manchuria with chilling efficiency.

He Zizhen understood that the revolution for which she had fought from the age of sixteen was now almost over, that victory was within grasp. Her commitment to the revolution was genuine and she considered herself no less a part of it for having been in exile for ten years and for not having been active in the field for some years before that. She spent her first few days in Harbin acclimatising to the idea of her new life, most of that time in tears. She said later that her ten years in Russia had been ten times more bitter than the Long March.[32]

'All I want,' she told an old friend during her first three days back in China, 'is to be accorded the same treatment as a mid-level cadre. That's all. And I do have two requests besides. First of all I would like to see Mao Zedong just once, maybe talk to him a little, even shake his hand—just once. The second thing I ask is to be set free.' The words to express her pain did not come as easily as her tears: 'I don't want to be imprisoned by being "the first wife"—I don't want that to mean I won't be allowed to remarry or have my freedom. I'm still young, and I'm not ugly. Surely I can find an ordinary worker or a peasant to live my life with? Surely I can have just this—the freedom to be an ordinary Red fighter instead of the ex-wife of the leader?'[33]

This cannot be taken at face value, but it does reveal the impasse He Zizhen found herself in. As Mao's ex-wife she was clearly at the mercy of Jiang Qing's jealousy, which it is generally believed had already been responsible for the last six of her nine years of Russian exile. Also, while Mao lived she was untouchable by any other man. And no other man could now give her what she had experienced during her years with the fabulous Chairman Mao, architect of the Chinese Revolution.

5

OUTSIDE, LOOKING IN

The Moslem soldiers who captured Wang Quanyuan at gun-point that spring morning in 1937 herded her and what was left of her little band of women and boys out of the mountains to a small desert settlement called Wuwei. This was one of the first stops along the Silk Road to Samarkand, a tiny dot just south of the western tail of the Great Wall. It was the last reminder of China glimpsed from train windows by the steady stream of travellers as they started their journey to Russia along the 500 kilometres of the Gansu Corridor. The Gobi Desert lay to the north, snow-capped mountain ranges to the south and east.

In this isolated frontier town the Moslem cavalry imprisoned survivors of the Western Route Army Women's Vanguard Regiment whom they had captured over the past few months. Wang Quanyuan told her story in 1986 to a researcher from Gansu, and it is from his interview and research that the following details are taken.[1]

Wang Quanyuan was incarcerated in a high-walled prison where she found herself reunited with about one hundred of the women soldiers she had once commanded. The long northern winter lingered almost into summer and the old prison compound was sunless and damp. The women shivered in their thin unlined uniforms and light coats, growing weak and ill on their diet of black bread and soggy, unsalted vegetables.

One day Wu Fulian arrived at the prison, flanked by soldiers and hardly able to stand. She had been starving when they found her in the mountains, having survived for many weeks on grasses and whatever other vegetation she had been able to find or dig up. When she had collapsed from exhaustion during the Long March her companions had revived her with a pear they found in a peasants' hut. Now Wang Quanyuan asked the prison guards for codliver oil for her sick comrade, who by this stage was coughing up blood. But codliver oil was not enough to save Wu Fulian and she died ten days later. She was twenty-seven years old and the second of The Thirty Women to die.

About a month after Wang Quanyuan's capture the women were paraded under heavy guard through the streets of Wuwei to the Hai–Zang Temple where they were allowed to bathe under the watchful eyes of guard dogs. When they returned to their cold prison yard some of the women decided to feign madness in the hope they might be released: they climbed trees, laughed and cried relentlessly in turns, sang at the top of their voices and generally created an enormous racket, all to no avail. Their Moslem captors for their part decided to experiment with bouts of kindness as a means of breaking the women's spirit. It soon became clear, however, that while the women were not going to respond to harsh words and lack of food, neither were they to be swayed by sympathetic treatment such as being issued with clothes or being taken out sightseeing or to the cinema.

Two months later they were escorted to a courtyard garden to the east of Wuwei where Commander Ma Buqing addressed them in the dialect of north China: 'You may not be aware that the KMT and the Communist Party have again joined in a united front. As an act of goodwill we have therefore decided to release the following prisoners . . .' The women fell silent as names were called out. They began to notice that as each woman's name was read out a soldier moved to stand beside her, and it soon dawned on them that they were not being released but assigned to individual soldiers, presumably as wives. Pandemonium broke out. The women clung together and shouted abuse as the soldiers tried to drag them apart. Eventually the soldiers managed to wrestle out of the garden the twenty or so women whose names had been called out. The rest were returned to their prison yard.

A week later the remaining women were summoned once more

into the presence of Ma Buqing and about forty of his turbaned bodyguards. This time he was less conciliatory: 'You may think of yourselves as soldiers but you are, after all, only women. And women should be wives. You are still young and we don't want to harm you—but we want you all to fulfil your womanly destinies. Starting tomorrow,' he raised his voice above their mutterings, 'all female prisoners will be allocated as concubines to my officers. Anyone who doesn't toe the line will be despatched to the Western Paradise in three days' time.'

Wang Quanyuan stood quietly among the angry women, her hands thrust into the sleeves of her old grey army overcoat. Because she had been their commanding officer and because of her age (she was twenty-four, older than most of them) the women turned to her for leadership. But when they clamoured around her this time she had no idea what to do. She recalled that she told them: 'Even if we have to go with these Moslem brigands we mustn't submit to them. Just keep your wits about you. See if you can get hold of a gun somehow and grab the first chance you can to run away.'

Over the next two months the women were taken away from the prison one by one; most of them never saw each other again. In the vagaries of war, one young woman, Yang Wenju, was released instead of being made a concubine. Yang Wenju had joined Zhang Guotao's 4th Route Army in the early 1930s in Sichuan, married a fellow soldier and given her first child into the care of local peasants. She became friendly with Kang Keqing during the time they spent in Tibet (1935–36) but was separated from her at the Yellow River when Yang Wenju and her husband crossed with the troops who then became the Western Route Army. She was pregnant at that time. Her husband was killed but she was captured and gave birth to her baby in prison. After her unexpected release she made her way with her son to a village near Wuwei where she lived until 1949 with a Moslem tanner.

It is considered shameful for a Chinese to be captured by the enemy and to survive. Those who do survive are automatically suspected of collaborating with the enemy. This is a traditional attitude that has retained a hold on people's consciousness. Soldiers who are captured are expected either to kill themselves or to submit bravely to execution. You will see this in countless films made in mainland China from the 1950s on, each with its variation on the scene of hero or heroine shouting defiantly, 'Long live the Communist Party!' as the firing squad takes aim.

The women who were captured by the Moslems in the Gansu Corridor in 1937 knew that unless they escaped immediately, as a small number managed to do, to attempt to return to China and their previous lives would be virtually impossible. Their comrades would censure them for not struggling hard enough before they were captured, for not trying hard enough to be killed after they were captured, and for having traded their survival for the death of others. Their families would be humiliated by the perception of the community that they had collaborated with the enemy politically, and possibly sexually. Most of the women who were captured submitted to their fate as concubines or found a man to live with and settled down in the north-west, because they knew they could not go back home.

In November, at the same time as He Zizhen was boarding the train for Russia, Wang Quanyuan was assigned as concubine to the commander of a regiment of engineers. She was taken about five kilometres east of Wuwei to a walled garrison town called Xincheng where Commander Ma Jinchang awaited her. He was a short solid man, cleanshaven, with a shaven head. He was no longer young (his nickname was 'Small Old Five'), but in Wang Quanyuan's eyes he was strong and fierce, every inch a brigand. He rose from his wooden armchair and walked towards her as she was brought into his rooms, placing his hands on her shoulders. She squirmed and shrank from him, silent and watchful, then asked to be allowed to go to the toilet.

Wang Quanyuan discovered when she crept from the toilet to look for a way of escape that the city gate of Xincheng was heavily guarded and that her every move was being watched. Her hostile attitude in remaining silent and in persisting in her attempts to escape enraged Ma Jinchang. When she was taken back to his rooms he circled her menacingly then suddenly kicked her in the back of her knee, sending her crumpling to the ground. 'Bring a rod,' he ordered, 'and we'll see how soon she submits.' Ma Jinchang beat her with a thick wooden rod, which he brought down hard on her body at least twenty times. This, Wang

Quanyuan's first of a series of beatings, lasted until she passed out.

In time, Ma Jinchang began to beat her systematically, alternating on different days between a wooden rod, a leather whip and a length of hemp rope. The beatings Wang Quanyuan was subjected to continued until it became clear that she would not submit. When he had beaten her to within an inch of her life he lost interest and turned his attention elsewhere. Wang Quanyuan did not talk of rape in her 1986 interview. Her decision to avoid the subject, insisting that she remained unbowed despite terrible beatings, is understandable in light of the treatment she later received upon her return to her hometown. Yet it is difficult to believe that a professional soldier would think twice about raping a female prisoner of war, especially one not of his religion and cultural background.

Ma Jinchang had her sent to his home in Yongchang County about 50 kilometres west of Wuwei where his chief wife, some domestic staff and about twenty guards maintained a residence which he visited periodically. Ma Jinchang's home was 300 kilometres from the closest Chinese city—Lanzhou, capital of Gansu Province, on the Yellow River—and that stretch of desert between Wang Quanyuan and the Yellow River was enemy territory. She may have tramped well over 13 000 kilometres during her Long March but then she had been with her comrades, whom she thought of as her real family; the much shorter journey of 300 kilometres to Lanzhou was impossible for a woman alone and without transit papers.

Wang Quanyuan was nursed back to health after her beatings by a maid whose name was Axi, and they became friends as they worked together at household chores. Wang Quanyuan was also befriended by one of the resident guards, a man called Mu Zhuren, and it was thanks to these two Moslems that she was eventually able to escape.

She appears to have had a certain amount of freedom in Yongchang County and was not entirely isolated from the Chinese community or from her fellow communists. She was in contact with at least two women from the Women's Vanguard Regiment, one of them a sixteen year old who had been given to the head of Yongchang's Chamber of Commerce. Wang Quanyuan was by this stage on sufficiently good terms with Ma Jinchang to ask him to arrange the transfer to his household of this young woman, Wang Xiuying. When Ma Jinchang obliged and accepted her into his home, Wang Quanyuan set up another beating by challenging his motives for this act of kindness: 'If you think this means I'll be your wife now, then you're mistaken!' Infuriated, Ma Jinchang threw a stool at her, wounding her quite badly on the leg.

Her last beating at the hands of Ma Jinchang resulted from her refusal to wear a long gown he had had especially made for her. Not only did she refuse to wear it, but the whole time she lived in Ma Jinchang's house she insisted on dressing in the remnants of her old Red Army uniform. Her stubbornness on this point was doubtless an irritating reminder to all about her, and especially Ma Jinchang, that she considered her imprisonment to be only a temporary state.

Wang Quanyuan went about her chores within the Ma household for eighteen months, never relinquishing hope that she might escape. In March 1939 Ma Jinchang's engineering regiment was transferred out of Yongchang County and he left a skeleton staff and guard at the house to care for his chief wife, Wang Quanyuan and Wang Xiuying, who was pregnant by one of his guards. About ten o'clock on a cold late-winter's night (fifty years later Wang Quanyuan claimed to still remember the date, 19 March) the maid Axi roused Wang Quanyuan from her bed and handed her two slips of paper. These were safe conduct passes to Lanzhou signed by Mu Zhuren, she said. They were made out in the names of Wang Quanyuan and Wang Xiuying, and if the Chinese women were to escape they should leave immediately.

With Axi's help the two Wangs gathered some clothes and food, scaled the wall of the courtyard and headed eastwards in the darkness. They covered nearly 50 kilometres that night, skirting Wuwei in the near dawn light. Knowing how vulnerable they would be walking alone through the desert in broad daylight, about daybreak they climbed aboard a horse and cart headed for Lanzhou, paying for the ride out of the twelve silver dollars Wang Quanyuan had tucked in an inside pocket of her uniform. Safely camouflaged from Ma clan horsemen, they nevertheless were still susceptible to the normal hazards of frontier travel, and while crossing Wuqiao Ridge the cart overturned. Wang Xiuying was not hurt but Wang Quanyuan fell badly and was knocked unconscious. Knowledgeable locals revived her with urine that had been heated by placing hot stones in it. Whether due to the treatment or to the thought that it might continue, Wang Quanyuan's recovery was rapid and complete.

The ancient city of Lanzhou had for centuries been a strategic military and trade centre along the Silk Road, safe behind thick brown walls on Chinese soil, on the eastern bank of the Yellow River. When the two Wangs saw Moslem KMT guards at the western end of the Yellow River Bridge, however, they were reluctant to test the power of their safe conduct passes. Instead they went to a prearranged destination in a nearby settlement to await the arrival of a fellow escapee who had been assigned as a concubine to one of Ma Jinchang's officers in Yongchang County. Wang Quanyuan then set out alone to attempt to cross the Yellow River Bridge. While she was waiting to have her papers checked a plainclothes security man from the Ma clan became suspicious and tried to take her into custody. She twisted from his grasp and threatened to jump into the river, causing such a commotion on the busy bridge that he was forced to let her go. Desperate to reach the safety of the Red Army in Lanzhou, she circled around below the bridge and followed the slow-flowing Yellow River until she found a ford and was poled across on a raft made of ox-hide. Once inside the city walls it was a simple matter to find the 8th Route Army office. But it was here that her real troubles began.

The communists had an official policy for dealing with personnel who had been captured by the enemy, and this included those who followed Zhang Guotao south in the autumn of 1935. Since Zhang was perceived as having deliberately flouted a Central Committee directive in order to wrest control from Mao, everyone who marched south with him was within his circle of blame and considered a potential traitor to Mao. The Communist Party had decided that people who returned to the Red Army within a year (Kang Keqing was one such) were to be accepted and re-assigned, if possible, to their original unit. People who returned within two years were to be investigated before any decision was made whether to take them back (Wu Zhonglian and Zhang Qinqiu were in this category). If more than two years had passed since an individual became separated from the main Red Army, she was to be rejected outright. Wang Quanyuan had been absorbed into Zhang's 4th Front Army in September 1935, and by the time she reached Lanzhou it was March 1939. She had therefore been separated from what became the mainstream and victorious Red Army for three and a half years.

Wang Quanyuan felt as though she was returning to her family as she walked into the 8th Route Army office. She poured out the story of how she had walked with the 1st Front Red Army from Jiangxi, been assigned to the Left Column, worked in Tibet, and been placed in charge of the Women's Vanguard Regiment which crossed the Yellow River and became part of the Western Route Army. The pleasant young man in Lanzhou's 8th Route Army office listened patiently to her story then explained the policy to her. Wang Quanyuan argued with him, telling him that she was a party member and was married to Wang Shoudao, a high-ranking party official. The officer shook his head. Her party membership was no longer valid, he told her, and he handed her five silver dollars—not even the dreaded eight silver dollars—as he escorted her to the door.

This rejection was Wang Quanyuan's most devastating beating. The tears of rage and frustration she had never shed while a prisoner of war in the north-west streamed down her face as she stood outside the 8th Route Army office in Lanzhou clutching her five silver dollars. Finally, broken in spirit, she retraced her steps and told Wang Xiuying that they had officially been abandoned by the Red Army.

Unattached and cut off from their community, they lacked any means of survival, economic or social. Lanzhou was a frontier city where several survivors of the Women's Vanguard Regiment in similar circumstances had managed through marriage to avoid both starvation and prostitution. Two of these women found partners for the Wang escapees. Wang Xiuying placed her baby, born late in April 1939, with foster parents then set up house with a barber. Wang Quanyuan married a man from Yunnan Province named Wan Ling who was a truck driver with the KMT. She was by then twenty-six years old and the hardships of the past few years had left deep physical and emotional scars, none more so than her rejection by the Red Army. No longer was she the joyous and enthusiastic Red soldier who had stepped out from Jiangxi nearly five years before; no longer was she Miss Floral Frock ready at a moment's notice to mount the stage and lampoon landlords and local bullies; no longer was she the lofty prisoner of war cloaked in her old army overcoat. Throwing in her lot with Wan Ling she became a vagrant with neither an acceptable profession nor a meaningful family context: they were not attached to the land, they were not soldiers, they were not merchants or tinkers or barbers. Their strange accents were further evidence of their foreignness and they were thus condemned to live on the fringes of society in an area where life was precarious even for native northerners.

With the war against the Japanese settling into its third year the government stripped the countryside of men, materials and food in an effort to keep the provincial KMT armies on their feet. Governments paid farmers as little as 20 to 30 per cent of the market price for the huge quantities of rice they commandeered. They justified their rapacious behaviour as a means to discourage hoarding and speculation, but in reality wealthy landlords were well able to hoard rice to wait for higher prices while small farmers had to take whatever price they could get. With shortages in the wind, those who could do so hoarded, which in turn created a genuine shortage. As rice supplies dried up, panic set in. There were rice riots. The price of rice shot up; in Chungking above the Yantze River gorges the price of rice increased 500 per cent in the second half of 1940.[2] Small farmers were forced off their land as inflation set in and land taxes soared.

Wang Quanyuan and Wan Ling stayed in Lanzhou for about a year before moving on to the small city of Hanzhong 600 kilometres south-east, halfway between Xi'an and Chengdu; whether through their own decision or because Wan Ling was sent there by the KMT is not known. Japanese bombers lacerated much of north China during the year Wang Quanyuan and Wan Ling spent in Hanzhong. Indiscriminate air-raids on cities and towns demoralised the people, as they were intended to do, so in the summer of 1941 Wan Ling responded to a call for drivers and mechanics to join the provincial anti-Japanese army in his native Yunnan Province. As a recruit, Wan Ling was possibly transported the 1000 kilometres home and Wang Quanyuan went with him; no mention is made of them walking this great distance. As soon as they reached Yunnan, Wan Ling was sent on a tour of duty to neighbouring Burma.

Alone again far from home, Wang Quanyuan nevertheless now had official status as the dependent of a soldier in a provincial army. Together with other dependent families she was moved east to Guizhou Province and assigned work in a cigarette factory. There she learnt a trade by which she could finally support herself, and for close on a year she worked in the factory rolling cigarettes and saving a little money. The instinctive need to belong, which had driven her to join the communists and then to marry Wan Ling, now surfaced as homesickness. She wrote to her family. Someone wrote back saying that her mother was seriously ill and needed her at home. Out of desperation, Wang Quanyuan quit her job and set off to walk the 800 kilometres home. She trod the footpaths and by-roads back across the mountains between Guizhou and Hunan provinces, buying and begging food along the way, then walked across Hunan to Jinggangshan, the mountains where the Red Army had come into being. In later interviews she gave no indication of how long this trek to her family took, but by July 1942 she had crossed Jinggangshan and returned to the lush green tea-growing hills of central Jiangxi Province to be back in her native place talking her own dialect. She forgot that she was a different person from the seventeen year old who had left there twelve years before, and she hoped the community she had been born into would not apply to her the traditional beliefs about captured soldiers who lived to escape.

The Red Army in Jiangxi Province had disintegrated by the early 1940s into isolated bands of 'rebels' and everyday life had returned to normal. Most of south-east China was under KMT rule and society ran in exactly the same way as it had for centuries. It mattered little that Generalissimo Chiang Kai-shek headed the country, he may as well have been an emperor for all the difference it made. Life for the mass of peasants remained a never-ending struggle to produce enough rice (or, for northerners, wheat) to feed the family and pay the taxes. And taxes, always plural, became a veritable cascade in wartime. When small farmers with little surplus grain and no savings couldn't pay, they were forced to take out further crippling loans from their land-lords or sell their land for a pittance. The number of destitute grew in leaps and bounds.

China's lifelines—the major roads and railways—were primary military targets throughout the war. When the Japanese severed these arteries the nation fragmented into a loose coalition of provinces each forced to rely on its own meagre production of food, with disastrous results. In 1942 there was a drought in the northern province of Henan. It was followed by frosts, hail and locusts. Reeling under this succession of natural disasters the province produced only a quarter of its usual spring and summer harvests. In normal circumstances this significant drop in food production would have caused shortages and made life rather more difficult; the authorities would have had to buy grain from neighbouring provinces and sell it to the people. What turned two bad harvests into a catastrophe, however, was that nearly one million KMT troops were garrisoned in Henan. Unable to ship in grain, the government requisitioned the entire local harvest to feed the one million troops. Starving farmers walked off their farms, many having 'sold' them for as little as the price of 8 kilograms of wheat.

By the spring of 1943 the Henan famine had claimed the lives of almost five million people. Even though Wang Quanyuan was not among the 10 000 who starved to death in her neighbouring province of Hunan in 1946, she was one of the 33 million people in central and southern China who never got enough to eat in those years.

At first she was relieved to be back home in her native village of Aocheng with people she knew, who ate the same food, followed the same customs and whose every word she under-stood. Yet she was an outsider even there. The success of the Long March had shifted the centre of the revolution with Mao from southern to northern China, and with it had gone any spirit of resistance. No propaganda teams tramped the Jiangxi country-side holding meetings, recruiting and stirring up the peasants. Although the communists' propaganda about their wholehearted opposition to the Japanese was winning them overwhelming support throughout the country, the KMT was in control of the south-east of China. Wang Quanyuan had put behind her the years she spent as a communist soldier and wanted only to settle into the familiar life of feeding the pigs and chickens, growing vegetables, tilling the soil and harvesting tea. Instead, she became the focus of the villagers' fears. She found that the people were not as welcoming as she had expected. They were suspicious of this apparently unattached 29-year-old woman who had been married out of the district twelve years before and who had then walked out of her husband's home to join the Red bandits. The locals knew something of the series of misfortunes that had dogged her since then and they were uneasy about her. Landlords and KMT officials in the district began to talk of her as 'ill-omened' (a description that Wang Quanyuan, in her heart of hearts, may have identified with) and tried to hustle her out of the area; they suggested she marry away and leave the district; she no longer belonged and they wanted her, quite simply, to go away.

Wang Quanyuan, however, refused to move. She had been out in the world and all her good work and good intentions had brought her nothing but pain: the party she had joined as another family had gone back on its promises and abandoned her. She always claimed that she never rejected the communists, she had retreated to her blood family out of sheer desperation. Once there, she wanted to stay.

She would not, however, countenance another marriage of convenience. Her first arranged marriage, when she was seventeen, had been a nonsense. Her second, impromptu, marriage to Wang Shoudao during the Long March had turned out to be a farce. She often asked herself if he might have intervened to rescue her after she contacted the 8th Route Army office in Lanzhou, when she might still have been considered to be his wife. At other times, however, she wondered if Wang Shoudao had been the reason she was turned away; if, in his position of some influence where he worked quite closely with Mao, he wanted *not* to be reunited with her. Perhaps on the Long March he had taken from her all he needed. She had no way of knowing where he had been when she needed him in 1939 or where he was in 1942. Edgar Snow says that immediately after the Long

March Wang Shoudao was heading guerrilla detachments on the Hunan–Jiangxi border; if that is so, he was working within 100 kilometres of Wang Quanyuan's village. Snow adds that in 1940 Wang Shoudao was 'Hunan Party chief and governor'. Other sources say he remained in the north-west at least until 1944, one having him in Yan'an about 1941 helping Mao edit party papers, after which he fought the Japanese and the KMT in Hunan and central China for several years.[3]

Wang Quanyuan told the villagers she was waiting for her husband Wan Ling to come back. Wan Ling had joined up to fight the Japanese in Burma and she owed it to him, a man fighting for his country, to be there when he returned, she said. It was not for the villagers to know that her liaison with Wan Ling had been forged out of desperation, that forming a union with him had been her only hope of survival.

To her surprise, Wan Ling did in fact eventually return. He arrived one day about two years later, apparently expecting to resume their relationship. Any pleasure she might have felt on seeing him didn't last long, however. 'I really don't know!' he responded when she asked him why he hadn't answered any of her letters. 'That woman,' he went on, as if to himself, 'she must have made sure they didn't get through to me . . .' He had not been much to start with, but still Wang Quanyuan could not bear this oblique admission of his duplicity at setting up house with another woman. She must have been aware that many men far from home set up house with whomever was at hand, but if it occurred to her that before her there may have been another wife left behind in Yunnan she failed to dwell on it. She accused Wan Ling of faithlessness and he offered no defence. He went back where he came from and they never saw each other again.

This left Wang Quanyuan in a precarious situation. She had had three husbands but she was no longer wife or widow to any of them; she was also childless, apparently barren as a result of the damage her reproductive system had sustained during the Long March. Her period in captivity in the north-west further complicated her status, for who was to say she hadn't shared her Moslem husband's bed willingly. The murmurings about her grew louder; she was sneered at for being a 'bandit's whore', a traitor and a deserter. Her brother and his family joined in the chorus of denunciation, claiming she had disgraced both them and the Red Army by allowing herself to be captured by Moslems.

A poignant story is told about a peasant woman who, like Wang Quanyuan, stepped on the cracks of traditional Chinese society and was relentlessly branded ill-omened. The story, written in 1924 by Lu Xun, a man universally respected as the pioneer of modern Chinese literature, is called 'The New–Year Sacrifice' and concerns a woman known as Xianglin's Wife.[4]

Xianglin's Wife was twenty-six and recently widowed when she was employed in early winter as a maid in the home of an ultra-conservative Neo-Confucian gentry family in southern China. Her sixteen-year-old woodcutter husband had died the previous spring and she still wore around her hair a white mourning band. The patriarch of the gentry family was initially reluctant to employ a widow but Xianglin's Wife came with a good recommendation and soon proved herself such a hard worker that the uncle put his doubts to one side. The uncle was finally convinced when Xianglin's Wife's worked so hard that she saved the family the cost of extra help during preparations for the New Year sacrifice ceremony. It appeared that Xianglin's Wife was also happy with her new situation: 'Little by little the trace of a smile appeared at the corners of her mouth, while her face became whiter and plumper.'

Then, one morning soon after New Year, this comfortable arrangement was shattered when Xianglin's Wife was abducted. She had gone to the river to wash the rice and two men, who witnesses said 'looked as if they came from the hills', seized her, tied her up then whisked her off up-river in their boat. It so happened that while this drama was being enacted on the river bank, a woman arrived at the house to explain to the uncle that she was the mother-in-law of Xianglin's Wife, who had run away from her dead husband's family the previous autumn. That being so, the mother-in-law had come to take her back, along with her wages and her clothes. The uncle considered this to be an indisputably correct course of action: 'If her mother-in-law wants her back, there's nothing more to be said.'

Xianglin's Wife was sold deep into the mountains where few families wished to send their daughters as wives, thus earning for her mother-in-law the sum of 80 000 cash. No-one expected

Xianglin's Wife to agree to this second marriage; after all 'Some widows sob and shout when they remarry; some threaten to kill themselves; some refuse to go through the ceremony of bowing to heaven and earth after they've been carried to the man's house; some even smash the wedding candlesticks.' But Xianglin's Wife put up a monumental struggle, according to the local go-between. She screamed and cursed and could not be made to go through with the ceremony at all. Then, as soon as the three men holding her momentarily loosened their grip, 'she bashed her head on a corner of the altar, gashing it so badly that the blood spurted out. Even though they smeared on two handfuls of incense ashes and tied it up with two pieces of red cloth, they couldn't stop the bleeding. It took quite a few of them to shut her up finally with the man in the bridal chamber, but even then she went on cursing.'

Xianglin's Wife—everybody still called her that, even though she was now the wife of another man—gave birth to a healthy baby boy nine months later and seemed to have accepted her new life. Then her second husband died of typhoid fever. She stayed in their house with her son, able and willing to support herself, but one morning her precious baby boy was carried off by a wolf. Her in-laws immediately reclaimed the house and turfed her out.

Xianglin's Wife wound the white mourning band around her hair again, came down from the hills and approached the gentry family once more for employment. As soon as she told the dreadful story of how her little Amao had disappeared after she left him to shell a basket of beans and how they finally found him 'lying in the wolf's den, all his innards eaten away, still clutching that little basket tight in his hand . . .' she was taken in again as a maid. But she was not the same as before, not as quick. She was preoccupied with her son's horrible death, telling the tale to anybody who would listen, until finally there was not a soul in the township who could not repeat it word for word. They grew bored with her.

The main trouble, however, was that because she had remarried after being widowed the uncle considered her unclean and refused to let her have anything to do with the ancestral sacrifices. A maidservant explained to Xianglin's Wife that the uncle considered her unclean because she had not remained a chaste widow. Xianglin's Wife listened in horror as the maidservant told her that when she died the King of Hell was going to have to saw her in half so that her ghost could be apportioned out rightfully to her two husbands. She quietly saved her wages for a year until she had enough to buy a threshold offering in a local Buddhist temple. Believing she was now cleansed and absolved, she began to recover her spirit and when it came time to prepare for the New Year sacrifices she expected to be able to take her part, as in the old days. The uncle, however, still forbad her to touch anything.

This rejection, which convinced Xianglin's Wife there was absolutely nothing she could do to save herself and re-enter society, was more than she could bear and within a year her hair had turned white while her 'sallow, dark-tinged face that looked as if it had been carved out of wood—had lost the grief-stricken expression it had borne before. The only sign of life about her was the occasional flicker of her eyes.' She began to lose her grip and could no longer do her work. The gentry family let her go. She turned to begging and died, inconveniently, in the snow during preparations for the following New Year. How did she die? 'Of poverty of course,' said the uncle's manservant. Reading between the lines, however, one can be sure that Lu Xun is telling us she died of Confucianism.

Wang Quanyuan did not die from having had three husbands and being taken by a Moslem, but she found it increasingly difficult to withstand the pressure of those around her to relinquish her status as an unattached woman. After the defeat of Japan in 1945, popular support for the communists swept through the country, and KMT supporters retreated towards the south-east. No doubt influenced by her having once been a Red bandit, the local landlord did all he could to intimidate her, including threatening to harm her brother's farm animals (and thus his livelihood) unless she moved away or married.

She held out for four years before relenting and marrying Liu Gaohua, a man from the nearby village of Heshixiang, in August 1948. Liu Gaohua's political history had a familiar ring to it. He joined the Red Army in 1933 after his father was killed and his mother was driven from their home by anti-communist vigilantes, but he was captured even before the communists set off on their Long March. Prisoners in Chinese prisons were not given meals and had to rely on family or friends bringing them food, otherwise they starved to death. Liu Gaohua fell ill after several months in prison and was released with a fine of one hundred eggs. Upon his release from prison he rejected revolution and returned to the soil. Wang Quanyuan said she married Liu Gaohua because, like her, he had tried to take part in the revolution. 'So many fine comrades sacrificed their lives for the revolution,' Kang Keqing once said, 'yet there were also those who cracked when their lives were in the balance, and those who were so demoralised they turned their backs on the world.'[5]

6

THE RED AMAZON

The communists who survived the Long March had already begun to assume legendary status in China by 1937, when the American journalist Helen Foster Snow arrived in Yan'an under a mantle of gold velvet, as she called the fine loess dust which drifted down upon everything and everybody in the best egalitarian tradition. With Japan in control of Manchuria and the Chinese Government unwilling to commit KMT armies to the field against Japan's mighty forces, the pervasive anti-Japanese propaganda of the communists made them the popular focus of national opposition to Japan's aggressive military presence in China. As they marched through north China, the Red Army painted slogans in large Chinese characters on the walls of houses and temples:

> Improve the livelihood of the people!
> The people must unite with the army to fight the Japanese!
> Decrease taxes!
> Drive the Japanese from China!
> We must never become homeless slaves!
> Arm yourselves; fight until the Japanese are all driven from China!
> Soldiers and people unite![1]

An ongoing recruitment campaign added tens of thousands of young men to the Red Army, while a steady stream of intellectuals, artists, actors, writers and students 'rushed to Yen-an from remote corners of the country, with their ruck-sacks strapped to their backs, defying long treks, dangers, and difficulties . . . They regarded Yen-an as the Holy Land of resistance to Japan. "Those who are for resistance to Japan go to Yen-an" had become the slogan among the young people.' So wrote Zhang Guotao of the early days in Yan'an.[2]

Kang Keqing shared with Zhu De one of Yan'an's ancient cave dwellings that were carved into the mountainside at the foot of Phoenix Mountain, just north of the small walled township. They often invited Helen Foster Snow to Phoenix Mountain Village to share their meals during the four months of her stay. Kang Keqing responded gravely in her throaty voice to Helen Foster Snow's eager questions. By candlelight at night they would sit together on the cosy *kang*, a raised brick platform stretching the length of the room and heated by a small fire in its base. Northerners use the *kang* as a bench during the day and sleep on it at night. On summer afternoons with the rains drumming down Kang Keqing and Helen Foster Snow talked in the pale daylight filtering through paper-covered lattice windows. Kang Keqing revealed her total lack of interest in feminism and the women of China. She saw no personal need for feminism: she had resisted an arranged marriage and ventured out into the world, had accepted responsible positions within the party and mixed daily on what she understood to be an equal footing with men, had applied herself diligently to the difficult task of learning to read and write, and had just enrolled at the Anti-Japanese Red University. She was working towards her goal of becoming a regular military commander in charge of male soldiers, and she was intent on doing this entirely on her own merit. Helen Foster Snow nicknamed Kang Keqing 'The Red Amazon'.[3]

For Kang Keqing, the Long March had been a challenge and an adventure. She was young and healthy, and after reaching Yan'an she was given the opportunity to attend university and the Party School where she was able to translate the experience she had gained into a career as an official—a cadre—of high rank. Few Long March women were so lucky, and, while Kang Keqing spoke of what she had achieved being made possible solely through her personal efforts and the goodness of the party, it is difficult to believe she would have been unaware of the privileges being the wife of Zhu De brought her.

For most of the women, especially the older ones and those who were pregnant or ill, the Long March was an ordeal from which they never completely recovered. They had left Jiangxi in order to survive, knowing they would have been captured and killed had they remained behind, and they were exhausted by the time they reached the relative safety of Yan'an. Some became pregnant soon after, as did He Zizhen and Liu Ying, which further drained them physically and emotionally. Many of their husbands began to neglect them and show interest in the sophisticated young students and actresses arriving from the east. The women became bitter, often preferring to ignore their husbands' affairs than suffer the loss of position and prestige a divorce entailed.

Kang Keqing blamed the women for finding themselves in this predicament, as she explained to Helen Foster Snow: 'Most of the troubles of the women with the Red Army are the babies they're always having. This is bad for their revolutionary work, and many of them are sick from the strain . . . Some women have the special characteristic of liking to be dependent on men and have babies.'[4] Kang Keqing did not have any children and in this she was exceptional, not only among the Long March women, but among the women of China. She put it down to her own good management: 'I like babies as an institution, but don't want any myself, because I want to keep in perfect physical condition for my work in the army,' she said. 'I keep in good athletic condition by playing basketball, tennis and jumping.'[5]

It is not surprising that such a personal matter has never been raised by Chinese commentators, but it was this crucial fact of remaining childless that allowed Kang Keqing to entertain the idea of becoming a soldier and permitted her to accompany Zhu De on so much of his command work in the field. No reliable method of birth control existed in China then, but it had been a subject of discussion for at least twenty years, and some women obviously practised some form of contraception. These women were able to remain active within the communist organisation. Cai Chang, for example, had only one child, born in Paris when she was twenty-three. Deng Yingchao, the wife of Zhou Enlai, did not bear any children after suffering a miscarriage in her early twenties, although this itself may have left her unable to conceive.

Several methods of birth control were available to Kang

Keqing: the rhythm method, coitus interruptus, Daoist sexual practices, and celibacy. Celibacy can be discounted because, although the 27-year age difference between them meant that Zhu De was already in his fifties and she in her mid-twenties when they reached Yan'an, no suggestion has ever been made that Kang Keqing's marriage to Zhu De was anything less than genuine. She told Helen Foster Snow: 'Since [January 1929] I have always been with Chu Tê except for the time when we were separated for one year after the occupation of Kian [ie, Ji'an] in 1930. Sometimes we don't live in the same house, of course, and we have no children because they would interfere with my work.'[6]

Certain Daoist sexual practices require the male to bring his partner to climax while he refrains from ejaculating. The latter feat is achieved by exerting pressure on the urethra between the scrotum and the anus at the moment of ejaculation, which diverts the seminal secretion into the bladder. This technique of *coitus reservatus* is known in Daoist terminology as 'making the sperm return' and its purpose is to husband the male's *yang* essence so that he may attain longevity. The man's purpose in bringing his female partner to climax, incidentally, is to absorb her *yin* essence.[7] Zhu De may have known something of these practices but the battlefield conditions under which they spent Kang Keqing's fertile years did not lend themselves to such sexual refinement. The rhythm method of abstaining from sexual intercourse during the fertile period of the menstrual cycle, and coitus interruptus, which required the male to withdraw before ejaculating, were both widely known if not commonly practised in China, where large families were almost de rigueur. Both required the cooperation of one's husband, something He Zizhen had clearly been unable to elicit from Mao but which Kang Keqing may have found was more forthcoming from Zhu De. While Kang Keqing and Zhu De might have practised the rhythm method, the most likely explanation for Kang Keqing's freedom from pregnancies is that she was infertile, but this must remain conjecture.

Kang Keqing was just three years younger than 29-year-old Helen Foster Snow but twenty years younger than Agnes Smedley, the other American journalist in Yan'an. The moment she arrived in Yan'an in January 1937, Agnes Smedley had fallen under the spell of that charming old warrior Zhu De, of whom she said:

> . . . I personally believe him to be the kindest, gentlest man I
> have ever known. He is a man of the utmost simplicity, and he
> does not know the meaning of pride. He is fifty and more now,
> but his mind remains alert, alive, and he is anxious to learn
> from all people. In no particular is he selfish or moved by
> personal motives. These qualities have won for him the
> devotion of the whole army which he commands.[8]

Edgar Snow had earlier claimed Mao Zedong as his chief communist biographee; Agnes Smedley decided on Zhu De for hers. She followed him about for three months to record his life story. She paid little attention to Kang Keqing, whom she referred to briefly while at the front in late 1937 as 'this simple, capable peasant girl from Kiangsi, one of the best trained women in the army. She has just arrived from the Anti-Japanese University in Yenan, in North Shensi Province, and she will soon take up political work in the army. She is a fine woman, not yet thirty.'[9]

Agnes Smedley and Kang Keqing had another common interest besides Zhu De. Each was intent on the war, Smedley on reporting it, Kang Keqing on being in it.

Kang Keqing's passion to become a soldier had not lessened in the nine years since she had joined the Red Army as a partisan. During her time in the Jiangxi soviet as a youth worker, director of the Headquarters Guard Regiment, political instructor, and communications inspector she had carried a gun for protection but had never been involved in the fighting—apart from the 'happy day' in 1934 that transformed her into 'the Girl Commander' when she led 300 men into battle. She told Helen Foster Snow that the only woman she admired was He Ying, sister of the flamboyant He Long of the 2nd Front Red Army, who had commanded 'a whole division of troops—all men soldiers' but had been killed in battle. 'My ambition now is to do real military work as Ho Lung's sister did. I am hoping to become a commander in the army.' She said: 'Comrade Chu Tê sympathizes with my ambition and wants me to perfect my military knowledge so I can be capable of commanding an army in the future. I think I will succeed—I am very good at military science. I have learned a great deal from Chu Tě and always listen when he talks to others.'[10]

Despite Kang Keqing's confidence in him, Zhu De's sympathy with her ambition does not appear to have ever been in danger of becoming more than just that. When Helen Foster Snow asked him why he had no women's regiments in his army, he replied:

> Many women are very anxious to join the Red Army, but we can't take them in. The main problem is one of discipline. Then, too, the Red Army is so mobile that they cannot keep up with such fast marching as our maneuvering requires in fighting, nor carry the necessary burdens easily, and also they get sick more often than men, as the life is extremely hard. However, their fighting spirit is good, and they would make good soldiers for any ordinary army. There have been many brave women in the partisan groups.[11]

Zhu De's determination to keep his Red Army free of women was reinforced by the new domestic ethos of Yan'an that reclaimed the Long March women as wives and mothers. Kang Keqing did not consider herself a wife, however, and she had the good luck not to become a mother. As in so many things, she thought she was different. She was disciplined, fast and strong enough to be one of the men, so she believed all she needed to become a soldier was a little more training. She took pride in her profession, as when she mastered the art of the puttee: first, how to wrap her lower legs securely in the cloth puttees of the soldier, then how to peel them carefully off into a rolled bandage. Each night she methodically placed the rolled puttees in her upturned cap on the *kang* bed beside her then placed her clothing neatly on top of the cap, first off on the bottom, last off on top. Only then would she sink into a deep sleep secure in the knowledge that she could be up and dressed, even in the dark, ready to go at a moment's notice.

In March she enrolled in semester two at the Red Army University, now renamed Kang–Ri junzheng daxue (Anti–Japanese Civil and Military University) and popularly abbreviated to Kang-da. The university song echoed her desires:

> Red Army University students,
> vanguard of the anti-Japanese fight, leaders of the people's revolution:

we're cadres resolving it all, studying hard, hard, hard!
Indivisible.

Working so hard, our life so fine, sticking to the rules we
charge ahead.
National Red Army spirit—that's what we are, in battle gear
heading off to the front![12]

She was assigned to Class Two with many other women and
was soon elected head of the Kang-da female student body. She
studied the only two subjects available to her class, politics and
military strategy. The latter covered partisan and artillery warfare,
topography and the science of arms; politics covered social science
and political work, the Sino–Japanese problem and the Chinese
struggle for liberation. Her lecturers were the very men who
shaped the Chinese Revolution:

- Mao Zedong lectured on dialectical materialism;
- Zhu De discussed party recommendations;
- Dong Biwu (52-year-old Chairman of the Communist Party
  School and long-time revolutionary) took modern Chinese
  revolutionary history;
- Zhang Wentian (Secretary of Communist Central Committee
  and new husband of Mao's protegee Liu Ying) analysed the
  problems of the Chinese Revolution;
- Bo Gu (Chairman of the North-West Branch Soviet Government and at that time husband of Liu Qunxian) filled them
  in on basic Marxist–Leninist theory;
- Otto Braun demonstrated military tactics through 'seminars,
  war games, and sandbox exercises'.[13]

Zhang Guotao also taught at the university, but his were the
senior students and his subject was economics. He was living just
outside Yan'an at that time, awaiting the arrival of his wife, Yang
Zilie, whom he had not seen since their work separated them in
Shanghai more than six years before, and his twelve-year-old son,
whom he had not seen for ten years.[14]

Universities and colleges were the communists' training ground
for cadres (*ganbu*), or office-holding party members. Cadres were
responsible for recruitment, and since it was essential that communist soldiers understood exactly what they were fighting for,
so that they were prepared to die for it (Helen Foster Snow's

admiring description of the communists' astonishing revolutionary elan was 'the pure in heart facing self-sacrifice for a purpose'),[15] cadres were the driving force of the revolution. They needed to be literate, to have the wide social experience and general knowledge necessary to convince the people that the party's direction and solutions were necessary to rescue China from the mire of its past and the predicament of its present.

Kang Keqing was already a cadre by dint of her years of experience in Jiangxi. Illiterate till she went onto Jinggangshan at the age of seventeen, she had diligently practised writing the complex written characters of her native language at every spare moment and had been spotted more than once during the Long March with her rucksack on her knees as a desk quietly concentrating on writing out messages. She was justly proud of her hard-won ability to take down even basic notes during class. Literacy was of major concern to the communists as the print media were a valuable means of spreading their message, and in Yan'an they published material for adults learning to read and write; Otto Braun used these primers, commenting that they 'were well illustrated and each character was accompanied by a corresponding romanization'.[16] Since the university had few textbooks, reading fluency was not so much an issue for Kang Keqing.

She was also proud of her sporting ability and kept physically fit as she was aiming for the post of commander. She played tennis and dabbled in athletics, but her greatest pleasure came from basketball, partly for the joy of teasing Zhu De. Most afternoons after class, in between rainstorms, the female students would play basketball against the male students. Zhu De sometimes turned up looking for a game and Agnes Smedley, who came to watch him play, later remarked: 'General Chu would often shake his head a little wistfully and remark that the young guards never liked him to play on their side because he wasn't a very good player.' Edgar Snow also described Zhu De's as 'a "wistful" game of basket-ball'.[17] If the women relented and took Zhu De on to their team, Kang Keqing immediately swapped over to play with the men so she could be assured of being on the winning side.[18]

Once Japan had occupied Peiping, Tianjin and Shanghai in mid 1937, its massive armies began to roll confidently down through north China. Zhu De left Yan'an in late August 1937 for the front, where as Commander-in-Chief of the Red Army he established 8th Route Army headquarters in the Taihang Mountains just south of the Great Wall. His immediate task was to halt the Japanese advance down the main north–south railway through the province of Shanxi.

Shortly afterwards, Kang Keqing requested and received special permission to travel to the war zone about twelve days to the north-east of Yan'an. This was another example of how effective was her *guanxi*, as Helen Foster Snow implied: 'At that time no Soviet women were permitted to go to the fighting front, but K'ang K'e-ching considered herself in a special category and was determined to be with her commander-in-chief husband in the thick of the fray.' Kang Keqing packed her few belongings, wound on her puttees, donned her army cap and set out from Yan'an on 7 September with about twenty-five others.[19]

Fording icy rivers and skirting fresh mudslides, the little contingent squelched south through the treeless and stony mountains for over a week till they reached Front Political Headquarters in the town of Sanyuan. From there Agnes Smedley and Helen Foster Snow made the four-day trip to the transit city of Xi'an where Edgar Snow had arranged to meet his wife. At Sanyuan Kang Keqing turned east and headed for the front. It had been raining steadily since June and the loess-drenched Yellow River looked magnificent when she crossed it by junk. China's Sorrow, it was called, this river that would not be contained between man-made walls, flowing in places twelve metres above the surrounding North China Plain. Its floods were catastrophic, the famines that followed worse. It caused colossal damage when it sought a new path to the sea 800 years ago, and over the last two centuries it has changed course three times on the Shantung Peninsula.

The sight of China's muddy Sorrow was soon followed by the further excitement of her first train ride. As the steam train trundled northwards, stopping at, and several times between, every small station, she looked out at a different landscape from that of the north-west she had just left behind. The sun shone from the clear autumn sky on a softer land of trees, mountains terraced with fields of cotton and millet, and an endless stream of refugees, including many wounded, making their slow way south just ahead of the invaders. The train brought Kang Keqing to the 8th Route Army in the city of Taiyuan, where Japanese aeroplanes defecated their loads of bombs over the already battered city several times a day. The city's few hospitals were crammed with thousands upon thousands of wounded soldiers, but the overworked doctors had no drugs, no equipment, nothing for their patients' pain, no hope of treating them; most of them would simply die from their wounds.

After two days' wait in Taiyuan, Kang Keqing received permission to travel north into the high Taihang mountain range that marked the dividing line between the highlands and the North China Plain. Deep in those soft green mountains 8th Route Army guerrillas confounded their enemy by repositioning themselves silently at night, disabling enemy aircraft (they had none of their own), and arming themselves with captured Japanese weapons. Agnes Smedley described Red Army men she saw moving through the mountains one early November evening:

Up this narrow, stony path came long lines of Chinese soldiers, marching with astounding swiftness. Their clothing was the blue-grey cotton which they always wear, their shoes were cotton cloth slippers with soft soles. Many wore string or rope sandals, and almost all had no stockings. Above their heads extended the ends of their rifles, with bayonets fixed. Some carried machine-guns, and behind them toiled mules, heaving under heavy loads of ammunition. In pockets about the waist of each man were many hand-grenades, and on their backs were small square packs with grey cotton blankets around them. Two battalions of the old Red Army from Kiangsi were marching to battle, marching with their two-hundred-li-a-day stride that has no equal on earth. They were out-flanking the oncoming Japanese.

The shadows of night deepened and the coiling line of men merged with the darkness of the ravines below. One by one the men stepped up out of the darkness and passed along the path, then plunged down into darkness again. For three or four seconds each man passed before me, and as he passed, turned his face toward me. He spoke no word, but passed like a shadow. His soft-soled shoes made no sound. Sometimes a rifle clanked against a shovel on a man's back. Some of the shadowy figures were heaving, and their faces gleamed with perspiration. But not one slackened that steady, swift pace that can cover twice or three times the marching distance of ordinary soldiers.[20]

A three-day journey by horse, passing through enemy lines at night and a steady fall of deepening snow, brought Kang Keqing to 8th Route Army headquarters on Wutaishan, at 3000 metres the highest peak in the Taihang range.

'I would like to be assigned to a fighting unit,' Kang Keqing told the officer in charge of organisation.

'Well, things are moving so fast just now, the Japanese are changing their strategy, and we still haven't worked out how to deal with them. We don't think it's the right time for women from Yan'an to go on duty at the front yet—I suggest we make you an organising cadre with GHQ's Political Bureau. Is that all right?'[21]

It wasn't what she had in mind but, willing to do whatever work would keep her in the war zone, Kang Keqing accepted the offer and devoted herself over the next two years to her job as an organiser. She lived with the local people, paying for her food and lodging; she explained the principles that motivated the 8th Route Army of opposing the Japanese and sharing the land out to the people; she called meetings at which the communists interpreted for the people the events of this war that had engulfed them; she organised peasants into groups to help transport the wounded; she organised the people into self-defence units and the young men into guerrilla units.

The Japanese Army, on the other hand, moved in highly mechanised waves: bombers first, followed by tanks and trucks then well-equipped foot soldiers. In the first ten-day period of November, just a few weeks after Kang Keqing had passed through the city of Taiyuan, it fell to the Japanese. Long lines of Chinese soldiers rose in the dead of night to pad silently over the mountains and back to the south and west.

They were heady days on Wutaishan, and Kang Keqing knew no fear. The weather was foul and the going was tough—heavy clouds piled up over the mountaintops, it rained, it snowed and the rivers began to ice over. Thousands of soldiers died, thousands more were wounded, civilians who were not driven from their villages were slaughtered by the Japanese, but Red Army spirits were high. Eighth Route Army headquarters (a fluid concept in guerrilla warfare) moved every few days: 'The 8th Route Army is like the fish, and the people like the water,' is how Peng Dehuai, Zhu De's deputy commander, described their way of operating. 'We move amongst the people, and the Japanese learn nothing about us. We have no traitors in our ranks.'[22]

Kang Keqing was in her element. The muted bugle would hardly have sounded across the snow at two o'clock in the morning before she was up and dressed in the pitch dark. Puttees, army cap (with winter earmuffs), heavy overcoat firmly belted, chest crisscrossed by pack and equipment straps, white enamel mug dangling at her belt: she was ready to go. She did not mention Agnes Smedley by name in her reminiscences, saying only that quite a few foreign journalists visited the 8th Route Army at this time, among them Russians, Britishers and Americans, and that these journalists placed their hopes of a victory over the Japanese in the Chinese Communist Party and the 8th Route Army.[23] Agnes Smedley wrote in absorbing detail of the two months she spent trailing after Zhu De's portable headquarters with a small troupe of Chinese and foreign newspaper reporters; she mentioned Kang Keqing once, maybe twice. She told of sheltering from the drizzling rain to watch Zhu De standing outside an old temple draped with welcoming banners to address a small crowd of people. She described the lively performances of the thirty-strong Front Service Group, that would publish 'living newspapers' for their entranced audiences, the actors strutting larger than life across red-curtained stages lit by hanging iron lamps, the singers chanting the tale of a recent battle to the rhythm of drum and clappers:

> One of the players appeared before the curtain, a pair of small clappers in one hand, to keep the rhythm of this talk. He spoke in old ballad form, telling the ten principles of the Communist Party of China. He told them in verse and he developed and interpreted them, sometimes sending the audience into gales of laughter. In another 'piece,' a blind minstrel, with his musical instrument, appeared in the home of a family and sang them the news from all the fronts of China. He brought news, he said, from the Eighth Route Army, which was 'the Chu–Mao, the Red Army of China.' He brought news

of the miner Partisans of Yangchüan, and he sang of their fighting against the Japanese.[24]

On 26 December 1937, with the Japanese war machine gearing up to overrun China from the top down, Agnes Smedley requested permission to accompany the American Evans Carlson to the front. She was infuriated when Zhu De refused to let her go because she was a woman. Kang Keqing watched as Smedley 'pouted for a day and, much to everyone's amazement, even tried tears'.[25] But there was no changing Zhu De's mind so Agnes Smedley packed her things and left Shanxi Province by train on 4 January 1938, reciting to herself Ruth's poignant words— 'Entreat me not to leave thee, or return from following after thee; for whither thou goest I will go . . .'.[26] Smedley never saw Zhu De or Kang Keqing again, although Zhu De wrote to her from time to time. She died in London in 1950, her biography of Zhu De still in manuscript form.

In mid 1938, 8th Route Army headquarters stabilised for a time in a valley to the south of Wutaishan. There the army set up a temporary hospital whose facilities were totally inadequate to deal with the thousands of military casualties. An unnamed Australian nurse who made her way to the valley reported the devastation of people's lives. In that small area she saw hundreds of bombed and burnt-out villages; thousands of new shallow graves; she could give no idea how many unburied civilian corpses she saw.[27] After it was over, officials tried to put some figures on the Sino–Japanese War that lasted from 1937 to 1945. They said that about one and a half million Chinese soldiers died and nearly two million were wounded; no-one was prepared to guess at how many civilians got in the way of it all and lost their lives, their homes, their families.

Eighth Route Army headquarters fell further back into the south-western heights of the Taihang range as the Japanese pushed down through Shanxi and Generalissimo Chiang Kai-shek tightened his blockade on the communists. The people suffered greatly; it cannot be otherwise with war. A dry winter caused a drought during the northern spring and summer of 1938; water had to be carried and wells dug. Kang Keqing saw starving peasants eating the bark and leaves off trees. She withdrew to the south and west of Shanxi Province and continued living and working with the people, calling meetings and training partisans. Although China was at war with Japan and the task of the 8th Route Army was to hinder the seemingly unstoppable Japanese Army, the bulk of the communists' efforts in the north was directed to mobilising the masses; Mao had directed cadres to devote 70 per cent of their efforts to building up party membership and establishing 'liberated areas' similar to the Jiangxi soviet. As Kang Keqing moved from place to place she first sought out the people she described as being 'progressive in their thinking and politically reliable'. These people were immediately admitted to the party and became the kernel of workers', peasants', youth and women's groups, which were further linked to a provincial network called 'national salvation confederations'. She helped set up literacy groups, which were placed in the care of an umbrella organisation called the National Salvation Association of Cultural and Educational Groups.

The communists had since 1930 concentrated on activating the peasantry, whom Mao believed to be the most fertile ground for revolutionaries. Peasants comprised the mass of the population in China, but the north was also a mining area, and the communists found there another ready source of disaffection. How the communists won the coal miners of Shigejie to their cause is a typical example of how they went about their work of propaganda and organising.

These miners had gone on strike at the end of 1937 and, although some improvement in working conditions had been won, they were unsure of their next move and called upon the army in June 1938 for further guidance. Kang Keqing was appointed to go and talk to them as a representative of the army. She brought back to headquarters the information she had gathered from her discussions with the miners, then a party cadre who had once worked as a miner was assigned to the task of organising them. Before long he had started up a party branch at the mine. When the Japanese took over the mine in July 1939 some of the men formed anti-Japanese guerrilla units and others carried on the work of the party branch in a clandestine manner. It was by thus becoming the pivot of the anti-Japanese war effort that the communists benefited tremendously from the Japanese invasion of northern China.

Each Saturday night Kang Keqing would travel to wherever Zhu De was billeted, usually only a few *li* away, to catch up on his week. Their work even gave them a genuine excuse to play basketball with the locals, who were terribly impressed at the earthy attitude of this Commander-in-Chief of the 8th Route Army, indistinguishable on the court from his men, and enjoying a game with his wife.

In 1939 Kang Keqing was assigned to the Northern Region Women's Committee to co-direct women's work in south-eastern Shanxi—an unexpected posting that threatened her long-cherished vision of becoming a military commander. Taking full advantage of her *guanxi* as the wife of the Commander-in-Chief, she gained permission to continue in her job as an organiser with headquarters instead of moving across to fill the honorary position of chair of the South-east Shanxi Women's National Salvation Confederation. Her contribution to this compromise was to agree to do as much as she could for the Confederation from where she was, which happened to be some 300 kilometres away, on the far side of the province.

In the spring of 1940 Zhu De was ordered to go to the ancient city of Luoyang in Henan Province to meet with KMT leaders in an attempt to shore up their precarious united front. Wanting to accompany him, Kang Keqing realised she could justify the trip by going in her capacity as honorary chair of the Confederation. Since the expedition brought them into KMT territory they took the precaution of surrounding themselves with a crack company of communist soldiers. They travelled south by foot and by horse along local foot tracks, through blockades, by night, around and over mountain peaks. On the southernmost edge of the Taihang range they halted briefly on Wangshi Mountain to gaze down at the muddy Yellow River making its broad unhurried way eastwards across the flood plain. In the time-honoured tradition of scholars Zhu De scrawled a poem on an old shrine on the mountaintop, to celebrate their 'Emerging from Taihangshan' on this mission so vital to the communists' survival:

Steep peaks crowd on Taihang—look!
Yellow River, wide mud-moat.
War reddens its banks—take heart,
let's drive off our common foe.[28]

Luoyang is an ancient city, built as a walled town during the Zhou dynasty about 1100 BC and made the Zhou capital nearly 400 years later; at various times in its 3000 years it has been the capital of seven other dynasties. When Kang Keqing arrived there in May 1940, it was a large city where the KMT had established their northern command headquarters and where modern trucks and cars sped through the broad streets. She had never seen anything like sophisticated Luoyang, and she felt she was a total misfit.[29] She spoke in later life of her experiences there, using them to illustrate what she considered to be the reactionary and reprehensible attitudes of the KMT. What is most striking about her recollections, however, is that this appears to be the first time she became aware that what she expected from her life as a communist, and what the communists, in the influential form of Zhu De, expected of her might not coincide.

She was driven straight to KMT command headquarters, where Commanding Officer Wei Lihuang stood in his yellow uniform and shiny leather boots at the head of a welcoming queue of generals and their wives. For Zhu De there was an element of homecoming as he warmly greeted smiling ex-colleagues from his days as a KMT general. Kang Keqing floundered in his wake, blindly shaking the proferred hands of men and women she didn't know, didn't trust, and had every reason to hate.

That evening, neatly dressed in her best uniform, she sat stolidly beside Zhu De through the official banquet Commanding Officer Wei had arranged in their honour. Along with the uni-formed generals and their sleek colourfully gowned wives she raised her glass when a toast was proposed to Commander-in-Chief Zhu De. Obediently she raised her glass again when a toast was proposed to somebody called Mrs Zhu. She was startled when her husband nudged her and whispered: 'They're offering a toast to you, didn't you hear?'

Flushed with embarrassment and not a little annoyed, she rose awkwardly to her feet: 'I'm sorry, I didn't realise. We don't use that form of address where I come from.'

Amid general polite laughter Commanding Officer Wei brought her to heel: 'It's the way we do it here,' he chided her through a civil smile. 'From now on, Mrs Zhu, there'll be no need for you to be perplexed by our formalities.'

Kang Keqing held her tongue for the rest of the evening and did not comment when Commanding Officer Wei presented to her the young, beautiful wife of one of his senior officers, saying she would be Kang Keqing's 'companion' for her stay in Luoyang; this woman was to perform the multiple duties of guide, chaperone and guard. As Kang Keqing returned with Zhu De to their quarters she sought moral support from her husband, telling him how uncomfortable she felt at being called Mrs Zhu instead of Comrade Kang, or simply Kang Keqing.

He said: 'A revolutionary can't be a Mrs Official, and a Mrs Official can't be a revolutionary—I agree with you absolutely. And you know I don't want you to be just my wife, either. However,' he went on, 'as Wei Lihuang said, that's the way they do things here.' Kang Keqing was surprised to hear her husband take the part of this man whom she had believed to be their common enemy. Baffled, she remained silent. 'Our main task here,' Zhu De explained, 'is to unify our military effort and of course we must remain vigilant; but we must also change some of *our* old customs. So long as our principles are not compromised we must subordinate everything to our main task.'

There was nothing Kang Keqing could say to this standard communist slogan of subordinating everything to their main task, even though it appeared that she was the one expected to make the changes. Zhu De did not need to compromise himself as he moved between communist and KMT society. He could remain a man and a soldier, both named Zhu De, while in KMT society the soldier named Kang Keqing would have to give way to a wife named Mrs Zhu.

And it was Mrs Zhu who became a silent pawn in diplomatic gamesmanship between Zhu De and Commanding Officer Wei. 'Mrs Zhu, it seems to me that pistol you're wearing is too big. It's a man's toy, it doesn't become a woman,' was Wei's first comment when he arrived the next day for discussions with Zhu De. 'Actually, I have a small German pistol, a "palm-of-the-hand thunderclap" and one hundred bullets to go with it which I would like to present to you as a gift.'

Instead of allowing Kang Keqing to defend her right to wear whatever pistol she chose, Zhu De indicated that she should gracefully accept this smaller pistol, immediately returning the compliment by presenting Commanding Officer Wei with some war trophies of his own: a Japanese pistol, sabre and pair of binoculars; a beautifully finished wool overcoat that had belonged to a Japanese officer; and a bundle of books and magazines.

From Luoyang, Kang Keqing and Zhu De travelled to the provincial capital of Xi'an, where they spent a few days in the second ten-day period of May 1940 consolidating KMT–Communist relations. Xi'an was the Casablanca of north-west China—the nearest railway junction to the communists' base area and the transit point for all communists making their way into or out of Yan'an. It was a city of spies, intrigue, checkpoints and high-level diplomacy.

By chance they reached Xi'an at the same time as Zhou Enlai, who was on his way to Chungking for negotiations with General-issimo Chiang Kai-shek. Taking advantage of Zhou Enlai's diplo-matic skills, Zhu De included him in his talks with various KMT generals. He also included Kang Keqing, to the extent that the words '. . . request the pleasure of the company of Assistant-Commander Zhu De and his wife' began to appear as a matter of course on invitations to the obligatory formal dinners. Kang Keqing's request to be excused on the grounds that she was unsuited to this form of social intercourse were ignored. Her husband told her that it was her duty, in fact part of her revolutionary work, to put aside her distaste for grand occasions and attend these dinners.

Zhu De also encouraged her to fulfil other official responsi-bilities, as when she was called upon to address reporters and KMT women's federation workers in her role as honorary chair of the South-east Shanxi Women's National Salvation Confeder-ation. Seeing how scared she was of facing her audience, his advice was: 'Don't think of the audience as educated intellectuals, just imagine they are ordinary people like you. They've asked you to tell them what's happening with the 8th Route Army and the women in the base areas because they want to know. Don't disappoint them by being nervous. Just be yourself, tell them the truth and you'll be fine.'

It is clear that Kang Keqing's purpose in recounting these episodes was to reinforce the image of Zhu De as the firm but fair senior communist father figure and of herself as a simple young peasant woman who overcame her dislike of the trappings of privilege as well as her feelings of inadequacy to carry out her sacred duty as a communist. Beyond these standard communist cliches, however, these episodes reveal that as the communists came of age and took their first steps beyond the charmed circle of Yan'an, old attitudes that had lain dormant while they lived as guerrillas now re-surfaced. Kang Keqing may have believed that Zhu De sympathised with her military ambitions, but his actions indicate that he never had any intention of allowing them to become a reality. She had been withdrawn from the Red Military Academy in Jiangxi before she finished her course, she was never appointed to a military post, she was not permitted to join a combat unit. For most of the Long March she was a political instructor, helping organise meetings, spread propaganda and recruit soldiers. At the anti-Japanese front she continued with this work of organising peasants into unions so as to more easily explain the administration, tax and land reforms the communists were undertaking. It was also at the anti-Japanese front that she began to experience pressure to attend to women's work, which she had assiduously avoided since joining the communists on Jinggangshan. Whether or not she noticed it, from the time the communists reached Yan'an their talk of equality and the liberation of women increasingly took on the mien of mere rhetoric.

Upon Kang Keqing's return to Yan'an on a warm spring afternoon in late May 1940 there were many familiar faces to catch up with after her nearly three years at the front. Joyfully she greeted Wu Zhonglian, her old friend from Jinggangshan. They had just missed each other in the autumn of 1937, Wu Zhonglian arriving in Yan'an as Kang Keqing left. Wu Zhonglian, not quite so athletic now with the passing of time and the hard lines she had been dealt, recounted the horrors that befell the doomed Western Route Army after it crossed the Yellow River four years earlier, all but a few of the female soldiers killed or taken prisoner. She told how she had given her baby son into the care of a sympathetic young couple before galloping off into the mountains of Gansu, only to be captured by Moslem cavalry three months later. She described her imprisonment as a worker in a felt-factory in Ningxia and her abortive escape to Xi'an with two other women, one of whom was Zhang Qinqiu, longtime head of political organisation with the 4th Front Army.[30] Zhang Qinqiu had given a false name when she was captured by Ma Bufang but local authorities sympathetic to the KMT suspected her real identity and betrayed the three women. They were arrested by the KMT as soon as they reached Xi'an and sent to KMT headquarters in the southern city of Nanjing. There they were interned in a 'self-criticism institution', where they would doubtless have remained but for Zhou Enlai. Wu Zhonglian's one piece of good fortune had been that the Communist–KMT united front was in its early stages with both sides releasing political prisoners, so Zhou Enlai had been able to arrange the immediate release of the three women. After Wu Zhonglian reached Yan'an she worked with the organisation section and the political department of the 8th Route Army in the north-east.

Another surprise for Kang Keqing was Han Shiying, who had been dropped out of the Long March in Yunnan five years earlier with folk-singer Li Guiying to build up a guerrilla force in the south-west. By the time the two women were caught by the KMT at the end of 1936 they had considerably depleted the grain stores of many local bullies and pasted up hundreds of inflammatory posters drafted by Han Shiying in her beautiful calligraphy. After her release in May 1937 Han Shiying was escorted home to Sichuan where her father tried to keep her under house arrest. She escaped to the KMT capital of Chungking, however, where she taught school for a time. By September 1937 she had made contact with the party once more, had married and gone with her husband to Yan'an where she was on a form of sick leave when Kang Keqing returned. Li Guiying had had a baby at the beginning of 1936 in Sichuan, where Han Shiying took her as a comparatively safe place for the birth. She returned to guerrilla work, having apparently left the baby in Sichuan, and in the winter of 1936 was arrested and imprisoned by the KMT. Released in October 1937, she travelled to central China whence she reported to Deng Yingchao, director of the women's work department and wife of Zhou Enlai, on the dangerous guerrilla work being carried out there.[31]

Other familiar faces were gone, however; a painful fact of wartime life. No-one could help her when Kang Keqing asked about Jin Weiying, who had travelled to Moscow with Cai Chang and several others in the autumn of 1938. Also missing, although Kang Keqing probably did not notice, was Zeng Yu, the maverick whose Long March baby had been the first to arrive and the first to be abandoned. Zeng Yu and her husband had been transferred to the south, she to work with a local unit, he to join the New 4th Army fighting south of the Yangtze River. It was later reported that Zeng Yu disappeared, presumed killed, as she attempted to return to her unit after taking her child back to the comparative safety of her family in Hunan in early 1941.[32]

Kang Keqing already knew she would not see He Zizhen on her return. Instead, she met Mao's new 27-year-old wife. Jiang Qing (River Green) had arrived in Yan'an in 1937 as the Shanghai actress Lan Ping (Blue Apple). She had gone by several different names during her short life, having been born Li Shumeng, become Li Yunhe when she started school, then adopted the name Lan Ping in Shanghai when she was twenty years old and starting rehearsals for her part as Nora in Ibsen's *A Doll's House*. She changed her name to Jiang Qing in Yan'an, apparently to mark another new phase of her life, although it is not certain whether this happened when she first arrived or, as many sources claim, after she started living with Mao.[33]

Kang Keqing's and Zhu De's new quarters were almost next door to the three-roomed cave of Mao and Jiang Qing, who had been living on Yangjialing since late 1938 and already boasted a baby daughter not yet a year old.[34] Mao Zedong had planted his own small vegetable garden on the apron outside his cave-home and Zhu De made a similar gesture towards simplicity.

Yangjialing, where the party leaders now lived, was about three kilometres from the town centre, while 8th Route Army headquarters had moved out to Wangjiaping, seven kilometres away. The truckloads of enthusiastic young people arriving almost daily in Yan'an to become part of the anti-Japanese war effort had created a population explosion and suburban sprawl. More serious than that, however, was that with the KMT blockading supplies to the north-west the communist community had become an enormous economic burden to the local peasants. When it became clear that the communists would have to start contributing to their own upkeep in a practical way, the party initiated a mass movement to reinforce official communist policy of

self-sufficiency and cooperation with the peasants. Mass movements remained a vital part of communist life well into the
1960s. They were so called because they were to appear as an
upsurge of popular sentiment so strong that the party could not
resist responding; in fact, they were engineered by the party
through slogans and meetings that effectively shamed the people
into participating.

During this Great Production Movement of late 1940 small
salt-producing, weaving and papermaking enterprises were
expanded, while communist soldiers entered into labour exchange
arrangements with local peasants and farmers. Most worthy of
celebration, though, was Zhu De's vegetable garden project at
Nanniwan, about 45 kilometres south of Yan'an. Soldiers from
the 8th Route Army ploughed and planted this desolate stretch
of land for four years before they were able to clothe and feed
themselves by their own efforts, transforming the barren earth
of Nanniwan into a fertile 'Yangtze valley on the frontier'. In
later years it became a symbol of the Yan'an spirit of self-sufficiency and the setting for several propaganda musicals.

In the meantime, 29-year-old Kang Keqing went back to
university. The Party School was an elite institution that aimed
to develop the political and cultural knowledge and skills of
trusted party members earmarked as future leaders. In other
words, party members were sent there as a reward for their loyalty
and hard work. Kang Keqing enrolled in May 1940 and spent
four years at the school, living on campus during the week and
returning home to spend Saturday night and Sunday with her
husband pottering in the garden and meeting friends.

It was normal procedure in Yan'an for couples to live in separate
quarters and see each other only on the weekend; Mao and Jiang
Qing were a noted exception to this general rule. A highlight of
the weekend for some was the Saturday night dance. This, a
leftover from Agnes Smedley's Western dance classes and now
ardently supported by Jiang Qing and other new arrivals from the
east, was one of Kang Keqing's least favourite activities. However,
it was something she could not avoid. Her protests that she
couldn't dance only entangled her in an awkward dancing lesson
one night from a supremely confident but equally stiff Mao.

The students and intellectuals who had recently come to join

The earliest known photograph of Kang Keqing (aged 20, far left) and He Zizhen (aged 21, far right), taken when they attended the first meeting of Chinese Soviet Representatives in Ruijin in March 1932. Qian Xijun (aged 27) is standing next to Kang Keqing; she married Mao's youngest brother Mao Zemin and took part in the Long March. The three other young women are Zhou Yuelin (next to He Zizhen), Zeng Biyi (seated left) and Peng Ru (seated right).

Kang Keqing, the Red Amazon, in Yan'an in 1937. Her cropped hair is covered by a winter cap with its ear-flaps pinned up, and her cadre status is underscored by the two pens in her breast pocket.

Yan'an, 1937. Agnes Smedley (left) and Kang Keqing (right) strike a pose in their Red Army uniforms, complete with puttees. Agnes Smedley's stance and shape are recognisably female while Kang Keqing, clothed in layers of padding against the cold, could easily be taken for a male soldier.

He Zizhen (left) and Kang Keqing (right) were never close but they look distinctly uneasy in this photograph taken in Yan'an in1937. He Zizhen's frail body is well concealed by her bulky clothes.

Some of the Long March women who attended the 1st National Woman's Congress in Beijing in 1949. Back row from left: Wu Chaoxiang (in cap), Zhang Qinqiu (partly obscured), Kang Keqing, Li Jianzhen, Li Zhen (in cap), Liao Siguang (partly obscured). Middle row from left: Deng Liujin, unidentified, Wu Zhonglian, unidentified (in cap, face completely obscured), Li Bozhao, Cai Chang. Front row from left: Liu Ying, Chen Qiongying (in bonnet), Qi Yunde (in cap), Zhou Yuehua (in cap), Wei Xiuying (holding cap).

Zhu De and Kang Keqing strolling in the snow at Zhongnanhai. Judging from their relaxed manner, this photograph was taken during the mid 1950s.

Towards the end of her life Kang Keqing's eyesight appeared to be failing. This photograph accompanied the announcement of her death in the *People's Daily* on 23 April 1992.

Mao Zedong and He Zizhen (and a stray chicken) outside a cave dwelling in Bao'an, 1936. The character *shou* above the door means 'long life'.

He Zizhen and her nurse snapped
outside a park in scenic Hangzhou
in 1964 by her niece He Haifeng.

He Zizhen photographed in Shanghai in 1980 by her niece He Haifeng.
About this time, as she entered her seventies, she was admitted to
Huadong Hospital to receive treatment for edema.

Wang Quanyuan, date and place unknown.

Wang Quanyuan aged 83, in 1996.

A woodcut of the famous incident during the Long March in which Xie Fei writes a note after leaving payment for the invisible owner of the juicy pear that saved the life of Wu Fulian.

A sketch of Luding Bridge, the 13-chain suspension bridge across the Dadu River, constructed by one of the Long Marchers.

the communists held a very different set of attitudes and values from those of their slightly older comrades who had experienced the bitterness and solidarity of the Long March. Theirs was an intellectual and untested communism of theories learnt mainly from translations of Russian books. It did not always sit comfortably with the pragmatic communism of Yan'an, which was based on Mao's perception of China's unique experience, and peopled for the most part by peasants like Kang Keqing. Mao was forty-eight by this time and, having already won leadership of the party several times over, he was sensitive to any new threats to his authority. He seized the initiative in the early 1940s by suddenly unleashing two major campaigns within a year, the first designed to weed out maverick elements and establish his political supremacy, the second to bring intellectuals, writers and artists firmly under party control.

Mao ignited his Rectification Movement in mid 1941 to correct 'unorthodox tendencies'; it spread through the ranks of high-level cadres before searing like a purifying fire through the Party School. With his Rectification Movement Mao established Maoism, in the process providing the means whereby those who did not abide by the wishes of Mao were labelled heterodox and branded enemies of the party and the revolution. The critical importance of the Rectification Movement and the Yan'an Forum on Literature and Art that followed is that they shaped the way Chinese communists related not only to the party, but to each other. The Chinese people were in the habit of conformity by virtue of living in an agrarian society, and the rigid familial relationships dictated by Confucianism had reinforced these habits through the centuries. Individualism made life difficult for everybody in China, and in the community of communism it was openly perceived as a threat. Communist propaganda was based on the belief that the only way the people could defeat landlords, the gentry, and the Japanese was by standing together. Unity in the face of their enemies was the ABC of Chinese communism, and in 1941 it was Mao who told them who their enemies were.

Zhou Enlai, Zhu De and Liu Shaoqi made it clear in a series of talks that orthodoxy now consisted solely of adopting Mao's 'objective' approach to Marxism and Leninism. Kang Keqing joined with her fellow students to criticise comrades who were not following Mao's formula of 'seeking truth from facts' (*shíshì qiú shì*). She participated in formal group discussions that condemned intellectuals for burying their noses in books and refusing to dirty their hands with manual work. In later years she did not express regret for her part in muzzling free thought and free speech in Yan'an. This remained to her the necessary means to achieve the survival of the Communist Party and the eventual victory of the Chinese people over their past.

As always, Kang Keqing was one of the lucky ones and she emerged from the Rectification Movement uncharred. She was clearly not an intellectual, and while she was protected by her *guanxi* to Zhu De, who was a model of devotion to Mao, the party and the Red Army, her blameless record of upholding unity by abiding by party policy would have made her difficult to fault. The illogic of how victims were chosen, however, was the ghost of things to come. Han Shiying, the guerrilla fighter who had written so many inflammatory posters in her beautiful hand and who was now a student at the Party School, came under suspicion for having let herself be arrested by the KMT after the Red Army left her behind in Yunnan in 1937. She and her husband escaped with 'a comparatively minor investigation'.

Kang Keqing stood passively on the sidelines a year later when Mao fanned the dying fires of his Rectification Movement by throwing open for discussion the proper philosophical framework in which communist writers and artists were expected to operate. The conclusion Mao drew from this month-long discussion during May 1942—known as the Yan'an Forum on Literature and Art—was that art for art's sake had no place in the Chinese Revolution. All art, Mao proclaimed, must centre on the masses and serve an overtly political purpose.

One of those who came under severe criticism for her radical views was the writer Ding Ling, who had recently returned from a tour of duty in the Taihang war zone with the Front Service Group. As one of the literary editors of the Yan'an *Liberation Daily*, Ding Ling wielded some influence, of which she wrote cynically but in her case not quite accurately: 'My views can be ignored, coming as they do from the pen of a woman.' In March 1942 Ding Ling published an article entitled 'Thoughts on

Women's Day 8th March' that has since become famous, not least because it was suppressed for thirty years. Responding to Mao's invitation to expose thoughts and voice criticisms, Ding Ling wrote of the difficulty of being a woman in Yan'an, that best of all possible worlds.

She looks forward to the day, Ding Ling wrote, when 'women' will no longer be an issue demanding special attention. As it is, she wrote, women in Yan'an are under constant pressure to marry, preferably a leader or a high-ranking party member, and spinsterhood is simply not an option: 'It's an even greater sin not to marry, for that makes you a legitimate target for rumour and eternal damnation.' Having succumbed to the pressure to marry, women then find themselves expected to have children (not wanting to have children because that would interfere with their work was the reason several of the Long March women gave for their reluctance to marry; all but one married). Once they become mothers, Ding Ling wrote, the women in Yan'an come under further criticism. If they place their children in the care of a nurse or a creche they are criticised for not being good mothers: 'Minding children is work, isn't it?' they are told. 'You never made much of a political contribution anyway, and now you're saying you don't want children and you're not prepared to look after them. Why did you get married in the first place?' If, however, they give in to their husbands' wishes and stay home to look after their children, they are accused of being politically backward and mocked as 'Noras who have returned home', a reference to the main character Nora in Henrik Ibsen's play *A Doll's House*. Then they are likely to be divorced by their husbands on the grounds of their political backwardness, she wrote. Ding Ling tactfully forbore to cite here the examples of He Zizhen and Xiao Yuehua.[35]

Mao Zedong was upset by Ding Ling's outspoken article. A fellow author, Wang Shiwei, was imprisoned that same week for publishing an article entitled 'Wild Lilies' that was a thinly veiled criticism of Mao's liking for beautiful women and his bourgeois lifestyle, the title a not very subtle reference to Mao's affair with Agnes Smedley's interpreter Lily Wu. Wang Shiwei was executed five years later as the communists prepared to withdraw from Yan'an under threat of KMT attack. Ding Ling was removed from her position with the local newspaper in 1942 but had the good political sense to recant, so she lived to fight on.[36]

Kang Keqing remained far more interested in guns than in the slick politics of Mao Zedong. At an exhibition of state-of-the-art small arms mounted in Yan'an by the United States Army she was entranced by gas masks and protective clothing, landmines, magnetic mines, and TNT. Gravely she handled the submachine-guns, automatic rifles and chunky pistols that were on display. What most took her fancy, however, was the stunning new pistol fitted with a silencer and demonstrated with impressive accuracy by a young American officer. If you were standing right up close when it was fired you could hear a slight 'Pok!' and that was all, she reported.[37]

The Americans to whom these weapons belonged were part of the Military Observers Mission, popularly known as the DIXIE Mission, that was stationed in Yan'an for over a year from July 1944. For a decade the United States had provided military and financial aid solely to the KMT, but towards the end of World War II Japan's entrenched position in the north of China and the threat of increased Russian influence in China forced a reconsideration of this policy. Hoping to prevent a civil war that would weaken China and thus make it more difficult to defeat Japan, the United States commenced negotiations in 1944 to bring about a KMT–Communist coalition. Allied to this was the DIXIE Mission, whose purpose was to explore the military potential of the communists in Yan'an. The credentials of this mission were impeccable: its leader, Colonel David D. Barrett, was fluent in Chinese, and its political adviser, China-born Foreign Service Officer John S. Service, had worked for many years in China. After protracted talks with Mao and Zhou Enlai, John Service reported that the communist leaders were competent, that they 'had established a viable government and could propose useful cooperation with the Americans under an "Allied" command rather than under a "bankrupt" Kuomintang command'. Ignoring Service's recommendation that the communists were clearly the better bet for fulfilling America's aim of securing a stable China, the United States Government clung to its old ally. By continuing to pour aid into the Generalissimo's coffers, the United States effectively ensured that China would collapse into civil war once the war with Japan ended.[38]

By the end of World War II the communists were in control of 'liberated areas' throughout China with a population of 100 million, and Kang Keqing was just one of almost one million party members ready to take up arms to liberate the rest of the country. She was thirty-four years old and had been fighting the KMT half her life. Having survived six years of guerrilla warfare, she had walked the brutal 13 000 kilometres of the Long March then turned around and crossed the Grass Lands and the Snowy Mountains twice more. She had been witness to the suffering of soldiers and civilians at the hands of the Japanese during the three years she spent in the Taihang war zone. She had never been wounded and, she said later, 'In those days I knew no fear.'[39]

In September 1945 Kang Keqing was appointed a member of the Women's Council of the Central Committee. She was more excited, however, by Japan's surrender and her part in the battle ahead with the KMT.

PART III
REALITY BITES,
AFTER 1949

PART III PROLOGUE

While the Long March had bestowed upon its survivors the status of invincible heroes, the Yan'an period and the war against Japan focused the hopes of the Chinese people on the communists, eventually winning for them a mandate to rule. The period immediately 'after Liberation' (that is, after 1949) became a race against time to create from the smoking ruins of almost half a century of war a functioning modern nation of healthy, productive individuals.

The Chinese Communist Party had always presented itself as the people's party. And yet no peasants rose to the leadership of the Communist Party, which was run from the start by intellectuals. Many of these intellectuals genuinely hoped to win for the people the rights they were fighting for; for others the revolution appears to have been a cynical exercise in gaining power through unleashing the massive power of the people. Mao Zedong graciously accepted the mantle of leader of the new nation. As Chairman of the Chinese Communist Party and architect of the revolution he expected nothing less.

With Mao playing the role of emperor and Premier Zhou Enlai his trusted minister, the party created a government in the shape of a pyramid. At the base of the pyramid were China's close to 600 million citizens. Apart from those who were labelled of 'questionable background', each citizen belonged to at least one of a network of local organisations: workers' unions, the women's federation, youth groups, professional organisations for intellectuals, and so on. These grassroots organisations reported up to the Central Committee, which reported up to the Politburo, whose seven-man Standing Committee reported to the Premier and the Chairman: a dictatorship of the proletariat. That, at least, was the theory.

In practice it worked the other way around, the pyramid becoming a means of passing government policy down to the mass of the people, while the local organisations became the means of persuading the people they should abide by the latest official policy. The party called upon the masses to reject the traditional Confucian values of loyalty to family, father and emperor and embrace in their place the Maoist values of loyalty to people, party and leader. In many ways this meant little actual change, as, for instance, when the party secretary of the local collective farm stepped into the shoes of the patriarch of the local wealthy Confucian family that had recently been driven out or executed. Other changes were more deep-seated and troubling, as when people were persuaded that they must put loyalty to the party before loyalty to their own family.

One of the first pieces of legislation brought down in new China was the Marriage Law of 1950. It guaranteed women full equality in marriage, divorce and property ownership, and released a flood of applications from women for divorce. The Marriage Law also outlawed the killing and sale of children, and abolished prostitution. Yet, although this law placed women on an equal legal footing with men, old attitudes were not so amenable to legislation and the local branches of the All-China Women's Federation were kept busy policing lapses.

Land reform also became a reality by 1952 when all peasants were given a hectare or so of land to work as they wished. Soon, however, they were told to work in mutual aid teams and share farm animals and implements. These teams were then absorbed into cooperatives the size of small villages, with peasants receiving wages for their labour and a nominal rent for the use of their land. In 1958, all cooperatives were subsumed by huge communes the size of counties and run along almost military lines. In real terms, within eight years of liberation the peasants had returned to being hired labour.

Yan'an-style mass movements with their mass criticisms and 'struggle sessions' became the primary tool for mobilising the people, based as they were on the Maoist belief that from chaos comes order, from struggle comes unity. After the outbreak of the Korean War in 1950, a 'resist America, aid Korea' campaign immediately swung into action. When the new communist broom was brought out to sweep away all KMT remnants and those of dubious loyalty, a 'suppress counter-revolutionaries' campaign was launched in 1951. A mass movement to 'increase production and be more economical' that same year was followed by a 'three antis' campaign to expose corruption, waste and bureaucratism in the party and administration. It was followed in 1952 by a 'five antis' campaign targeting bribery and tax evasion by businessmen, industrialists and merchants. Intellectuals were subjected from 1950 to an ongoing 'thought reform' campaign and made to study the classic books of Marx and Mao.

With Chairman Mao at the helm the mass movements kept coming, with economic disasters never far away. The First Five Year Plan announced in 1955 was supposed to transform China within a few years into a modern country along Russian lines: in reality, industrial production initially doubled but agricultural production slumped, leading to food shortages. The famous slogan 'Let a hundred flowers bloom together, let the hundred schools of thought contend' trumpeted a campaign in 1956 to bring intellectuals on side and tap their research skills and creativity: all this campaign unearthed, however, was trenchant criticism of the party. Mao dreamed up the Great Leap Forward of 1958 which he claimed would instantly make China self-sufficient. Instead agricultural production plummeted, food shortages turned into a three-year famine, and millions of peasants starved to death.

Mao continued to be dismissive of experts, claiming to have utter faith in the wisdom of the people to solve even the most intricate problems: 'When it comes to economics,' he announced at the 1959 Lushan Conference, 'even the illiterate can also do it.'[1] He was nevertheless forced to acknowledge his responsibility for the disasters of the 1950s, and in 1958 declined to serve as Chairman and Head of State, his executive role taken over by Liu Shaoqi, a colleague of Jiangxi soviet days. While Mao held no immediate power and withdrew from most public commitments in late 1959, he remained Chairman of the Communist Party.

In old China, education had been pivotal in maintaining the orthodoxy. The sons—and quite often the daughters—of the rich learnt to read and write by memorising a dozen or so sets of ancient books known as the Confucian Classics, then young men (and only men) competed for jobs in the bureaucracy through a series of examinations based entirely on those texts. Like countless patriots before him, many of them women agitating at the turn of the century, Mao rejected this notion of an education for the privileged few. But he went further. His dream was not only to cauterise China of the text-based rote-learning Confucian education system, but also to destabilise society so that it could never again settle into a rut, any rut whatsoever, good or bad. He wanted to create what he called 'perpetual revolution'. The irony was that he replaced the Confucian orthodoxy with a Maoist orthodoxy called Mao Zedong Thought, and cast out the Confucian Classics only to replace them with the Maoist classic *The Thoughts of Mao Zedong*, available in bookshops everywhere.

Mao regained power in the 1960s and eventually, in May 1966, initiated his last and greatest debacle: the Great Proletarian Cultural Revolution. The people welcomed this new mass movement enthusiastically with processions, drums and gongs, but it soon got out of hand when Mao sent eleven million young Red Guards rampaging through the countryside on his perpetual revolution. He told them they were to attack 'the Four Olds'—old ideology, old thought, old habits and old customs—and this they did by beating up individuals who in their eyes represented 'the Four Olds', and destroying 'old' property such as temples and statues. Schools and universities were closed; intellectuals were plucked from their desks and sent to the countryside to work alongside peasants.

The air grew thick with recriminations as Mao transformed the Cultural Revolution into a personal vendetta against those who had criticised his economic (mis)management in the 1950s. Liu Shaoqi became one of his chief targets. Mao turned against his Long March colleagues because they stood between him and his perpetual revolution. He accused them of being 'rightists', 'rightist opportunists', 'capitalist roaders': these terms should not now be taken literally, but were then razor-sharp political weapons. For the next eleven years it became dangerous to challenge the Maoist notion that the primary concern of all citizens must be politics rather than knowledge or technical skill. In other words, it became safer to be 'Red' than 'expert'.

From 1949, as the Long March women approached middle age, they negotiated the politics of their individual lives and the changes that came about in the lives of Chinese women in very different ways. While He Zizhen was still waiting to be let in and Wang Quanyuan was buried somewhere in its base, Kang Keqing found herself at the top of the Chinese pyramid.

7

UNTOUCHABLE

Sometimes when you travel by boat on Lake Tai (Taihu) near Wuxi in the southern province of Jiangsu a dense mist will swirl out of nowhere and obliterate the landscape. Suspended in white air you feel as if you have stepped into a Chinese painting, unable to see anything but the wooden deck upon which you stand and the timber railing upon which you lean, as if in a dream. From time to time solid objects will materialise: small islands and long junks with angular black sails will suddenly appear, then dissolve back into the mist after a few moments.

The tale of He Zizhen's later life is a little like Taihu, a life swathed in mists, seemingly of no certainty and little outward substance. What we hear of her as she grows older is vague and contradictory. We begin to doubt things; to wonder about the story of her early life and speculate how much of it was created in retrospect by those eager to make of her a more acceptable mate for the demigod Mao and a mirror so pure it would splendidly reflect the vulgar actions and nature of his new mate Jiang Qing.

He Zizhen returned to China in 1947 and eventually went back to the south, living first in Shanghai, then in her native Jiangxi Province and in Fujian Province. She returned to Shanghai, where she spent her last years under a form of house arrest during the Cultural Revolution and after that in hospital. These are the facts that are surrounded by swirling mists of uncertainty about the state of her mental health and her relationship with Mao.[1]

186

In mid 1947 He Zizhen and her daughter Jiaojiao arrived in Harbin, the far northern city of ice-sculptures and capital of the province of Heilongjiang. Jiaojiao was ten by then and spoke better Russian than Chinese so that mother and daughter must have communicated in an awkward mixture of the two languages. They waited in Harbin for about twelve months before receiving permission to travel further south into China.

Jiang Qing is usually blamed for this long delay, sources claiming that she pulled obstructive strings because she was apprehensive at the prospect of the return of Mao's previous wife. He Zizhen was only three years older than Jiang Qing but she had borne Mao a son (Little Mao) and as a veteran of Jinggangshan, the Jiangxi soviet and the Long March she was far senior to her in terms of revolutionary experience. However, Jiang Qing was not in a position of power at that time, and her marriage to Mao appears to have been in some difficulty; she was sent to Russia for an enforced rest of more than six months in 1949, and in 1952 spent an unhappy year in Moscow, obviously against her will. While it is indeed possible that Jiang Qing tried to prevent He Zizhen returning, it must be kept in mind that after her fall from power in 1976 Jiang Qing was made a scapegoat for just about everything that had gone wrong in China, so other reasons must be sought for the treatment of He Zizhen.

During the long, dark winter in Harbin He Zizhen had little to do. Some biographies say that she attended a labour conference and that she commenced reading science textbooks in an effort to catch up on her lost years, but this is not convincing. She made contact with some old friends and revolutionary comrades who tramped in and out of the city doing propaganda work and mopping up after the fifteen-year Japanese military occupation, but it is unlikely that she would have been fit enough mentally or physically after several years in a Russian sanitorium to join them in this work. Cai Chang, for instance, spent a great deal of time in Heilongjiang from about 1946, organising women cadres and persuading them of the importance of women's work. She gave talks to women university students and carried out investigations into women's working conditions in factories and on farms, and was elected secretary of the north-east region women's committee. She and her husband were stationed in Harbin from May 1947 till the end of the following year, this period coinciding with He Zizhen's sojourn there. As with her time in Moscow, however, Cai Chang does not appear to have mentioned meeting He Zizhen in Harbin.

The civil war between the communists and the KMT was not quite over when He Zizhen received permission to move on from Harbin in 1948. It is generally accepted that she was intent on going to Peiping with Jiaojiao but that she was prevented. By whom is not clearly stated. One source claims that while travelling from Harbin she was approached by two people who said they had been 'sent by the organisation'; in other words, they represented the Communist Party. They told her she was not to go to Shijiazhuang, where Mao had established his base while preparing to enter Peiping in triumph, but could 'only go to the south, to your brother's'. They also told her: 'This has been decided by the organisation.'2 This seems unnecessarily melodramatic, given the absolute power the party had exercised over He Zizhen's movements for so many years. It may have been Mao who forbad her to remain near him, but all indicators point to the other party leaders, who may have decided that the presence in the capital of the leader's ex-wife—his 'first wife' in terms of seniority and still, in the eyes of many older comrades, the faithful wife he should not have discarded—would cause problems.

Another source claims that He Zizhen and Jiaojiao broke their journey from Harbin at the dirty industrial city of Shenyang, about 600 kilometres north-east of Peiping. He Zizhen is said to have fallen ill in Shenyang and asked the party to assign her work, but the detail of this story is also questionable. He Zizhen would have been aware that her application, revealing a wealth of revolutionary experience gained during her ten years as Mao's wife, would be referred to the highest level. This would indicate that she was testing the waters of her relationship with Mao. If, as this source suggests, she was offered a junior position within the Ministry of Finance then Mao was guilty of dealing her a studied insult.

Both sources, however, agree that He Zizhen's sister He Yi played an important role at this time. It was He Yi to whom He Zizhen had entrusted two-year-old Xiao Mao, her only son, the day she left Ruijin on the Long March, and the sisters had not seen each other in the fourteen years since then. In that time, all trace of Xiao Mao had been lost, and He Yi's husband (Mao Zedong's brother) had died, killed in the aftermath of the Long Marchers' retreat from Jiangxi. In 1937 or 1938, not long after He Zizhen went to Russia, He Yi travelled to Yan'an with her new husband to confront Mao about his shabby treatment of her sister, accusing him of shucking her off on the eve of his political success. Mao gave her short shrift, ensuring that she and her husband were assigned to separate locations, both far from Yan'an. Whether or not it was He Yi who was instrumental in obtaining permission for He Zizhen to leave Harbin, she appeared in Shenyang in 1948 to take charge of He Zizhen's affairs. Enraged by the cavalier manner in which the party (and, by implication, Mao) had treated her sister by abandoning her to a minor post in a provincial northern city, He Yi took Jiaojiao and marched off to confront her brother-in-law.

Mao was approachable enough. He seemed taken by this Russian-speaking daughter he hadn't seen for eight years, calling her his 'foreign daughter' and joking that he might have to call upon the urbane Zhou Enlai (who apparently spoke Russian and French) to interpret for them. He didn't quibble when He Yi assumed Jiaojiao was to be placed in his care, and could not have been more pleasant when He Yi told him he must do something to regularise his ex-wife's status. Straightaway he turned to his desk and with a bamboo pen wrote on his personal notepaper a few lines to He Zizhen.

Soon after delivering Jiaojiao over into her father's care, He Yi embarked on an odyssey to Ruijin to find Jiaojiao's lost brother, Xiao Mao. There can be no doubt she did this for her sister but her journey may not have been wholly altruistic. He Yi could not help but profit from her position as the double-aunt of Mao's Number Three son, if he were still alive. Unfortunately, her efforts were fruitless. The boy was never found and she was killed in a car accident in 1950 while still engaged on the search.

He Zizhen had moved one step closer to Peiping and was in the coastal city of Tientsin just 150 kilometres to the east by the time she received Mao's note. It said simply that he liked his daughter Jiaojiao and was happy to have her stay with him.

He Zizhen should take good care of herself, he added, and hold fast to the revolution, to her health, and to others while 'remaining mindful of the overall situation'.[3] There was nothing about what help she could expect from him or the party, or what she was supposed to do with the rest of her life; she was thirty-eight years old at the time. What distressed He Zizhen most, however, was not the perfunctoriness of the note, nor even its impersonal air, but the message he had sent between the lines. Mao had addressed the note to 'He Zizhen', choosing to write the word 'Zi' with a character that meant 'self' so that his note was actually addressed to 'Congratulatory Self Treasure' instead of 'Congratulatory *Little* Treasure'. This clever pun underscored his message that he had done with her and that from now on she was on her own—she was going to have to 'treasure her*self*' or, in other words, to look after herself because he clearly was not going to.

He Zizhen headed to the south whence she came and stepped off the plane at Shanghai's Rainbow Bridge Airport on 1 October 1949, just in time to hear the national broadcast from Beijing of the ceremony proclaiming the People's Republic of China. She found it simply too much to bear when Mao's voice, the voice she had not heard for over ten years, suddenly blared from the loudspeaker—'The Chinese people have stood up at last!'—and she collapsed on the tarmac.

She fell into kind hands in Shanghai, those of a loyal old comrade from the days of the Ruijin soviet. Red Army Commander Chen Yi was so severely wounded that he had been left in charge of those who stayed behind when the Red Army marched out of Ruijin in 1934. He had survived the shocking massacres and privation of the next few years only because of his optimistic nature and strong constitution. His reward for leading the troops that eventually captured Shanghai was to be placed in charge of the city, where he stayed until he was made a Vice-Premier in 1954, then Foreign Minister in 1958. Now he stepped forward to take care of He Zizhen, assigning the best doctors to look after her and arranging a comfortable residence for her to live in.

The mists swirl over He Zizhen's life in Shanghai, revealing a tantalising glimpse from the recollections of others of a slender, still good-looking woman in her early forties visiting an old friend in hospital in the summer of 1954, her oval face and fine deep-set black eyes calm and assured. There are other recalled glimpses: of recurrent bouts of fainting followed by illness; of schizophrenia. It was taken for granted that she remained devoted to Mao despite being excluded from Beijing and having no contact with him. She was not assigned work. She lived a quiet and lonely life with few friends.

He Zizhen requested and received permission to leave Shanghai for a time to visit her home province of Jiangxi and in May 1958 moved to the provincial capital, Nanchang. The authorities installed her in a two-storey house within a large, quiet courtyard and provided her with a cook, a nurse, a vehicle and a driver. She received a substantial salary because she was a Long March veteran and because of her past *guanxi* with Mao, but remained without work. Her schizophrenia manifested itself in more frequent episodes of unreality when she would become paranoid and refuse to eat or drink for days at a stretch, frightened 'they' were trying to poison her. She would withdraw into an almost trance-like state.

At other times she was quite clear-headed and would chat brightly with visitors, but she tired quickly, her conversation becoming disjointed, her words hard to follow. She was approaching fifty and had aged considerably in the last four years, her short black hair now streaked with grey and with deep lines around her eyes. When she was well she took great delight in the visits of her daughter Jiaojiao who, since becoming a member of the Mao–Jiang Qing household, had been given the name Li Min; Li was Jiang Qing's original surname. Li Min at twenty-two was an uncomplicated young woman, not terribly bright, some said, but considerate and honest. She would bring gifts of foods and medicine and once she brought her young man along to introduce him to her pleased mother.

The summons from Mao did not come through Li Min, though, and it is not even certain in what year it happened. One woman, Shui Jing, who claims to have been the only witness, said it was in 1959 while Mao's personal physician, Dr Li Zhisui, claims it was in 1961 and that he was present. Both agree that He Zizhen's meeting with Mao took place on Lushan in the summer. Lushan (Mount Lu) is on the northern border of Jiangxi

Province. A lush, spiky mountain of great beauty, it towers over Lake Poyang where the lake pours its fresh waters into the Yangtze River. Upon assuming the mantle of the nation's leader, Mao had installed himself in a sprawling complex on Lushan and retreated there to relax, swim, hold meetings, and plot.

Shui Jing has recounted Mao's meeting with He Zizhen in a highly romantic manner, but elements of her account fit well with Mao's behaviour—he has since been described as 'a narcissist with a borderline personality' who had 'a driving need to manipulate and use others, while always guarding [his] own feelings and being constantly alert as to who is controlling whom'.[4] Shui Jing was married to the party secretary of Jiangxi Province, and one afternoon in the first ten-day period of July in 1959 she visited He Zizhen, suggesting they spend a few days enjoying Lushan, which is about 100 kilometres north of Nanchang. Mao was not mentioned.[5]

Shui Jing collected He Zizhen the following afternoon and drove up the twisting road onto Lushan, where she settled her in a comfortable twin room in a quiet corner of the almost deserted Mao complex. The next night, on Mao's orders, Shui Jing led the unsuspecting He Zizhen to Mao's second-floor rooms at nine o'clock and waited outside in the bodyguard's office. After an hour or so Mao ushered He Zizhen out of his rooms mumbling to Shui Jing something like, 'It's no good, her mind's gone—she doesn't make sense.' He instructed Shui Jing to put He Zizhen to bed and take her back to Nanchang the next day, making sure nobody in the Lushan complex caught sight of her.

It had always been the prerogative of emperors to cast women aside and several of the nine adult emperors of the recently departed Qing dynasty had done just that, sometimes on a whim or out of deep hurt, at other times for reasons that will remain a mystery.[6] He Zizhen had not lived the luxurious and privileged life of an empress, nor had she been subjected to the Machiavellian family pressures notoriously placed upon imperial women. She had, however, once been wife to the man who was now China's paramount ruler and, as had many an empress before her, she had been ousted from the imperial bed while still in her mid-twenties. He Zizhen didn't collapse in shock at her sudden encounter with Mao, as one might expect, but came away extremely animated. She was so high she couldn't stop talking and Shui Jing claims to have spent the rest of the night listening to her tell from beginning to end the story of her years with Mao. He Zizhen acknowledged that she had been wilful and sometimes bad-tempered, especially when they were first married, but she had been very young, she said. She also mentioned in passing that she had been pregnant ten times in her ten years with Mao, which would mean she had four miscarriages in addition to the six live births that are recorded.

The reason He Zizhen gave for leaving Mao twenty years before was that she had felt inadequate and naive when confronted with the foreign journalists and sophisticated young students who poured into Yan'an. She realised that Mao's behaviour towards her had changed—she did not say in what way—because he was no longer interested in her. Her heart had finally broken, she said, when she realised that Mao did not care enough to see that her temper tantrums were her clumsy attempt to get him to pay some attention to her. When instead he turned his back and moved out she knew it was all over. This version of He Zizhen's flight from Yan'an has little to recommend it, echoing as it does the official line that she was young, flighty and unstable while Mao was completely blameless for the breakdown of their marriage.

Mao was in serious political difficulty in 1959 after the failure of his Great Leap Forward, and this may have been why his thoughts drifted nostalgically back to He Zizhen, the devoted second wife, and mother of most of his children, whom he had abandoned as he approached his years of great prestige and power. In supreme disregard for her feelings or needs, he ensured that she had no time to prepare herself for the rendezvous he set up on Lushan, even though the most stable of personalities would be unsettled by having such a momentous meeting sprung upon them. 'Don't tell He Zizhen you are bringing her to see me,' Mao warned Shui Jing. 'It's better that she doesn't get excited, we don't want to bring on a bout of her illness.' To her credit, He Zizhen stood up remarkably well to the shock, but at nearly fifty she was obviously not what Mao had hoped for and since he had nothing to gain by renewing their relationship in any form they never met again.

Dr Li Zhisui, who wrote his book *The private life of Chairman Mao* from memories after having wisely burnt his diaries in 1966 at the start of the Cultural Revolution, does not mention Shui Jing in his version of He Zizhen's meeting with Mao in 1961 but claims to have been present throughout. The accuracy of Dr Li's recollections has been the subject of controversy, and the glaring errors in his references to events before his time do not inspire confidence. He says, for instance, that Mao and He Zizhen were 'hundreds of miles away in the Jiangxi soviet' when his wife Yang Kaihui was executed in Changsha in 1930 (Mao was almost outside the city walls, having not long since abandoned a military attack on Changsha, and the Jiangxi soviet did not come into being for another year, in late 1931); and that 'Mao lost interest in He [Zizhen], shortly after their arrival in Yanan in 1935' (the communists did not reach Yan'an until January 1937). Dr Li was not concerned with the past but with the time he spent with Mao after 1952, and these slips may simply reveal that he was not overly careful when he repeated hearsay. Was it hearsay, however, or fabrication when he claimed that 'He Zizhen's younger brother, an officer in the garrison command' in Shanghai was used as an intermediary in setting up her meeting with Mao when her only younger brother was killed in 1927?[7]

He Zizhen was just fifty then, but Dr Li described her as elderly, with silver-grey hair and 'the unsteady gait of the aged'. He said that He Zizhen was emotional during her meeting with Mao, her face showing delight at first, then her eyes filling with tears. 'Her voice was barely audible,' he recalled, 'and after the brief flash of recognition her words became incoherent. She seemed flushed with excitement, but her face had gone blank. Mao invited her to have dinner with him, but she refused.'[8] After He Zizhen left, having said little during the encounter, Mao asked Dr Li the nature of He Zizhen's illness. Schizophrenia, Dr Li told him, is 'a condition in which the mind cannot correctly relate to reality'. It was the same illness that Mao's second son, Mao Anqing, was believed to have suffered.

It is taken for granted by Chinese and Western writers that He Zizhen was mentally unbalanced from the time of the Long March. Dr Li repeated in his book the popular opinion that 'He

Zizhen's mind had gone sometime after she and Mao were separated' and said that she had been diagnosed by Russian psychiatrists as schizophrenic. However, the behaviour labelled schizophrenic in China would not always be so classified in the West. Anne F. Thurston, the American editor of Dr Li's book, notes that "The Chinese definition of schizophrenia is clearly much broader than that given in the *Diagnostic and Statistical Manual of the American Psychiatric Association*, used in the West. The psychiatric profession [in China] was nearly devastated after 1949, and there were few practicing psychiatrists.' Professor Lucian W. Pye laments that Dr Li's psychological assessments were not more professional and that Dr Li was not trained in psychiatry.[9]

Schizophrenia was a convenient catch-all in China for aberrant behaviour, as was the term neurasthenia which, according to Professor Pye in the article just quoted, is 'a quaint Victorian classification which has no standing in modern psychiatry'. Both Mao and Jiang Qing were said to have suffered from neurasthenia, whose symptoms Dr Li described as 'Insomnia . . . Headaches, chronic pain, dizziness, anxiety attacks, high blood pressure, depression, impotence, skin problems, intestinal upsets, anorexia and bad temper'.[10] Dr Li's description of one of Mao's anxiety attacks—'Once, in an open field, [Mao] suddenly became disoriented and would have fallen except for the help of his bodyguards'—sounds very much like He Zizhen's collapse at Shanghai airport, except that she had no-one to prevent her fall. Mao's physician did, however, understand that neurasthenia was not a mental disease. He spoke of Jiang Qing's imaginary illnesses as being 'linked to her thwarted ambitions. Her neurasthenia was political.'[11] He saw that neurasthenia was a reaction to stress: it is, he wrote, 'usually induced by some sort of psychological malaise, but because admitting to psychological distress is simply too shameful for most Chinese, [neurasthenia's] manifestations are usually physical'.[12] The line between being diagnosed as suffering from schizophrenia with Chinese characteristics rather than neurasthenia must have been no more than a razor's edge; on the other hand, in many cases it may have been purely illusory.

Traditional Chinese medicine considers pain in specific organs and parts of the body to be indicative of a larger imbalance. So, too, unacceptable behaviour is considered indicative of a person's imbalance within the larger society.

When He Zizhen stepped beyond the bounds of 'normal' behaviour and berated Mao that summer night in Yan'an in 1937, she was seen to be unbalanced. Her 'abnormal' behaviour in Russia then earned her the diagnosis of schizophrenic. When she returned to China as the abandoned imperial wife she was not assigned work but was left to rot in loneliness and inaction. Whereas in old China people's identity had been determined by their status as peasant, scholar, student, gentry official and so on, in new China it was people's jobs that gave them an identity and allowed them to play their part in rebuilding the nation. That job belonged to them and they in turn belonged to their work unit, be it a commune, a factory, a mine, a shop, a school, a university, a hospital or a government department. In other words, when the state assigned work to people it gave them something to which they could belong. The only people who were not assigned work in new China were intractable 'bad elements' such as counter-revolutionaries and KMT agents.

Almost without exception the Long March women who had survived the years of warfare up till 1949 were assigned work or given a title and appointed to some committee or organisation. They all belonged somewhere.

Kang Keqing's friend Wu Zhonglian, who had handed her new-born baby into the care of peasants just before being captured by the Moslems, had remarried and moved to the province of Zhejiang after 1949. There she became prominent within the public security and people's court system, rising to the position of Director of the People's High Court in Zhejiang.[11] Zhang Qinqiu, the head of political organisation who had given birth to a boy child while besieged by the Moslems in 1937, was also allowed to go on with her life despite being taken prisoner by both the Moslems and the KMT in the late 1930s, and having been married to Zhang Guotao's right-hand man. She was appointed Vice-Minister of Textiles in 1949, the highest ranking position of any woman, and sat on the major Women's Federation committees. Even Han Shiying, who, despite not having made her way back to Yan'an until 1940 after being dropped out of the Long March in Yunnan in 1935 and being harassed in the

Yan'an Rectification Movement, was assigned work. From 1950 she served on several official party, women's and legal organisations in her home province of Sichuan and in the south-west.[12]

All three of these women, incidentally, became victims of the Cultural Revolution, during which time they were all persecuted to death. This phrase 'persecuted to death' was commonly used to explain the death of thousands of people during the Cultural Revolution: it covered suicide, death from stress-related illness, and death due to lack of medical aid. Liu Shaoqi, for example, was a diabetic and he was 'persecuted to death' when his guards confiscated his medication, leaving him to die in prison.

He Zizhen was one of the few people not assigned any work after 1949. Although allocated a generous salary, she was not given a job, or even appointed to a sinecure. Without a job she could not belong to a work unit, and not belonging to a work unit she stood outside society. She was completely without status and her only identity became that which she had dreaded: the untouchable 'first wife'. Her only surviving child had been taken from her and she was condemned to live alone.

He Zizhen appears to have been a pawn in her later life, offering no resistance as she was moved about by others. It is not difficult, however, to see how the feisty young woman who stood atop the south gate of Yongxin and shot two men, the brave young rebel who ran the blockade of Jinggangshan, became so passive. Her ten years with Mao, whom Dr Li described as 'devoid of human feeling, incapable of love, friendship, or warmth',[13] left her emotionally and physically battered. When she fought back and attacked Lily Wu and Agnes Smedley, Mao abandoned her and had her exiled to Russia. Then, when she returned to China, she was confronted by a wall of silence. The Communist Party, 'the organisation', directed that she be paid a salary and provided with a comfortable place to live, south of the Yangtze River. The organisation's decision that He Zizhen had lost her mind and that she was to be kept quiet and well away from Mao and Jiang Qing was just as binding. It was made difficult for friends to visit her; she was prevented from working; she had no means of reconstructing her life. There was nothing He Zizhen could do about it.

In 1962 she went to live with her older brother He Minxue, who was Deputy Governor of Fujian Province and lived in the provincial capital of Fuzhou. The last time she had been to Fujian was in 1932 when she gave birth to Xiao Mao in a hospital in Changting. The time before that was the year she spent as a guerrilla with the fledgling Red Army soon after coming down off Jinggangshan as a pregnant nineteen year old. It was in Fujian in 1929 that she gave birth to her first baby, whom she passed into the care of a peasant family somewhere in the west of the province before moving reluctantly and tearfully on with the Red rebels.

He Zizhen did not remain in Fuzhou with her brother and his family but returned to Shanghai; perhaps she came and went between the two cities over the next few years. There are not many photographs of He Zizhen and most of them were taken in Yan'an: standing smiling beside Mao Zedong with her hands behind her back, or standing awkwardly alongside Kang Keqing, always in her padded army uniform and peaked cap. A rare photograph taken in 1964, however, shows her standing on a white gravel path outside a park in the glorious city of Hangzhou, just south of Shanghai. On the back of the photograph someone has written that it is of He Zizhen and her nurse and that it was taken by her brother's daughter He Haifeng. Patient and nurse are both smiling at the camera.

The Cultural Revolution began not long after this photo was taken. It is not clear how badly He Zizhen fared during this time. She does not seem to have been physically harmed by Red Guards as some Long March women were and she had no workplace colleagues to criticise her. It is rumoured that Jiang Qing ordered her placed under house arrest in Shanghai. She was kept isolated and it was difficult to obtain permission to see her. She did, however, manage to slip away from her guards from time to time and walk the streets of Shanghai with her niece to read the big character posters pasted up all over the city criticising her old comrades-in-arms. Her niece tells of how she tried to quieten her aunt, who was fiercely defending the chief targets: Liu Shaoqi, Deng Xiaoping and Peng Dehuai. Unafraid of the repercussions of her outspoken comments, He Zizhen's indignation would grow louder with each poster she read until she was declaiming: 'Jiang Qing is a bad woman! The Central Committee ought to be told that she is an evil witch.' Her niece also told of rushing to shut doors and windows when, hospitalised with fever, He Zizhen began shouting as she regained consciousness: 'Quickly! Hurry and save Chairman Mao—Jiang Qing is going to harm him!'

These incidents sound suspiciously apocryphal, designed to show how perceptive and loyal He Zizhen remained during those years of terror. She does, however, seem to have always retained her courage and feisty spirit, apparently unafraid of cursing Jiang Qing in front of her nurse–guards before poking her tongue out at them and walking off. He Zizhen is credited with having harboured a deep hatred for Jiang Qing—to the extent, some said, of detesting the colour blue because Jiang Qing's stage name had been Blue Apple.[14] Nothing is said of how she felt about apples, but then apples are hard to come by in southern China.

In 1973 He Zizhen's first-born child was found. Periodic searches had been undertaken over the years for the babies and children farmed out by the roving communist revolutionaries. Mao's two sons by Yang Kaihui, for instance, had been discovered in Shanghai in the late 1930s and sent to Yan'an to eventually become part of his patchwork family. Xiao Mao, the first born son of Mao and He Zizhen, was never found even though he was sought several times. But, somehow, someone in authority officially identified a 44-year-old party member living in Fujian and named Yang Yuehua as the long-lost first daughter of Mao and He Zizhen.

Yang Yuehua lived in Longyan in the south-west of Fujian and had been passed around as a child to three families before one decided to keep her. She had married at the age of eighteen and produced six children (as had He Zizhen): three girls and three boys, all of whom were assigned work in or around Longyan as they grew into adulthood. Dubbed by one journalist 'The Unfortunate Princess', she nevertheless appeared to be perfectly content with her lot working in the local cinema deep in the countryside of one of China's more hardpressed provinces.[15]

The party summoned Yang Yuehua to Shanghai in the autumn of 1973 to meet He Zizhen and confirm the identification. This was the first in a series of meetings that went strangely awry. Yang Yuehua was taken to the designated place, outside her new-found mother's residence, but was refused entry. She was not allowed in, she was told, because the person appointed to vouch for her at the gate had not arrived. Since that person was a member of Mao's extended household and, given the cómplex power plays within the Mao–Jiang–He relationship, could not possibly have been considered an unbiased go-between she was indeed a perplexing choice. Be that as it may, having failed to bring mother and daughter together the party took Yang Yuehua to Fuzhou to meet her maternal uncle He Minxue, Deputy Governor of Fujian Province. Her uncle suggested it would be unwise to upset He Zizhen by putting her under too much strain. He told Yang Yuehua he would arrange for her to meet her mother another time, and then niece and uncle spent several hours talking, apparently enjoying one another's company before Yang Yuehua was taken back home to Longyan.

An attempt was made to reunite Yang Yuehua with her father in early summer 1974. This time she went with a family member and her adoptive mother to Beijing to meet Mao. They stayed in the house of the woman who had failed to turn up in Shanghai the year before and, not surprisingly, this rendezvous was equally unsuccessful. Mao was in his eighties and very ill; he had had pneumonia in 1970, had nearly died from congestive heart failure in 1972, and he had suffered bronchitis, depression, oedema, cataracts and a rare motor neuron disease called Lou Gehrig's disease. Quite possibly Jiang Qing was instrumental in preventing the meeting between Yang Yuehua and Mao, as some claim, but Mao's minders were doubtless happy not to have to bother Mao with such an inconsequential matter as the new-found daughter of an abandoned wife.

For the next few years Yang Yuehua went on working in the cinema in Longyan, He Zizhen lived her lonely life in Shanghai, and Mao began to disintegrate physically at an alarming rate. He died on 9 September 1976.

The year after Mao died He Zizhen went to Fuzhou for medical treatment. As usual she stayed with her brother, intending to go to Longyan to meet her daughter but this did not happen, for 'several reasons'. What these several reasons were is not specified but they could not have been orchestrated by Mao, who was now dead, or by Jiang Qing, who was in jail. Perhaps

Yang Yuehua on her side was disillusioned or fearful, perhaps He Zizhen was too ill; she suffered a stroke that year—she was sixty-seven years old—that left her paralysed down the left side and bedridden for some time.

The last attempt at a reunion failed because of the streak of stubborn pride that He Zizhen seems to have passed on to both her daughters. Unable to get to Longyan herself, He Zizhen asked Li Min to go there with her husband and see what she could do. Li Min arranged to sit in on a meeting at which Yang Yuehua was scheduled to present a report on her work, but she asked to remain incognito, her presence explained as her being a 'leader' from provincial cultural headquarters. Yang Yuehua, however, soon recognised Li Min from a photograph of her she had seen when she was in Beijing. Yang Yuehua stubbornly ignored her sister and walked out of the meeting room without a word as soon as she finished her report. She resented Li Min's devious behaviour, as is evident from her later explanation of her actions to her uncle: 'I'm older than her. She could have said something, why should I be the one to have to do it?'

Even though He Minxue eventually announced publicly that Yang Yuehua was indeed his niece and the daughter of Mao and He Zizhen; even though the party promised to arrange a meeting in Shanghai between mother and daughter; even though the party promised to provide a car, the gap was too great. Yang Yuehua never went to Shanghai and she never met He Zizhen.

Once Mao was dead and Jiang Qing had been incarcerated as the wicked witch of the Cultural Revolution, the party could rehabilitate her: suddenly He Zizhen's schizophrenia no longer mattered and she was after all capable of being assigned work. The national feeling of relief that followed Mao's death marked a period of remorse and reconciliation. During this time He Zizhen was invited to Beijing and elected to the 5th Chinese People's Political Consultative Conference, of which Kang Keqing was Deputy Chair. The same year, 1979, she joined the endless queues in Beijing and silently made whatever internal peace was possible as she gazed upon her ex-husband's body, laid to rest in the massive mausoleum that had been built to house it. There was little to keep her in the capital once she had been allowed to rejoin society, had lived to see the detested Jiang Qing overthrown and had viewed Mao's body, so she returned to Shanghai.

Now that He Zizhen was, in a sense, back at work people were prepared to listen to the resentment and frustration she felt at what was a life half-lived. It depressed her immeasurably, she said in 1980, to compare her wasted life with the achievements of women who had worked and studied to make a success of their lives these past forty years that she had been locked away. She was convinced she had possessed the ability to become a leader in her own right, even without the flying start of being Mao Zedong's wife and confidential secretary, a privilege that had come to bedevil and destroy her. Her regrets were valid. She had been shackled from the beginning, by motherhood and by the sheer bad luck of falling in love with Mao, charming and powerful but ultimately manipulative and destructive.

She was aware, of course, of the double-edged nature of *guanxi*. She knew it was not ability alone that allowed women to rise towards the top. She knew that no matter how capable were the women who held positions of influence, they were there only because they were the wives of prominent men. Kang Keqing would not have been placed at the head of the women's movement if she had not been the wife of one of the nation's leaders; Madame Song Qingling would not have been elected Vice-chair of the Central People's Government if she had not been the chaste widow of Dr Sun Yat-sen; Deng Yingchao would not have been elected to national councils if she had not been the wife of Premier Zhou Enlai; even Cai Chang, respected revolutionary that she was, would have languished in the middle ranks if she had chosen to divorce her husband Vice-premier Li Fuchun when she discovered his dalliance with another woman.[16]

The negative effects of *guanxi* were, however, equally strong. No matter how great her ability, a woman who was married to a prominent man could not rise to a position of real power for fear of charges of nepotism or concern that too much power would be concentrated in the hands of a single family; Jiang Qing's manipulative role in the Cultural Revolution was a case in point. In terms of education, experience and party credentials, both Deng Yingchao and Cai Chang were exceptionally well qualified to fill ministerial positions but because their husbands were in the top echelon of power they were never considered for such posts. They were invited instead to fill purely ceremonial positions that allowed them little opportunity to exercise their considerable abilities. To forestall criticism of their husbands, they became figureheads, not executives. In a country where Mao said they held up half the sky, women were still outsiders who could only approach the top if their husbands were already there to give them a hand up. He Zizhen's fate was so intimately tied to her marriage to Mao, however, that she may not have seen the unfairness of it all, of how the early communists' talk of equality had not translated into the women of her generation receiving their due when the jobs were handed out after liberation.

Another photograph of He Zizhen was taken in Shanghai by her niece He Haifeng in 1980. He Zizhen has put on a little weight and her face has filled out. She is standing by herself and she is not smiling. Her friend Shui Jing, who had not seen her since taking her to Lushan nearly twenty years before, tells of how she visited He Zizhen in Shanghai's Huadong Hospital about this time and found her an alert white-haired old woman, puffy in the face from oedema, sitting propped up in bed. 'I'm old now,' 70-year-old He Zizhen told her, still able to joke and muster a smile. 'I'll soon be meeting Marx.'

He Zizhen spent her last years in hospital and the precision with which the date and time of her death at the age of seventy-four are given—5.17 pm on 19 April 1984—stands in stark contrast to the murkiness that obscures the last fifty years of her lonely life. She was laid in state at the Longhua Revolutionary Cemetery in Shanghai, where the flag of the Chinese Communist Party was draped over her coffin in a posthumous gesture of respect and the hall was full of flowers from fellow Long Marchers and old comrades: Kang Keqing, Cai Chang, Deng Yingchao, Deng Xiaoping, Wang Shoudao. All that remained of her life—the two battered suitcases she had carried home from Russia, an army blanket, alarm clock and her tea jar from Jinggangshan—was donated to a state museum in Shanghai.

When they cremated her body they found a piece of shrapnel. Her ashes, and the shrapnel shard, were interred along with those of most of the nation's respected revolutionaries in Babaoshan Revolutionary Cemetery in the western quarter of Beijing.

8

NEVER SAY DIE

The difficulties Wang Quanyuan experienced throughout her life arose from the fact that nobody stood by her. The Communist Party labelled her politically unreliable and abandoned her when she approached the 8th Route Army office in Lanzhou after escaping from her Moslem captors in 1939, then her family and the people of her native village did their best to get rid of her when she returned after the disturbing and exciting years of her Long March. She brought trouble to her brother and was suspected of having collaborated with the enemy. When Wang Quanyuan eventually agreed to marry Liu Gaohua in 1948 it was made clear to her that she was expected to leave the village, and towards the end of the year the couple moved to neighbouring Taihe County.[1]

Taihe County straddled the Gan River just north of Kang Keqing's native village and nestled in the eastern foothills of Jinggangshan south of the city of Ji'an. This was not a prosperous region but it rewarded the toil of its inhabitants with rice, sweet potato, rapeseed and sugarcane; tea plantations provided work and income, while the area's bamboo and fir trees were sought after. At some time in the distant past local artisans had begun to make oil-paper fans and screens, which remained a famous speciality of Taihe. Wang Quanyuan and her husband set up house deep in the mountains near the small township of Heshixiang. They drew their water from the village well and there was no electricity, but on those rare nights when they stayed up much after dark they could see the lights of Jinggangshan from

204

their two-roomed, wattle-and-daub shack. They went about their lives in the way of peasants, turning their hands to the soil to eke out a living.

The cheerful young Wang Quanyuan of Jiangxi soviet and Long March days had become a thin and worn woman of thirty-six by the autumn of 1949 when she learnt that the victorious Red Army was approaching Ji'an. Although her party membership had been cancelled from the time she had been separated for over two years from the 1st Front Red Army in the north-west, she decided to walk into Heshixiang to catch her first glimpse for ten years of the liberators of the nation who had once been her comrades.

Wang Quanyuan's trip to Heshixiang is presented in her biographies as evidence of her loyalty to the communist cause and her overwhelming love of the party. Just as she had been one of the first in her district to join the revolution in the early 1930s, so too she stepped forward to welcome the Red Army and lead them back to her village in triumph on the eve of liberation nearly twenty years later, the story goes. Her real motives were probably less noble but equally compelling. Wang Quanyuan was a simple peasant girl whose life had been transformed by her seven years with the communists, and there is every reason to believe that she remained genuinely committed to communism despite her devastating experience in the north-west with the Western Route Army and the party's implicit accusation that she was a traitor for having survived capture by the Moslems. However, her own people had dealt so harshly with her upon her return home that she undoubtedly saw the coming of the Red Army as an opportunity to regain her status in the community. Thus she strove to renew her relationship with the communists, who had turned out to be the winning side in China's long ideological war.

Little information is available on Wang Quanyuan's life after 1949. As a peasant woman in her middle years living deep in the countryside, her everyday life held few surprises and was little different from that of millions of others. Her political life, however, was fraught with difficulties. Because of her valuable experience with the Red Army, her hardwon literacy and her political commitment, Wang Quanyuan was assigned to work in

the district office in Heshixiang soon after liberation. She and
her husband became leading figures in the new administration,
Wang Quanyuan in charge of women's affairs and Liu Gaohua
the village head. When a death in the family made it necessary
for Wang Quanyuan to return to her village to fulfil her filial
duties, she was immediately replaced as district head of women's
affairs. This was no reflection on the quality of her work, but
simply an indication of the importance the new government
placed on consciousness-raising work among local women
throughout the country. When she returned to Heshixiang after
the mourning period she was transferred to the position of
production team leader in charge of land reform. Her knowledge
and experience gained with the communists before and during
the Long March would have been invaluable for this responsible
work. She travelled about the district gathering details of the
rents peasants were paying to local landlords then negotiated
reductions in both the rent and the amount of interest landlords
were permitted to charge on loans and late payments.

Wang Quanyuan's work in the women's movement and her
righting of wrongs in the land reform movement were an integral
part of the Communist Party's vanguard into the newly liberated
areas of south-eastern China. This region had remained under
KMT control until 1949, and after the Generalissimo evacuated
across the Formosa Strait (soon to become universally known by
its Chinese name of the Taiwan Strait) to Taiwan his ghost
lingered in the form of underground agents and covert loyalists.
The Chinese Government labelled the landlords and other
middle-class, anti-government 'counter-revolutionaries' who
retained some local influence in the south-eastern provinces a
'remnant reactionary clique' which they targeted through mass
movements. The 'resist America, aid Korea' campaign in 1950
had little impact on Wang Quanyuan and her fellow villagers but
the several 'anti' campaigns of 1952 bred fear among the most
isolated peasants.

An American woman, Miss P. Lum, described the 'Three antis,
five antis' campaign she witnessed in Beijing as a hideously wrong
way of carrying out admirable objectives. She suggested with
great perception that its main aim seemed to be to single out
individuals as targets against which the party and people could

unite, and her description might apply equally well to dozens of similar campaigns that ran their course over the following two decades:

> Speeches are made on the evils of corruption, waste and bureaucracy, and then each member of the staff [of a workplace] must get up and confess his own faults and criticize the shortcomings of others. The most successful technique is to confess just enough when it comes to your turn so that it sounds convincing and you may get off with a show of repentance and a small fine, but this is a matter of the utmost delicacy. You must try to cover all the points that anyone might conceivably bring up against you later, either out of spite or because they hope by accusing you to keep suspicion from falling on themselves . . . The one thing you must not do is to claim to be innocent . . .
>
> These meetings go on and on, not only for hours, but for days and weeks and sometimes already months on end . . .
>
> Meanwhile the Government sends 'investigators' to every shop, firm or institution to go through their books for the last twenty years, conduct interminable interrogations and try to find some sort of irregularity. [These investigations] are therefore carried out by men and women whose 'political consciousness is high', students, workers of good standing in the Party, activists and so on, young fanatics who know only that all business and all profit-making institutions are wicked and that they must find something wrong. China being what it is, and has been, they often do find some irregularity, but if they cannot unearth anything they must nevertheless procure some kind of a confession or they themselves may be accused of imperialist sympathies, capitalism or an insufficiently heightened political consciousness . . .
>
> According to the seriousness of the offence, a confession and apology may eventually, after hours or weeks of 'criticism and self-criticism', be accepted, or a fine may be imposed. A few of the real 'tigers', as the large-scale offenders are called, have been executed. But the average man, whether he works in a shop, office or institution, is still just waiting, attending meetings, confessing, thinking, confessing again, going over and over his books, with no idea of what is to come.[2]

Wang Quanyuan may have been deprived of the best kind of *guanxi* when she lost her party membership, but that's not to say she lacked it entirely. As village head and one who had not been active in the revolutionary struggle of the 1930s and 1940s against the KMT, her husband, Liu Gaohua, was a choice target for charges of corruption, waste and bureaucracy—or perhaps bribery, or cheating on government contracts—and he was inevitably accused, convicted and imprisoned. As his wife, Wang Quanyuan had to be guilty of something and, given her patchwork background as a Red Army soldier, it took little investigation to come up with the verdict 'Political history unclear'. She was called a defector for having marched under Zhang Guotao's banner towards the end of the Long March and traditional attitudes to prisoners of war ensured that her family and friends blamed her for having let herself be captured alive by Moslems. She was suspected of having collaborated with the Moslems and criticised for not having continued to involve herself in revolutionary work after her escape, despite being turned away by the party in Lanzhou. Determined to redeem herself, in the early 1950s she asked to be allowed to apply for party membership. Her request was rejected. She was removed from her job and sent back to her village to work on the farm.

Wang Quanyuan had had enough by this stage. She was only forty years old but she had already experienced a lifetime of injustice, from her birth as a peasant to her abandonment by the Red Army to being pilloried by her natal community, and she was no longer prepared to sit quietly while undeserved dishonour was heaped upon her. Not for her the suicide that was increasingly common among those who could not stand the strain in Beijing, or in Shanghai where it was not safe to walk along the Bund by the river because of the falling bodies, or so the joke went. Wang Quanyuan's dander was up, and with it her courage. It was not only her honour that was at stake, but her livelihood and the rights and privileges associated with belonging to a work unit and being an accepted member of the community. She decided to appeal against the double blow of losing her job and her income, and the imprisonment of her husband on what she claimed were false charges.

She wrote to the provincial authorities and to the party but, because she was under surveillance, one after another the letters she posted 'went astray'. Eventually she wrote to her old Long

March comrade Kang Keqing, now a woman of some influence living in the leadership compound in Beijing, and appealed for help. Knowing the letter would not get past the village limits if she tried to post it in the normal manner, she entrusted it to a reliable friend who promised to mail it in the major industrial city of Wuhan on the Yangtze River. Still nothing happened, however, and she never found out if her letter reached Kang Keqing. Her husband languished in jail, she occupied herself in her vegetable garden.

She did receive one letter, in 1958. Wan Ling, her husband from the early 1940s, wrote to her enclosing a photograph of himself and telling her he was now the proud father of four sons. He also mentioned having taken a trip to Tibet. Despite the harsh memories of Tibet and the north-west that must have flooded back with the arrival of Wan Ling's letter, Wang Quanyuan politely wrote back saying that she, too, had remarried but that she was childless. That was her last contact with Wan Ling.

Wang Quanyuan remained under a paralysing political cloud for ten years, the decade of her forties. Then, one day in 1962, Kang Keqing passed through Ji'an on her way with Zhu De to pay a visit to Jinggangshan. News of the arrival of two such well-known comrades swept through the countryside, reaching even Wang Quanyuan in her isolated village. This time she did manage to get a letter to Kang Keqing, who rose to the occasion. Resorting to her considerable *guanxi*, Kang Keqing requested the local party authorities to locate Wang Quanyuan, whom she referred to as her fellow provincial and old Red Army comrade. A car was immediately sent to Heshixiang to fetch Wang Quanyuan who was whisked into Ji'an and the welcoming arms of Kang Keqing.

It would be difficult to exaggerate Wang Quanyuan's relief at seeing the broad reassuring countenance of Kang Keqing, committee member of the All-China Women's Federation and wife of Commander-in-Chief Zhu De, who was also a vice-chair of the Central People's Government. On the verge of tears she answered Kang Keqing's questions about everything that had happened to her in the twenty-six years since they had last seen one another. She told how her latest husband, Liu Gaohua, had been imprisoned and of how she had been labelled 'Political history unclear' and stripped of her job. She had worked so hard before and after liberation for the revolution, she said, that it was unreasonable for the party to deny her re-admission, especially when the party's refusal itself added fuel to the galling accusation that she had once been a counter-revolutionary.

Kang Keqing summoned the local authorities immediately. 'This is not right,' she told them. 'Wang Quanyuan is a good comrade and I will vouch for her. It was not her fault she did not complete the Long March by going all the way to Yan'an. I urge you to put this matter right immediately.' Kang Keqing also arranged for Public Security to release Liu Gaohua and publicly exonerate him. She extracted from the local authorities a guarantee that Wang Quanyuan would be assigned work appropriate to a woman of her abilities and age (she was forty-nine, six years short of retirement age). Then, seeing how thin and sallow Wang Quanyuan was and recalling the problems she had had with her menstrual cycle on the Long March, Kang Keqing arranged for her to be admitted to hospital.

The scant biographical material that has been published in China on Wang Quanyuan quote her as mouthing standard propaganda statements such as: 'I have never doubted that I was born to be a communist and that, no matter what, I would die a communist.' They talk of the strength and endurance of her faith shining through the many hardships fate dealt her. Again, this may indeed be how she felt, but it cannot be denied that a more pragmatic explanation for her determination to re-unite with the Communist Party would have been to forestall her becoming a non-person, discarded once more as a social outcast. Kang Keqing rescued her from this, holding out to Wang Quanyuan the hope of returning to her spiritual home by regaining a foothold in the communist fold. Kang Keqing was not able, however, to erase from the record Wang Quanyuan's unjust dishonourable discharge from the party in 1939 or erase the more recent verdict of 'Political history unclear'. It was only Wang Quanyuan's native optimism that led her to believe it was just a matter of time before her dishonourable discharge was erased, thereby restoring to her credentials unbroken party membership from the time of her joining the party in 1934.

Wang Quanyuan's husband, Liu Gaohua, fades from sight after

his release from prison and rehabilitation in 1962; given his history as a peripheral revolutionary, this is not surprising. He probably returned home and simply kept his head down, as so many others tried to do. If he had already reached retirement age, he would not have had to concern himself with attachment to a work unit.

Wang Quanyuan and her husband must have had some form of income, however, because they adopted several small orphaned children over the years. To be childless in a peasant society founded upon the extended family was to face an extremely difficult and desolate old age, so they took in an eight-year-old boy, whom they named Liu Ren. Over the next few years Wang Quanyuan gathered under her wing seven orphaned children. They all left home as they reached adulthood except Liu Ren, who married another of Wang Quanyuan's brood of orphans, the couple staying on to care for their adoptive mother.

By the time the authorities got around to assigning work to her, Wang Quanyuan had reached the retirement age of fifty-five. She was placed in charge of the district old people's home in Heshixiang in 1968 at a salary of 25 *yuan* per month. Her salary was only slightly above subsistence level but her expectations had never been very high and she was happy to have work at last. She enjoyed the job and soon became thoroughly involved with the home and its occupants. She moved a step closer to regaining her rightful status in the community when she was elected to the local council of the Chinese People's Political Consultative Conference, a body of which Kang Keqing had been a member at the national leadership level since 1949. Her party membership credentials had not been restored, however, so she started on another letter-writing campaign, determined to see this injustice righted and with it her privileges.

She was settling back into the community when the Cultural Revolution began and again she found herself in the line of fire. Long Marchers were a primary target during the Cultural Revolution, their main ostensible crime being that they had turned into reactionary bureaucrats who had lost their revolutionary zeal and concerned themselves only with raising the people's standard of living. So effective was Mao's manipulation of political campaigns and mass feeling that senior party members who proposed the development of technical education and industrial skills, for example, were accused of not relying on the revolutionary potential of the masses but instead of trying to create an elite class of specialists.

Wang Quanyuan was neither bureaucrat nor technocrat, she was born of the masses and had returned to the masses. The Cultural Revolution should not have touched her. However, she had taken part in the Long March, and random justice evaded her again. She was accused of being a traitor for having been absorbed into Zhang Guotao's 4th Front Army in September 1935, for having been placed in command of the Women's Vanguard Regiment of the Western Route Army and, the final ignominy, for having been taken alive and held prisoner by Moslems sympathetic to the KMT. As before, she objected to the unfairness of the charges against her, emphasising the extent of her resistance to her Moslem captors. She sent off more letters explaining her position and requesting correction of her party membership credentials. Her letters went unanswered. Somebody decided to withhold her salary and she was not paid for twelve months. Kang Keqing could not be called upon for help this time since she herself was persona non grata during the Cultural Revolution. At least Wang Quanyuan kept her job during those ten catastrophic years and was not caused actual bodily harm.

Mao died and with him the Cultural Revolution, but Wang Quanyuan's crusade for justice continued. In 1981, five years after the Cultural Revolution drew to a close, she was still sending off letters about her party membership credentials. It was then that she received a welcome invitation through the local branch of the Women's Federation.

She was contacted by her fellow provincial Wei Xiuying, who had answered to the name of 'Shortie' throughout the Long March. Wei Xiuying was exceptional in that she had never married, which had left her free to concentrate on her work. She had attended the Party School in Yan'an and despite her peasant origins held various reasonably high-level posts on provincial committees after 1949. In this, too, she was exceptional: she was the shining example of the way the communists had said it would be for peasant women, especially those who had taken part in the Long March. Wei Xiuying told Wang Quanyuan that the

Women's Federation had embarked upon a program of reconciliation and rehabilitation, and that they were inviting Wang
Quanyuan to a meeting of veteran cadres.

Wang Quanyuan, now aged sixty-eight, requested leave from
her job to attend the meeting. By foot, bus and train she travelled
the 200 kilometres north along the Gan River to the thriving
provincial capital of Nanchang, which since 1949 had become a
revolutionary shrine to the successful 1927 uprising led by Zhu
De and Zhou Enlai. It was the farthest she had travelled since
returning home from the north-west in 1942.

Meetings such as this were being held throughout the nation
as part of the process of washing the party and the people clean
of the fear and mistrust that had poisoned the country from the
early 1950s. Wang Quanyuan made full use of the opportunity
to present her case where it would do the most good and told
her story from beginning to end to an audience sympathetic to
her righteous indignation. Women's Federation cadres organised
the necessary paperwork and outlined the bureaucratic steps
necessary for her to be awarded her rights as a citizen. In this
new climate of cooperation the civil administration office in
Heshixiang processed Wang Quanyuan's forms without delay and
within a short time she was issued with all the privileges of a
Red Army veteran, including food and grain rations and a pension
of 90 *yuan* per month. One thing remained undone: she still had
her sights set on re-admission to the party and restoration of her
continuous party membership credentials.

Later that year Wang Quanyuan borrowed 100 *yuan* for
another train fare. This time she was going to Beijing to attend
the 1981 Women's Federation reunion, accompanied by her
faithful adopted son, Liu Ren. They prepared several days' worth
of food and sat up in 'hard class' for the several days the trip
took, unaware until then that modern trains had sleeping com-
partments, which in any case would have been beyond their
means.

At the Red Army women's reunion, Wang Quanyuan was
confronted in the foyer by a sea of unknown faces from which,
one by one, old comrades she had not seen for nearly fifty years
came towards her. She was warmly greeted by Liu Ying, who in
her youth had been categorised as a student and assigned during

the Long March to the Women Workers' Group. Despite the great misfortune she suffered before and during the Cultural Revolution, Liu Ying appeared to hold no grudge against the party, believing that communism had fulfilled its early promise to her as an intellectual and a woman by allowing her to participate in the nation's affairs and rewarding her at the end of her life with a responsible bureaucratic position.

Deng Liujin, 'The Cannon', reminisced with Wang Quanyuan about the exciting days of the Long March and expressed deep satisfaction at the fulfilling work she had been able to do since 1949 despite being born an illiterate peasant. Zhong Yuelin, too, had been born a peasant and she offered no complaints about her life, having been assigned ever since 1949 to work alongside her husband of forty-six years who rose to high rank within the Communist Party. Xie Fei, on the other hand, had remained single after her brief marriage in 1936 to Liu Shaoqi and felt both gratitude and pride at having carved out through her own efforts a successful academic career in the second half of her life.

One other person approached Wang Quanyuan in the foyer, a man she had not expected to see: Wang Shoudao. It was an awkward meeting, with Wang Quanyuan full of resentment at what she believed was her Long March husband's abandonment of her.

'Leaving everything else aside,' she said to him, 'there's just one question I want to ask you. When I got to Lanzhou from the north-west that time, did they refuse to take me back because you didn't want me?'

Wang Shoudao, vice-president and vice-chair of several national bodies, ex-Governor of Hunan and ex-Minister of Communications, shook his head. 'No, it wasn't that,' he told her. 'I waited three years for you in Yan'an before I found someone else. And I don't believe those malicious rumours about you, either.'[3]

Whether Wang Quanyuan believed his pat answer or not, many people privately considered Wang Shoudao's treatment of her shabby from beginning to end. He was certainly not to blame for her political exile and the poverty that accompanied it, but he had always been in a position to extend a helping hand by acknowledging their past relationship and the ten years of good work she had done. He had chosen not to, evidently preferring to distance himself from a comrade who had fallen out of favour. The Red Army reunion was nevertheless an exercise in Women's Federation reconciliation and Wang Shoudao had been invited to add his considerable political clout to clearing Wang Quanyuan's name by publicly vouching for her good character, no matter that it was several decades too late.

The story of Wang Quanyuan's early Red Army days, her Long March contribution and the unfortunate circumstances that led to her separation from the main march and subsequent tribulations in the north-west was thoroughly aired. It was unanimously agreed that she had done absolutely nothing to harm the party or the people. She was exonerated for what had befallen her and the labels of traitor and defector that had shackled her for forty years were dismissed as totally unwarranted. She walked from the meeting with her reputation restored, as she had believed all along would eventually happen.

Liu Ying sent to the Jiangxi provincial authorities testimonials on Wang Quanyuan's good character and unswerving loyalty. The Central Committee's Organisational Bureau received a letter from the office of General Xu Xiangqian, who in 1936 had been co-commander of the doomed Western Route Army. Wang Shoudao wrote to the authorities in Taihe County confirming that he and Wang Quanyuan had been married during the Long March. In his letter he said:

> Wang Quanyuan is a good comrade. She has been subjected to unfair treatment for some decades. Given her seniority and her experiences, Wang Quanyuan would have been justified in making any number of demands. That she made none is in itself proof of her absolute sincerity towards the party and the army. Even though she has lived in poverty she has been extraordinarily respectful of party organisation.[4]

Wang Quanyuan's persistent pursuit of justice had been rewarded; her rehabilitation was almost complete. There remained only the matter of 'Political history unclear' written into her record and the gap in her party membership credentials.

She was not the only woman to be still chasing that last vestige of justice. Many of the women with the Women's Vanguard Regiment in 1936 who survived but had not been able to escape had made a new life in the north-west. They, too, had been labelled traitors and deserters during the Cultural Revolution. Yang Wenju, who had remained in the north-west with her baby and lived with a Moslem tanner until 1949, had been agitating since 1962 to have their official status changed from 'Red Army personnel who became destitute wanderers' or 'Personnel with whom contact was lost' to something more realistic: she was suggesting 'Veteran Red Army soldiers of the Western Route Army'. Yang Wenju regained her original party membership in 1978.

Wang Quanyuan and her son caught the train to Jiangxi and made their way to their village near Heshixiang across the river from Jinggangshan. She settled back into her small house, still without electricity or running water, and returned to work as head of the old people's home.

With a resurgence of interest in Long Marchers after the Cultural Revolution she gained respect as one of The Thirty Women. She was portrayed as a Red Army heroine in a film, *Echoes of Qilian Mountains*, which told the tragic story of the Western Route Army and the Women's Vanguard Regiment, and she was admired in the north-west for her courage in resisting and escaping her Moslem captors. The extraordinary litany of mismanagement, bad luck and victimisation that had dogged her since then became known through a series of books and articles written in the mid 1980s. In 1985 she was re-admitted to membership of the Communist Party. The same year she was elected to the county and provincial committees of the Chinese People's Political Consultative Conference. It was another two years, however, before her membership credentials were fully restored and her slate was wiped clean.

A photograph was taken of Wang Quanyuan in August 1986, the year before she ceased work at the Heshixiang old people's home. Reproduced on bad quality paper, it is so grainy her face is hardly more than a grey blur. She stands slightly off the vertical, feet apart, hands hanging by her side, thin wrists poking out from the long sleeves of her shirt. She is looking straight at the camera, not smiling, and looks as though a gentle breeze might blow her over. The man who took the photograph travelled all the way from the north-west to interview her and found her reserved and distant, not given much to talk.[5] He described her as tall and thin with greying hair, a thin face and a 'stupefied look'. She picked at her food, he said, when they ate in the local canteen and during the banquet put on by the local branch of the Women's Federation, but looked healthy and claimed to have nothing wrong with her apart from the gynaecological troubles she had developed on the Long March.

In August 1996 a Beijing newspaper carried an article about Wang Quanyuan. The point was made that her life had turned full circle: from illiterate impoverished peasant girl to regimental commander with the Red Army to impoverished peasant woman. Asked if she had any regrets at being unable to fulfil the dramatic promise of her experiences with the Red Army, she replied: 'No, I have no regrets. It is the greatest honour of my life that I was able to go on the Long March. I am very content just to have been a part of it.'[6] Such loyalty in the face of rejection and vilification is difficult for Westerners to come to terms with, and it is tempting to suggest that it sprang not so much from love as from the justifiable fear of being excluded from the dominant group, in this case the Communist Party. What motivates loyalty may as often be fear as it is love, a distinction that is difficult to draw. That loyalty as unshakable as Wang Quanyuan's is not unusual among people of the Long March generation, however, says as much about how deeply convinced of the rightness of the revolution were the rank and file early communists as it does about its cultural origins. When the communists called on the people to replace traditional Confucian values with the Maoist values of loyalty to people, party and leader, they were not really asking them to change; they were simply shifting the people's gaze from the family to the party.

The stuff of Wang Quanyuan's life clearly remained little changed by communism, and the victimisation she suffered sprang from a traditional way of thinking that it suited the communists for many years not to challenge. The Long March women were well aware that reality fell far short of the promise of early communism, but because doors that had previously been firmly closed to them had begun to open they appear to have been willing to accept that reality. It is evident that Wang Quanyuan's pursuit of justice was unsuccessful until the other

Long March women supported her, but, more importantly, it is also evident that never before had it been possible for a group of women to wield such public influence on behalf of other women. This, to them, was an important symbol of hope.

Wang Quanyuan was still living in her village in Jiangxi Province as this book went to press.

9
ABOUT TURN

'I'm really not suited to this kind of work,' Kang Keqing told the meeting held in Xibaipo in Hubei Province.

> It's obvious that to be a member of the Women's Council you should have experience working with women and I haven't. I've been with the army for nearly twenty years now, and that's where my expertise is—with the military. I'd be prepared to work with army veterans, but I really don't believe I'd be of any use to the Women's Council. I therefore formally request to be released from the Women's Council.[1]

The meeting of women delegates at which Kang Keqing was speaking was the first of three meetings of the Central Committee's Women's Council, called between September 1947 and the summer of 1948, on the eve of the communists' victory. Their purpose was to prepare for the 1st National Women's Congress that would be held once the communists were in power and which took place in March 1949.

Not a soul supported Kang Keqing's request. One by one her old friends spoke out against it. From the chair, fellow Long Marcher Deng Yingchao called on her to stop her nonsense: 'You have been chosen by the Central Committee to be a member of the Women's Council; I trust you will re-think your position,' she said crisply. Zhang Qinqiu, who had crossed the Snowy Mountains and the Grass Lands twice with Kang Keqing during her time with the 4th Front Red Army, reasoned with her: 'It will be impossible to resolve the difficulties women will face in going out to work unless we first deal with the issue of what happens to their children. I trust you will do all you can to facilitate our work with children.' Other women rose to address the meeting: 'This is a crucial time. We're on the brink of victory throughout the country and it's terribly important to have strong commanders for the women's movement. Kang Keqing must not be allowed to leave the Women's Council.' Even her husband publicly disclaimed her in his address to the conference, without naming names, of course. Stressing the importance of working with women and children, Zhu De criticised the attitude of female cadres who were not willing to become involved in women's work.

So it was that Kang Keqing was led to see the error of her ways. The peasant girl who told Helen Foster Snow just ten years previously, 'I don't care much about the women's problem; I always work with men, not women', was directed to work with the Women's Council; the revolutionary soldier whom Agnes Smedley described as 'one of the best trained women in the army' was instructed to relinquish her military work; the childless soldier who grudgingly admitted she liked babies 'as an institution' but said she didn't want any of her own because they would interfere with her work found herself responsible for establishing creches, nurseries and child-care centres.

The communists' insistence on obedience to party decisions and policies clearly runs counter to Western ideals of personal independence and the rights of the individual. The Chinese communists, however, had their genesis in a pluralist society founded on Confucian values and centred on the family. In addition, the Chinese lived in an agrarian society so that they were accustomed to adhering to traditional ways and abiding by group decisions dictated by outside considerations, such as the seasons and the weather. In the early twentieth century, the communists believed that China's problems stemmed from Confucianism, which had long oppressed women and reduced peasants to the status of slaves. They proclaimed that solidarity alone could transform China, repeating over and over their simple message that people working as individuals were helpless, and that only 100 million peasants working together could overthrow the traditional landlord system. 'Workers of the world unite' became 'Peasants of China unite'. Individual dissent within their ranks was therefore widely recognised as problematic because it threatened the entire revolutionary process. Only much later did it become evident that solidarity with the party was not in fact synonymous with the much desired dictatorship of the proletariat, but merely served the dictatorial ends of those who sought power for themselves.

In her memoirs, Kang Keqing referred without apparent rancour to the criticism she received at the Xibaipo meeting, acknowledging it as an event which awakened her to her responsibilities as a faithful member of the party. It is difficult, however, to believe she would not have been distressed at what was effectively an order to undo her life's work. For nearly twenty years she had happily strapped on her side arm, taking literally the communist rhetoric about women being revolutionary fighters. From the beginning she had believed it was her destiny to be a soldier. Although she was aware that once the fighting was over she might have to relinquish active duty and become a desk soldier, it was her not unrealistic expectation that she would continue to be involved in what she called 'the exciting life of the army'.

There appears to be but one reason for the anonymous decision to remove her from an area in which she had considerable expertise to a field about which she knew little, and at that stage cared even less. Women were not barred from the military, and many continued to serve in the Red Army, which after 1949 was renamed the People's Liberation Army (PLA). One woman— Li Zhen—who had marched with He Long's 2nd Front Army from Hunan to Tibet in 1935–36 was the first of several women to rise to the rank of general.[2] It is also unreasonable to suggest that Kang Keqing was prevented from following an army career simply because her husband, the Commander-in-Chief, had never really approved of women in the army. On the other hand, it is certain that her husband's high profile and the spectre of nepotism worked against her. A revealing remark once made by Premier Zhou Enlai confirms this. When asked whether his wife Deng Yingchao would, like her male colleagues, be rewarded for her years of loyal revolutionary work with a ministerial position in the new government, Zhou Enlai replied: 'Deng Yingchao will never be a minister while I am Premier.'[3] So too, with Kang

Keqing. Negative *guanxi* ensured she would never become a commander in the army.

Kang Keqing had taken the stirring slogans about equality between the sexes so seriously over the years that she considered herself to be one of the boys. As such, she had never hidden the fact that she was unwilling to become involved in work that was associated with women, and it is not hard to see why she felt this way. Despite their rhetoric, the communists' behaviour left no doubt that they believed man was born to rule, woman to clean up after him. From the first, certain work associated with women was done solely by women. This consisted mainly of explaining communist policy on marriage, divorce, footbinding, women's and girls' education, and recruiting women and girls to the party. Such work was carried out through discussion, and talks to individual women and groups in the community, at schools and in workplaces. The practical reason why women did this work was that the traditional gender segregation within Chinese society made it easier for them to contact and move freely among other women. The women found, however, that once they became part of the separate women's bureau that was set up to oversee women's work they were, in the main, unable to assume positions outside the bureau. This meant they were all but excluded from the decision-making process since the bureau had no place in the power structure of the all-male party hierarchy. Gender relations within the party were so traditional, in fact, that 'a somewhat modified type of court politics reminiscent of the imperial period emerged at the center of the CCP. A central characteristic of this type of court politics was the development of an informal power structure for women premised on the notion that women did not require access to formal decision-making positions.'[4] In other words, if women were to take part in politics they should do so through their husbands.

Once Kang Keqing's request to be released from the Women's Council was refused, she had no option but to give in. She certainly was not the best woman for the job. Nevertheless, she put on a brave front (continuing to wear her uniform for as long as she could) and did as she was told with good grace, conscious always of her duty to display exemplary loyalty. Till the end of her life, however, she harboured regrets that she had not been allowed to remain in the army.

Kang Keqing appears never to have considered her election to women's committees and child-welfare committees at various times during the 1930s and 1940s as more than a formality bestowed upon her because she was a leading communist and the wife of Zhu De. Practically all the top people, both in and out of Yan'an, were elected at some time or another to a committee in an honorary capacity. In 1938, for instance, arch-enemies Generalissimo Chiang Kai-shek and Chairman Mao were both on the board of a child-welfare association in the city of Wuhan in central China, along with Zhou Enlai, Helen Foster Snow, Zhu De and Agnes Smedley. The Generalissimo's wife, Madame Song Meiling, was the association's director.[5] That same year Madame Song Meiling and her older sister Madame Song Qingling were appointed as honorary board members of a branch child-welfare association set up to serve three north-western provinces. Kang Keqing was a member of this board, as were Cai Chang, Zhang Qinqiu and the writer Ding Ling. Kang Keqing treated these as largely ceremonial positions.

It was the same with creches. These had existed in Yan'an from the early days but Kang Keqing's involvement had been peripheral, to the extent that when Zhu De showed an interest in creches and education for young children in the early 1940s she was merely obliged to tag along occasionally on his visits. The closest she came to day to day involvement was in 1947, when she was left in charge of a child-welfare association that served all of China's liberated areas after Cai Chang's departure from Yan'an. However, her duties were shelved when more important matters of survival intervened.

KMT bombing raids on Yan'an had almost reduced the settlement to rubble by March 1947 when Kang Keqing was ordered to cease her studies at the Party School and evacuate with the Central Women's Council. She headed east and forded the Yellow River by truck. For the next two years she was stationed in and around the smallish city of Xibaipo, about 300 kilometres southwest of Peiping on the banks of the Hutuo River in Hebei Province.

Kang Keqing accompanied Zhu De on his rounds as Commander-in-Chief, attended conferences on land reform, dabbled in women's work and played a small part in a 'lifting rocks' campaign intended to expose corruption among local cadres. She did not fail to mention in her memoirs the leading role she played during that period in clearing the streets of a small town of civilians caught in an air-raid. Quickly assuming command as people ran about in panic at the sound of approaching aeroplanes, she ordered two militiamen to shepherd the people to cover. Then, standing calm and firm in her 8th Route Army uniform, she called out loudly: 'Everybody off the streets! You mustn't give away our position! Obey instructions and take cover in the air raid shelters!'

She was eventually recalled from the field, and by April 1948 was back among the cypresses in Xibaipo as a member of the working party charged with organising the inaugural National Women's Congress. By September she had been appointed Acting Director of the Council for Children and Welfare in the Liberated Areas and the die was cast. One of her last tastes of the outdoors was a fieldwork trip to the city of Jinan on behalf of the Women's Council. She walked and hitched the 500 kilometres from Xibaipo and spent a happy two weeks in Jinan in the company of an old friend from Yan'an, visiting factories during the day and enjoying performances of a travelling theatre company in the evenings.

Her final adventure of this sort was a nostalgic trip to her birthplace in Jiangxi Province in the summer of 1951. This was just two years after the communists had come to power, and bandits and KMT loyalist remnants were still a danger in out-of-the-way places such as her native Wan'an County. Accompanied by an armed bodyguard, Kang Keqing strapped on her revolver and walked on to the mountain tracks of her childhood. She arrived at dusk, unannounced, in the tiny backward village on the bend of the river and stayed for a week. The first night she cooked dinner for her widowed foster father and tried to remedy several years of his neglect by tidying up. She slept so well she didn't hear the pig and the water buffalo squabbling during the night. In the morning they discovered that the buffalo was covered in bruises where the pig had bitten it, and by midday the buffalo was dead. This was not just a small family tragedy, it was a communal buffalo which her foster father had bought a share in with three other families. Kang Keqing's foster father only owned one leg and now the whole buffalo was dead. Fortunately for everybody Kang Keqing bought them what she described as 'a better water buffalo'.

People flocked from all around to stare at this fortunate local girl who had made good by marrying the Commander-in-Chief of the PLA. Her foster father enumerated for her the deaths in the family: her birth parents had died in the 1930s and her foster mother and grandmother had died in the 1940s; none of her three brothers had lived beyond the age of eleven, and only one sister was still alive.

Two photographs of Kang Keqing were taken in 1949 in Peiping (the capital reverted to its old name of Beijing on 1 October 1949). She was thirty-eight years old.

One photograph, taken in September, shows about seventy women who were attending the 1st Chinese People's Political Consultative Conference, at which Kang Keqing and her husband, who was then in his early sixties, represented PLA Headquarters. Kang Keqing stands gravely in the back row, one of the few women wearing Red Army caps. It was at this Consultative Conference that the law was passed enshrining the right of women to full equality with men in all aspects of life—listed as political, economic, educational and social. It was also at this conference that Madame Song Qingling and Zhu De were elected vice-chairs of the Central People's Government. Even though Kang Keqing thus became the wife of one of the leaders of the new nation, she was determined to remain the straightforward peasant she had always been. When the transition period from revolutionary to national leader was deemed to have expired and it was no longer proper for her to wear her Red Army uniform, she switched to a simple grey cotton Lenin jacket and trousers, which remained her basic outfit for the rest of her life. Amid much encouraging laughter she tried, but failed, to walk in the high-heeled shoes the stylish Madame Song Qingling sent her for her new role as a public figure. Instead, she continued to wear the flat, slip-on cloth shoes of the ordinary Chinese people.

The other is a lively photograph of seventeen of the Long March women who were attending the 1st National Women's Congress which opened in Peiping on 24 March 1949 and welcomed some 466 delegates representing workers, peasants, militiawomen, soldiers of the PLA and intellectuals. It was at this congress that the All-China Democratic Women's Federation was formed. Its name was later changed to the All-China Women's Federation and it is usually referred to as the *Fulian*, or Women's Federation. This first national conference had nothing new to say to the women of China, calling upon them to join in the democratic revolution that had succeeded in driving out foreign imperialists and the reactionary KMT and winning China for the communists. In effect, the Women's Federation was simply embarking on a public relations exercise by declaring its existence and revealing to the nation the presence of the many capable and dedicated women of various political affiliations who were part of the Federation—although few of them were part of the nation's decision-making process.

At this congress Kang Keqing began her new career with the Federation's Children's Welfare Department when she addressed hundreds of women in Huairentang, a large hall inside the Zhongnanhai complex. Reading from a report prepared during the preliminary meetings held at Xibaipo, she told her audience that ten million children were in crisis in areas that had been held by the KMT, and that shortages of food and medicine meant that the death rate among children in newly liberated areas exceeded 450 per thousand children. Without quoting figures, she contrasted this appalling situation with communist-held areas such as Yan'an, where no effort had been spared in child-welfare work. With victory at hand and the work of rebuilding China ahead, child-welfare work had become one of the nation's most urgent tasks. Relief had to be provided for vast numbers of orphans and children in crisis. Child care and education were needed for the children of urban women workers and professional women, who must be free to concentrate on playing their part in national reconstruction. The major problem in the countryside affecting women and their babies was lack of hygiene: besides training and despatching large numbers of paramedics and child-care workers, it was crucial that harmful superstitions be eradicated and doctors practising a pragmatic mix of Western and traditional Chinese medicine be seeded throughout the countryside. Nursery facilities of every conceivable style and size must also be popularised, and here Kang Keqing called upon the delegates to make child-care facilities a priority in their organisations' work of constructing a new China.

These became recurring themes for many years and Kang Keqing soon found herself working closely on these issues with two women she knew from Yan'an. Cai Chang was elected Chair of the All-China Democratic Women's Federation. This position dovetailed nicely with her other job as head of the female workers' branch of the All-China Federation of Trade Unions. With the two organisations working together, plans were immediately laid to provide special nursing rooms in factories where working mothers could breastfeed their babies, and creches for women with slightly older children. The other woman was the former singer and actress Li Lilian, who in 1937 had travelled with Jiang Qing to Yan'an and had married Otto Braun. Li Lilian had left Yan'an after Otto Braun was whisked away to Russia, never to return. She had worked hard in the 1940s to set up the first creche in a fishing-net factory in the northern port of Dalian (on the promontory in China across the water from Korea). She became Kang Keqing's valued colleague in the 1950s when it was government policy to establish creches, child-care centres and kindergartens throughout the country.

The early 1950s was a period of mopping up after four decades of social and economic instability and crippling wars. Food was short, families were shattered and scattered, and old ideas had not yet been challenged in most parts of the country. The Women's Federation saw their part in the rehabilitation of the nation as helping women crawl out from under the burden of the past so that they could learn to stand on their own unbound feet. This meant that the Federation was not only expected to establish creches and kindergartens but, through local cadres in the cities and the countryside, was also responsible for re-educating its 76 million members in all things traditionally considered women's business: childbirth and breastfeeding, menstruation and family planning.

The traditional Chinese attitude towards these matters differed little from that of people in the rest of the world from time immemorial: they happened to women, they should not be talked about, and whatever needed to be done should be done quietly and discretely so that everyone could pretend they weren't really happening. The Women's Federation wanted to change that culture of shame and secrecy.

The infant mortality rate was still very high in 1949 and there was a saying that: 'A woman having a baby already has one foot in the coffin.' In some areas birthing mothers were allowed only a few spoonfuls of thin rice gruel for three days after the birth and were convinced they should stay off solid food for a month after that. An additional problem was that the feeding rooms and creches that sprang up all over China were often staffed by older women who resisted change. Diarrhoea, caused by eating food that was not clean and not fresh, and measles killed too many young children in those early years. These were relatively straight-forward matters, however, and soon fixed through education programs about how to sterilise hands, scissors and rags before a birth, and classes in proper nutrition for new mothers and babies. By 1954 it was claimed that the infant mortality rate had dropped to nearly zero.

Women in the countryside traditionally dealt with menstrua-tion in the following way: they filled with dead ash from the stove any old piece of cloth they could find lying around and girded their loins with this dirty cloth pad for the duration of their menstrual flow. They did not dare tell anyone when the infections they caught caused menstrual problems, or when they experienced other gynaecological problems caused by going straight back to work in the fields after birthing. Menstruation was a topic that Kang Keqing, in her outspoken way, became determined to rescue from its shroud of secrecy. From the rostrum of a Welfare Department meeting she insisted in her Jiangxi drawl that women must make sure that 'menstrual pads, whether cloth or cotton, are spotlessly clean and bone dry. You must wash your private parts thoroughly after menstruation, and there is to be no sex while you are menstruating.' She was becoming accus-tomed to being in charge.

Family planning and birth control were much more difficult issues, given both the rural predisposition to large families (with a preference for male children) and the new government's policy in the early 1950s of encouraging population growth, to provide workers and to stimulate the economy. Abortions were outlawed and a ban was placed on the sale of contraceptives of any sort, while sterilisation was rejected outright. As a party organ, the Women's Federation did not support birth control at this time. By 1956, however, many intellectuals, including Zhou Enlai and Deng Xiaoping, realised that the country could not support such a rapidly growing population and a policy of birth control was approved on economic grounds. Mao's disastrous Great Leap Forward of 1958, which was in turn compounded by a horrific three years of famine in which millions perished, saw a collapse of the issues of family planning and birth control. The Women's Federation began at last to discuss family planning in the mid 1960s, but the topic again fell by the wayside when the Cultural Revolution engulfed the country in 1967. China's population had by that stage passed 1100 million.

In the early 1950s, Kang Keqing and Zhu De were assigned an apartment in Zhongnanhai. The twin lakes of Zhongnanhai, with their pavilions and palaces, were located within the old Imperial City in Beijing and belonged to the pleasureland of lakes and hills built during Genghis Khan's Yuan dynasty (1271–1368). In 1949 this pleasant spot was appropriated as a residential and administrative area for the top leaders. Beihai, just to the north, lay beyond the high security wall, now painted a brownish-red that was but a distant cousin to the original rose-red vermilion of imperial times. The people of Beijing rowed in Beihai Park on summer days, skated there during the winter, and all year long climbed to the top of Emerald Isle to take a closer look at the White Dagoba, 'a mighty monument glowing like a phantom lotus bud in the sunshine' that had been built in 1651 to mark the tributary visit to China of Tibet's Dalai Lama.

Kang Keqing and Zhu De were photographed walking arm in arm in the snow, Zhu De sporting a cap and a knurled cane, Kang Keqing bare-headed with a shawl draped across her broad shoulders. She had let her hair grow and now pulled it back off her handsome face into a loose bun low on her neck, in a style reminiscent of Madame Song Qingling's. In the summer they escaped Beijing's oppressive heat and spent several weeks at the beach, with the other leaders, at Beidaihe on the coast. Kang Keqing had become both the wife of the nation's Commander-in-Chief and a woman of some national prestige in her own right within the Women's Federation. She and Zhu De were looked upon as a model couple among the leaders in Zhongnanhai, along with Zhou Enlai and Deng Yingchao, and Kang Keqing seemed to be enjoying her new life of contentment and privilege.

As a representative of the Women's Federation she began to travel overseas. In October 1950 she travelled by train to Warsaw as a member of a delegation to a peace conference. In April 1953 a Russian aeroplane flew her to Vienna where she gave a paper at an international child-welfare conference. Her paper, entitled 'What does peace mean for our children?', seems to have been a fairly standard anti-American diatribe. She travelled back through Moscow, bringing with her a group of women—Japanese, Korean, Vietnamese and African—whom she had invited to China for a visit. The Russians protested that these women must be spies. Kang Keqing told them not to be ridiculous and convinced them to give permission for the women to travel on. When she returned to China, however, she was accused of distributing largesse in the manner of large (unnamed) foreign nations instead of restricting her contacts and invitations to fellow communist countries. She was told she would not be allowed to travel outside the country if she continued in this way. 'If I can't leave the country, then so be it!' she later claimed to have replied grandly. 'And if this accusation against me is not cleared up, I have absolutely no desire to leave the country again.'

She weathered these criticisms, and a year later was allowed to go to Korea. There as deputy head of a delegation she travelled through a still-smoking wasteland not long after the cease-fire was signed. This trip brought memories of her army days. The head of the delegation was the flamboyant General He Long, the younger brother of He Ying, a woman Kang Keqing had long admired. Trained in the martial arts and a brave warrior, He Ying ranked in Kang Keqing's mind as 'the only other' female commander besides herself in the main Red Army, high praise indeed.[6]

She also travelled widely with Zhu De on his official visits within China and continued her work in the Women's Federation, which was holding a national congress every four years. The second was held in April 1953, the third in September 1957 with Kang Keqing as Deputy Chair. From about 1955 she began to focus her efforts on the Chinese People's Council for the Protection of Children of which she was Secretary-General and Madame Song Qingling was Chair. It was this organisation that for many years published the popular propaganda magazine *Zhongguo jianshe* (*China Reconstructs*), a companion to the long-running Women's Federation magazine *Zhongguo funü* (*Women of China*).

Kang Keqing's comfortable life as a member of the ruling elite also exposed her to politics, however, and in her naivety—or was it foolishness, for in hindsight she blamed herself that she should have known better—she became entangled in an affair that toppled several progressive female writers and journalists.

By 1956 Mao no longer held sway over the Communist Party, whose more moderate leaders had begun to oppose his radical proposals for rapid economic development. Mao retaliated by initiating a mass movement designed to challenge what he saw as an increasingly conservative party leadership. In May 1956 he let it be known that the nation's scientists were invited to 'let a hundred flowers bloom together' by openly debating competing scientific theories, while writers, artists and scholars were invited to 'let the hundred schools of thought contend' through open debate and 'a free "battle of ideas"'.[7] By summer, the Hundred Flowers Movement had blossomed into virulent criticism of the communist bureaucracy as repressive and dogmatic, and the following spring 'a torrent of social and political criticism' poured forth. Among the criticisms were that the leaders were taking unto themselves such privileges as luxurious cars and expensive clothing while allowing the people to remain poor, and that the Women's Federation 'demonstrated little concern for the continued oppression of women'. Therefore, in early June 1957 the party, with the full support of Mao, uprooted the Hundred Flowers Movement and launched an 'anti-rightist' rectification campaign against those who had spoken out.

Littered as it is with '-ists' and '-isms', Chinese communist jargon is bewildering to many Westerners, ludicrous to others. However, terms such as rightist, rightist opportunist, capitalist roader, great-nation chauvinism, commandism, major vicious elements, anti-revisionism, anti-bureaucratism, anti-factionalism and anti-subjectivism are neat and concise in the Chinese language. They are also extremely effective political weapons in a regime ostensibly founded on unity of purpose because they brand as enemies of the people those the party does not want as members. Individuals thus accused must not only bear their labels as metaphoric 'hats' but are also often forced at meetings and in parades to wear real dunces hats on which are written their labels. People's lives, and deaths, were ruled by such phrases for a good twenty years during this period. The terms themselves, however, should not be viewed as an accurate measure of an individual's political philosophy so much as a signal as to where that person stood in relation to the current policies of Mao: in the late 1950s 'rightist' was shorthand for conservatives who did not wholly agree with the policies of Mao, while 'leftist' was for the time being a much more acceptable position.

In April 1957, Kang Keqing was the person responsible for statements issued by the Women's Federation's 3rd National Congress. Then, as the anti-rightist witchhunt swung into action, she was appointed a vice-head of the Rectification Movement subcommittee as well as being placed in charge of the Rectification Movement office within the Women's Federation. This was seen by many members as a conflict of interest, a view that was confirmed when the proceedings of the September 1957 Congress were published: over one-third of the text was devoted to the party's pronouncements on the anti-rightist campaign, and another third documented the criticisms levelled at women participating in the Congress who were accused of being rightists. This made clear how little attention the Federation was paying to the concerns of the women of China.

In retrospect, Kang Keqing claimed to have been uncomfortable with the personal attacks within the Women's Federation and to have regretted her part in them. 'I said and did wrong things,' she said thirty years later in her memoirs.

> But I genuinely tried to keep a grasp on reality and I tried to give my own point of view when I could, even if it differed from the official line. As far as I could, given the circumstances and the pressure that was brought to bear, I argued strongly for protecting some of our colleagues. Even though what I did was not always how I would have wanted it, I did come to realise that you can't tamper with history and that hard times bring out the best in friends.

Left-wing writers and artists were the major target of the rectification movement, and the Women's Federation became a convenient vehicle for destroying three such women. The most common method of criticising individuals, used since Yan'an days, was 'struggle sessions'. This was because unity, whether personal, ideological or social, was impossible without struggle, or so said Mao: 'What is correct always develops in the course of struggle with what is wrong.'[8] Individuals were 'struggled' at meetings where their ideas or actions were criticised with varying degrees of acrimony for causing disunity, until they responded by acknowledging their wrong thinking and promising to reform. Several women accused of rightism were struggled repeatedly during the 3rd National Congress.

Foremost among the women attacked was Ding Ling, the radical and outspoken writer who had been in similar trouble fifteen years before in Yan'an. Ding Ling had won the Stalin Prize in 1951 for her novel *The sun shines over Sanggan River* but now, at the age of fifty, she was accused of fomenting anti-party activities and branded a rightist. Expelled from the party, she was effectively exiled by being sent to Heilongjiang in China's frozen far north, across from the northern tip of Japan. Her writings were taken out of libraries and banned. Nearly twenty years passed before she was declared not guilty and allowed to move back to Shanxi Province in 1975, but it wasn't until 1979 that she was completely exonerated and welcomed back to Beijing, where she died seven years later from illness.

Two famous journalists—Peng Zigang and Pu Xixiu—and another woman well known in women's circles—Liu-Wang Liming—were also accused of being rightists and were severely struggled. All three were expelled from the party and prevented from working for over twenty years. Kang Keqing was ashamed of what the Federation did to these women and later in life admitted that she held herself responsible for their suffering, saying: 'We were wrong to criticise and struggle those comrades then.' While Pu Xixiu and Liu-Wang Liming died 'full of hatred' never knowing that they were eventually rehabilitated, Kang Keqing was able to make her peace with Ding Ling and Peng Zigang, who was also rehabilitated in 1979, and publicly pay her last respects to them when they died.

Kang Keqing came to realise, she said later, that 'everybody has their own limits as to what they ought to do and what they ought not do'. She reached her limit soon after the congress, obviously distressed at the unfair treatment of her colleagues, and in November objected to the decision to place her in full charge of the Women's Federation Rectification Movement. She managed to withdraw from the movement and avoid further involvement.

The Great Leap Forward of 1958 signalled the beginning of an appallingly wasteful twenty years for China. Doubtless influenced by Zhu De's moderate attitudes, Kang Keqing found herself increasingly at odds with Mao's radical policies. She and Zhu De opposed the drive to push peasants into forming cooperatives and communes, criticising as impractical the campaign to make people eat in common mess halls as though they were soldiers. Zhu De let it be known he believed that everybody should be free to prepare and eat their own meals in their own homes if they wanted to, and that people should be encouraged to build their own houses and make their own furniture. Kang Keqing began to re-think the policy of placing new-born babies into community care, believing that the people were entitled to a family life of their own.

Mao's campaign against rightists suffered a minor setback in the early 1960s, when the country began to recover from the famine caused by the Great Leap Forward. This reaction against Mao was set in train by an old Red Army colleague from the days of Jinggangshan who angrily criticised him at a meeting of the Central Committee held on Lushan in late 1959. Defence Minister Peng Dehuai spoke out against Mao's mismanagement, specifically his policy to force peasants into communes, and the disastrous Great Leap Forward. The people were receiving just 250 grams of rice a day, he told the Lushan Conference, exactly half the amount they had been getting in 1933, and he and his comrades had not spent their lives fighting to see the people sink back to that level of poverty. Zhu De was one of the many leaders who sympathised with Peng Dehuai's righteous anger. The astonishing outcome of the Lushan Conference, however, was that it was not Mao who was brought down but Peng Dehuai. He was removed from his post as Defence Minister and replaced by another old Red Army colleague, Lin Biao.[9] Zhu De was also accused of having turned against Mao, and Kang Keqing found she was labelled a rightist with capitalist tendencies.

For a while Mao took a political back seat, and during this time the economy gradually improved and people began to relax. The Women's Federation pardoned some of the women they had criticised, although they were not able to recall Ding Ling from Heilongjiang.

Zhu De had developed tracheitis and his throat was giving him trouble, so he and Kang Keqing took to spending their winters and springs in the south. Their marriage had turned out to be one of the few lasting and apparently happy unions among the communist leaders, no doubt cemented by Kang Keqing's straightforward simplicity and Zhu De's placid nature. Kang Keqing told Helen Foster Snow in 1937 that Zhu De was 'extremely kind by nature', this being his 'primary characteristic'.[10] She also said that 'He has no temper ordinarily, and I have never had a quarrel with him', a state of affairs that appears to have continued throughout the years. In 1962 Kang Keqing took a last trip home to Wan'an County then passed through the city of Ji'an. She took the politically courageous step of contacting Wang Quanyuan, whose citizen's rights she insisted the local authorities reinstate. Then, with Zhu De, she visited Jinggangshan, where it had all begun. She found it changed, the huts and villages she had stayed in long gone, the museums and memorabilia strangely foreign. That was the year Zhu De turned seventy-six, and Kang Keqing (then aged fifty) wrote a poem for his birthday, asking Zhu De's more literate secretary to tidy it up before she presented it:

> From great ambition and lofty ideals
> and heavy burdens you refuse to retire.
> Not relinquishing poetry you study theory
> to rebuild our nation and our people.
> In your magnanimity overlooking only yourself,
> an amiable self, heart's delight of the masses.
> A life of strict obedience to the party,
> of piled up years and piled up effort for the communists.[11]

Following a slow build-up of campaigns from about 1964, the Great Proletarian Cultural Revolution took shape in early 1966 when a series of cultural works, including plays and books, were criticised as thinly disguised attacks on the person of Chairman Mao—as indeed they were. From May 1966, *dazi bao* (big character posters) full of slogans and vitriolic criticism of rightists were slapped up on walls all over Beijing and Shanghai. These posters were messages, statements or exposés written by hand on very large sheets of paper by individuals, work units or committees; once a big character poster campaign got under way everybody was expected to take part. Everyone was encouraged to criticise party cadres through these posters and public meetings, with the intention of 'exposing contradictions', another favourite ploy of Mao, who claimed that contradictions could only be resolved by bringing them out into the open where they could be 'struggled'. The Cultural Revolution became a mass movement to smash elitism (a derogatory term for 'expertise') in any form, and it spread like wildfire. Schools were closed and millions of teenage Red Guards surged happily out of their classrooms and into the countryside where many of them indulged in months of vandalism.

Kang Keqing, Zhu De and the Women's Federation all became targets. 'Down with Zhu De!' and 'Throw Zhu De out of Zhongnanhai!' screamed the big character posters; the slogans 'Turn the cannons on Zhu De' and 'Zhu De is a black commander' were splashed in large whitewash characters on the icy January earth outside their compound. A public meeting was organised in the 10 000-seat Beijing People's Stadium to 'struggle' Zhu De and Kang Keqing but was cancelled at the last minute through the intervention of Mao and Zhou Enlai. The faithful old warrior Zhu De was nevertheless accused of being anti Mao, anti the party and anti socialism. He treated the charges with disdain, but Kang Keqing watched him grow increasingly morose and claimed to have heard him mutter from time to time: 'They have evil intentions . . . evil intentions.'

Kang Keqing was also subjected to a big character poster attack. Hers brought up the old charge of capitalist tendencies but added the new twist that she was antagonistic to Mao's wife, Jiang Qing. She probably was. Doing her best to ignore the posters Kang Keqing went on with her life, catching the bus to work every day at the Women's Federation, until one day in

February 1967 when a group of ten or so people, whom she described simply as 'of the masses', made her put on a dunce's hat bearing the sign 'Capitalist Roader' and paraded her and another woman from the Federation through the streets of Beijing on the back of a truck. These were anarchic times and she decided to stay home after that.

She was among the old leadership of the Women's Federation that was replaced by cadres more amenable to the aims and methods of Mao and the anonymous leaders of the Cultural Revolution. The new cadres arranged a large meeting at which she was 'struggled'. 'Struggle sessions' became extremely violent during the Cultural Revolution, often involving physical as well as verbal abuse. Succumbing to the pack mentality that was rampant at that time, the meeting stripped Kang Keqing of her dignity by forcing her to 'do the jet plane': this involved her bending forward low to the floor with arms upraised behind as she made her awkward way around the room. Kang Keqing said as little as she could, about herself or others, during this mental and physical ordeal but came away deeply shaken. From then on, the new cadres of the Women's Federation had permission to monitor her movements within the confines of Beijing.

This bullying took place in the first few months of 1967; after that Kang Keqing and Zhu De were pretty much left alone. They sat tight in their Zhongnanhai apartment for two years, prepared to wait out the political upheavals. Then, under the pretext of ensuring his safety during a looming military conflict with Russia, but in fact because he belonged to the moderates who posed a threat to the political ambitions of his old Long March colleague Lin Biao, Zhu De was ordered out of Beijing. Kang Keqing accompanied him, thanks to Zhou Enlai who, with his usual strange magic, conjured up the necessary exit papers for her. They flew out of Beijing in October 1969 and spent a lonely and frustrating winter and spring confined in pleasant surroundings at a convalescent hot springs resort in Guangdong. The political traumas they had witnessed over the previous fifteen years had seriously affected Zhu De, and upon their return to Beijing they asked to be allowed to move away from Zhongnanhai into a smaller apartment in a less prestigious leadership complex on Wanshoulu in the west of the city near the Babaoshan Revolutionary Cemetery.

Zhu De, who was eighty-four years old by this time, was deeply depressed and in indifferent health, but he continued his work as a member of the Central Committee and the National People's Congress. The Women's Federation had gone into recess by 1967 or 1968, however, and Kang Keqing remained idle for the whole of the Cultural Revolution. So when the Federation showed signs of coming to life in 1975, Kang Keqing was ready to get back to work; she was then aged sixty-four. The new leftist management had different ideas, however, and explained that they didn't need her any more. 'As far as possible we intend bringing in new staff and younger people. We won't be keeping any of the previous Women's Federation cadres,' they told her with a wave of the hand. 'Not that we're going to hustle you out the door, but it's up to you to find work elsewhere. When you do we'll gladly provide a car to see you off the premises.' Kang Keqing's fury knew no bounds but she could do little but fume for another two years.

Zhou Enlai died in January 1976, and the nation was determined to mourn this enigmatic and cultivated man who had devoted his life to the revolution. Those in control of the Cultural Revolution were equally determined that he not become a focus for rebellion. The word came down to step up 'struggle sessions' against rightists and with the word came a dreadful sense of approaching inquisition. Kang Keqing sat sullenly through meetings to criticise Deng Xiaoping, another fellow Long Marcher, not daring to speak out against charges she said later she knew in her heart were wrong. When pressed she mumbled the required slogans then slunk back home. As with events in 1957, she was not proud of her behaviour and could only console herself that she participated marginally without actively causing harm. This is a difficult stance to accept, smacking as it does of opportunism, yet it was fairly typical of those caught up in the Cultural Revolution.

Dr Anne F. Thurston, the China scholar who edited Li Zhisui's 1994 book *The private life of Chairman Mao*, also published a book called *Enemies of the people: The ordeal of the intellectuals in China's Great Cultural Revolution*.[12] Writing about her research, Dr Thurston says:

The majority of the people I interviewed had lied, confessed to crimes they had never committed, betrayed families, colleagues

and friends. Only one of my nearly fifty interviewees had
emerged from the experience of victimization as innocent at the
end of the Cultural Revolution as when it began. Only one
never confessed to crimes she did not commit, did not lie, did
not betray family, colleagues or friends.

Many of these people felt guilty for what they had done. One
man said:

> All of us, at one time or another, have had to speak words that
> we did not really believe . . . I don't mean to suggest that we
> *should* feel guilty that we really did something wrong. But still,
> I feel that this guilt is a good thing. It shows that we still have
> a conscience, that our consciences are intact. And so long as we
> have our consciences, so long as they work, there is hope.

Kang Keqing had lost her innocence in 1957, when she
realised she had unwittingly collaborated in the campaign to
destroy Ding Ling, Peng Zigang, Pu Xixiu, and Liu-Wang Liming.
When she in turn became a victim of the Cultural Revolution,
she did not have to turn on others but was able to retreat to
the sidelines, as she says she did in Yan'an in 1942. While her
behaviour fell far short of the heroic, her conscience appears to
have remained in good working order till the end of her life.

Zhu De went on as before, receiving overseas visitors as part
of his official duties. One hot summer's day in late June he caught
a chill from sitting too long in a badly airconditioned room. His
chill worsened; he reluctantly agreed to go to hospital, fully
expecting to be sent home the following day. Complications set
in and over the next ten days he gradually slipped away. He died
on 6 July 1976, just six months after Zhou Enlai. He was ninety
years old. Kang Keqing's fifty years with her husband ended thus,
quietly and without any fuss, and he died not knowing that the
Cultural Revolution was within months of ending.

Three weeks after Zhu De died, a massive earthquake flattened
the coastal city of Tianjin, and six weeks later Mao died, compounding the national turmoil. In short order Jiang Qing, Mao's
wife, was arrested a month later, labelled a member of the
infamous Gang of Four and accused of being the now-spent force
behind the Cultural Revolution. It was all over.

Kang Keqing was sixty-five years old when her husband died.
Speaking later of Zhu De's death she said: 'The best memorial

you can offer somebody is to complete their work when they die and make their dreams a reality.' And so she did for her Commander Zhu.

Events moved slowly at first as the nation felt its way, unsure of the official line after this sudden end to the Cultural Revolution or, as it came to be known, 'The ten-year catastrophe'. The first sign that Kang Keqing was to have a new lease on life came in March 1977 when it was announced that:

> The working party formed to plan the 4th National Congress of the Women's Federation has been dissolved. Kang Keqing has been appointed to head the new leadership team. The prestige and universal respect Elder Sister Kang enjoys will stand her in good stead as she takes charge of the work of the Women's Federation. Members of the now-defunct working party are to return home to their original units.[13]

Kang Keqing found it hard to suppress a satisfied smile as she moved back into her old office.

One year later, to thunderous applause, she officially opened a massive meeting in the Great Hall of the People in Beijing to celebrate International Women's Day. There were also joyous and noisy reunions of Long March veterans who had been victimised during the 'The ten-year catastrophe'. Deng Yingchao, now aged seventy-five, was there, as was 78-year-old Cai Chang, white-haired and losing her sight. Singer–songwriter Li Bozhao, sixty-seven years old, had carved out a new career as a playwright in the years before the Cultural Revolution and she mustered her considerable fighting spirit to attend the celebration. Once she had shepherded Kang Keqing across the Snowy Mountains but now she had trouble walking, having spent much of the Cultural Revolution on her hands and knees cleaning toilets in a six-storey building.[14] He Zizhen did not attend this meeting, nor did Wang Quanyuan travel up from her home in Jiangxi.

The Women's Federation held its 4th National Congress in Beijing the following September, welcoming nearly two thousand delegates. Cai Chang opened the congress; Deng Yingchao gave the opening address; Kang Keqing presented a report outlining the tasks ahead for the Chinese women's movement as it entered this new phase and was then elected the Federation's Chair;

Madame Song Qingling, aged eighty-five, closed the proceedings. The women were back in business.

Their next step was to try to repair the damage done to the Federation during the previous ten years. Kang Keqing called a large meeting to express sympathy for those women who had been accused, and grief for those who had been persecuted to death during 'The ten-year catastrophe'. As was happening all over the country, the women at the meeting were asked to focus their hostility on the Gang of Four. This cathartic process of scapegoating was then shored up by making persecutors admit publicly what they had done and suggesting they seek out and apologise to their victims.

Kang Keqing was wearing thick black-rimmed spectacles in Copenhagen in 1980 when she presented a paper at the United Nations Women's Conference and represented China at the signing of the UN Charter on eliminating all forms of discrimination against women. Her sight was fading and her health was deteriorating but she pressed on with public appearances, speeches and committee work now that she was a national figurehead for women and children. There was still much to do, she found, despite the rhetoric of positive changes that had been made in the two decades after 1949.

She realised that Chinese attitudes towards women and children were still fundamentally the same. Men were still practising bigamy, it was reported, and girls were still being sold or given away as child brides. Wives were being exchanged or rented out, young people were committing suicide (or being murdered) because of insoluble affairs of the heart, while there was still a trade in abducted women. The steady flow of reports of how the Marriage Law of 1950 was being flouted led Kang Keqing to initiate wide-ranging national discussion on how to amend the law. When the new Marriage Law was brought down in 1981 it was the Women's Federation that was given responsibility for telling the people about it. This in itself was an indication that the men in charge of the country still had no interest in how and whether marriages worked. To their mind marriage remained a matter of the 'inner quarters', which they believed to be the sole province of women.

One of the provisions of the new Marriage Law, which raised

the minimum age for marriage to twenty-two for males and twenty for females, was that both partners had to agree to family planning. The Women's Federation had given only lip service to the issue of birth control in the late 1950s, but in the 1980s as the population blew out towards the 2000 million mark the nation's survival depended on it. Here again it was women and children who suffered from attitudes that had not changed significantly. With boy babies still valued over girls, peasants in particular seemed to prefer to drown or abandon their girl babies rather than practise birth control, and the cruel chase after boy babies meant that women who bore girls were themselves often beaten or killed.

Kang Keqing had no doubt that it was attitudes such as this that perpetuated discrimination against women. Wife beating, physical and mental violence towards women and children, and unequal treatment of girls and boys in schooling as well as employment were all examples of this. Having been a signatory to the UN Charter, Kang Keqing felt duty bound to do something about this discrimination. When discussions began on amendments to the national constitution, the Women's Federation requested a clause be inserted outlawing the concept of male superiority. If nothing else, this signalled women's awareness of and dissatisfaction with the status quo. The clause was included in the new Chinese Constitution brought down in May 1982. Three years later the right of women to possess, inherit and bequeath property was enshrined in the Inheritance Law. Equal pay for equal work and an assurance that work units must not reject women for any suitable work were covered in a set of regulations issued in 1988. These attempts to legislate change in Chinese society clearly indicate the disjunction that continued to exist even in the late 1980s between communist rhetoric and the reality of women's lives.

Kang Keqing's hair was now beginning to thin and turn grey and she was wearing thick spectacles all the time, not just for reading. She was still Chair when the Federation held its 5th National Congress in 1983 and she was still reporting on the 'new phase of the women's movement'. This time she was encouraging women to develop self-respect and dignity: if it's going to start anywhere, it will have to be with us women, was her message. The new laws didn't seem to be helping to change attitudes. Men continued to consider themselves superior and discriminate against women: how many women were in the top layer of government, for instance? Very few: one member of the Politburo, fourteen of the 211-member Central Committee, two ministers and seven vice-ministers.[15] While this was an astonishing advance on having no women at all in public office, it was another example of the gap between communist rhetoric about gender equality and the real world. Female illiteracy was still at an unacceptably high rate, and it was now acknowledged that prostitution had made a big comeback, which was, among other things, a serious threat to women's health.

It was not that the Federation was actually being sidelined—the male leaders all attended the opening of the congress: Deng Xiaoping, Hu Yaobang, Li Xiannian—it was more that the men at the top had agreed to leave women's problems entirely to the women to resolve. This, of course, was the Women's Bureau of the 1920s revisited. Kang Keqing decided the Women's Federation should stop publishing books such as *Marx, Engels, Lenin and Stalin on women* and *Mao Zedong, Zhou Enlai, Liu Shaoqi and Zhu De on the liberation of women*, and start to develop some theories of their own by which the women's movement could direct their practical work. She made her opinion known then handed the running of the Women's Federation and the youth organisations over to the next generation.

The previous thirty years had seen very real successes. The Women's Federation, which had been headed until the 1980s by Long March veterans, had also been largely responsible for fostering women in all fields, thus creating an illusion of reality. In more recent years, a small minority of women had been promoted solely on merit to ministerial level in the bureaucracy, to the rank of brigadier-general in the PLA, and to leading positions in education, the diplomatic service and the sciences. Well-known writers were now as likely to be women as men, in contrast to the days when a woman writer was a curiosity. Younger women writers and intellectuals took advantage of the freedom after the Cultural Revolution to gain a new perspective from Western publications and to travel to Europe and the United States. Many of them also settled overseas. From these women's

writings a less than flattering assessment of the Women's Federation emerged. This younger generation perceived the Women's
Federation as just another arm of the party, and criticised the
'political woman' lauded by the Federation as a 'revolutionary
who had reached an elevated status through commitment to class
politics and wholehearted support for state policies'. In other
words, someone who had at heart the interest of the patriarchal
Communist Party, rather than of women. This criticism may be
simplistic, given the enormous complexity of the problems China
has faced this century, but it does evoke those proud words of
the young Kang Keqing: 'I don't care much about the women's
problem; I always work with men not women.'

Kang Keqing's lifetime spanned a chain of events that almost
transformed the lives of Chinese women. Towards the end of the
Qing dynasty many courageous women of the gentry class challenged tradition by entering the public arena to fight for the
rights of Chinese women to education, equality and the vote, but
they were unable to rend the fabric of the patriarchal Confucian
system. The Long March in which Kang Keqing took part ensured
the survival of both the Chinese Communist Party and Mao
Zedong as its leader, and it is to Mao and the party that the
eventual success of the revolution was due. Kang Keqing was one
of several Long March women who reached relatively high positions in the new bureaucracy, which would have been impossible
in traditional China. In this it seems they had the Long March
to thank, because few other women have since been appointed
to similar positions. For the mass of Chinese women, 1949
brought some immediate improvement in their status, with their
rights to education, freedom of choice in marriage and the vote
enshrined in law. Real equality, however, continues to elude them
in the man's world that is China.

Kang Keqing's health worsened and she began to use a cane.
She made her last overseas trip in 1984 but continued to receive
overseas guests, sometimes in a wheelchair. On International
Women's Day 1989, when Cai Chang was awarded a commemorative medal in recognition of her lifelong work for the Chinese
people, Kang Keqing accepted the medal on her behalf because
89-year-old Cai Chang was already blind and unable to attend
the ceremony. Kang Keqing was also awarded a commemorative

medal that day for the commitment she had shown over the years in her work for the Chinese people. This medal was essentially an acknowledgement of the special position she occupied in the annals of Chinese womanhood, in particular of her remarkable journey from impoverished and illiterate peasant girl to elder stateswoman of the women's movement.

After she retired, Kang Keqing remained in her apartment on Wanshoulu and would go for walks when she could, taking pleasure in picking the delicious red berries of the Chinese wolfberry bush along the way. She had her own secretary for correspondence—she wrote to Helen Foster Snow congratulating her on receiving a literary prize in September 1991—and kept up her own daily discipline, listening to the 6.30 news on the radio in the morning and watching the seven o'clock television news at night.

It is impossible to know how she reacted to the dramatic events in Tiananmen Square, sparked by the pro-democracy movement of spring 1989 after the death of her fellow Long Marcher Hu Yaobang. As a member of the party elite, she may have known something of the political struggle among the top leaders that caused Deng Xiaoping to send army tanks into Tiananmen Square in the early hours of 4 June 1989, massacring unarmed students and at least a thousand unarmed civilians under the pretext of quelling a 'counter-revolutionary rebellion'.[16] The censored television news broadcasts she watched would have told her the lie that few civilians had been harmed, and that the army had used force only in order to maintain security. Knowing something of the extent of the tragedy from the news that spread quickly throughout Beijing by word of mouth, she must have struggled to reconcile loyalties that had once been identical: her loyalty to the party and her loyalty to the people. Her loyalty to the party told her that unity remained of paramount importance during the large-scale economic reform of the late 1980s, which was to ensure China's future as a strong, modern world power. Her loyalty to the people, however, was what had made possible the revolution that created the People's Republic of China in the first place. She had been with the Red Army, the people's flesh and blood, from the beginning, and had believed that its sole purpose was to serve and defend the people. For the

People's Liberation Army to fire on unarmed civilians and students was an unprecedented betrayal of the people's trust as well as all that Kang Keqing and Zhu De had stood for. This must have tested to the limit her lifetime loyalty to the party, but she remained silent, as did Deng Yingchao, Zhou Enlai's widow, whether out of disapproval or despair is not known.

Kang Keqing's memoirs, published in 1993, made no mention of the 1989 Tiananmen Massacre, not surprising when one notes that the preface to her memoirs was penned by fellow Long Marcher General Yang Shangkun, husband of Li Bozhao but also one of the men believed to be responsible for ordering the army into Tiananmen Square in 1989.

Kang Keqing celebrated her eightieth birthday quietly in September 1991; a photograph shows her serious and unsmiling amidst a group of smiling women friends. On 23 April 1992, *The People's Daily* carried on the front page an official Central Committee obituary of Kang Keqing accompanied by a recent photograph:

> Comrade Kang Keqing Dies.
> Comrade Kang Keqing, proletarian revolutionary, outstanding leader of the Chinese women's movement, Deputy Chair of the 7th National Council of the Chinese People's Political Consultative Conference, and Honorary Chair of the All-China Women's Federation, failed to respond to medical treatment and died in Beijing at 12.04 pm on 22 April 1992. She was in her 81st year.

'I am hoping to become a commander in the army,' Kang Keqing told Helen Foster Snow in Yan'an when she was twenty-six. 'Comrade Zhu De sympathises with my ambition and wants me to perfect my military knowledge so I can be capable of commanding an army in the future. I think I will succeed . . .'[17]

Some say that Kang Keqing did finally succeed in commanding an army—an army made up of the women of China—and there is little doubt she reached the end of her life justifiably satisfied with what she had achieved. She had been fortunate in marrying a decent and honourable man, and her personal long march from peasant girl to respected stateswoman had been dignified, if entirely dependent in this man's world on having married that decent and honourable man.

As a young soldier she had thought she was above women's business: she had believed she could transcend her gender and take her rightful place alongside men. We can only admire the grace with which she carried off the harsh realisation that they hadn't quite meant it, and that, all along, in their eyes she had only ever been a woman.

APPENDIX
THE THIRTY WOMEN

A XIANG, see *Xie Fei*

AH HSIANG, see *Xie Fei*

AH CH'ING, see *Jin Weiying*

AH JIN, see *Jin Weiying*

CAI CHANG, 1900–1990, was born in Xiangxiang County, Hunan Province, to an impoverished gentry family. Her mother encouraged Cai Chang in her revolutionary activities from an early age, and Cai Chang and her brother Cai Hesen had become close friends with Mao Zedong by the time of the 1919 May Fourth Movement. Cai Hesen later married the famous revolutionary Xiang Jingyu; they were both executed by the KMT. Cai Chang travelled to France with her mother and brother in 1919 on a work–study program and helped set up the French branch of the Chinese Communist Party in 1921. In 1923 she joined the Communist Party, married Li Fuchun and gave birth to a daughter, whom she passed into the care of her mother. Cai Chang did underground work and propaganda work, was elected to the Central Committee in 1928 and was for many years in charge of women's affairs. She is remembered on the Long March as having been inspirational, many of her comrades recalling not only her good humour but her singing of the *Marseillaise*. Cai Chang went to Moscow for bouts of medical treatment, and during the Yan'an period worked in the organisation department of the Central Committee. She was elected to the Central

Committee in 1945, the only woman member. In 1949 she was elected to the committee charged with planning the new republic and was the same year elected to the Central People's Government. Cai Chang was elected the first president of the All-China Democratic Women's Federation, a position she held from 1949 to 1979, after which she became honorary president until 1988. She also headed the female workers' branch of the All-China Federation of Trade Unions. She was in disgrace during the Cultural Revolution because her husband Li Fuchun had tried in 1967 to derail the movement. After 1978, however, she undertook many ceremonial roles and was elected vice-chair of the standing committee of the National People's Assembly. Her eyesight deteriorated over the years and although by 1984 she was blind she did not retire fully until 1989, the year before she died. Cai Chang is regarded as a model revolutionary, a woman of the privileged classes who devoted her life to overthrowing tradition and improving the lot of the Chinese people. The positions she held and the work she did would never have been possible had she not taken part in the Long March and the revolution that it spawned.[2]

CH'EN HUI-CH'ING, see *Chen Huiqing*

CHEN HUIQING, 1909–1983, was born in Hong Kong to a family who came from Panyu County, Guangdong Province. Classed as a 'proletariat', she had worked from the age of fourteen in a factory in Hong Kong; she took part in the 1925 Hong Kong strike and joined the Communist Party in 1926. Chen Huiqing worked in Guangdong for three years, at one stage as a member of the KMT's propaganda department, and was involved in the Canton Commune uprising of December 1927. In 1929 she married Deng Fa and worked with him from then on, first in the labour movement then in the security office, Deng Fa holding the post of head of Security throughout the Long March. Chen Huiqing was pregnant when she set out on the Long March and gave birth to her baby in April 1935 in Yunnan; the baby was abandoned. Little is known of her after this, except that Helen Foster Snow met her in Yan'an and that she died, presumably of illness, in 1983.[3]

CHEN YU, see *Zeng Yu*

CHIEN HSI-CHÜN, see *Qian Xijun*

CHING WEI-YING, see *Jin Weiying*

CHING YU-LIN, see *Zhong Yuelin*

CHOU YUEH-HUA, see *Zhou Yuehua*

CH'U YI-HAN, see *Qiu Yihan*

DENG LIUJIN, 1912–, was born in Shangkang County, Fujian Province, and given soon after by her impoverished peasant parents to an itinerant barber and his wife. She joined the Communist Party in 1931, having no real idea what it meant, as a means of avoiding marriage. One year later, however, she was head of Shangkang women's bureau, in 1933 had become head of Fujian provincial women's bureau, and in 1934 enrolled in the Party School in Ruijin. Deng Liujin was a political fighter on the Long March, hiring bearers, carrying litters, doing propaganda work and arranging food supplies. In Yan'an she worked for the women's bureau, then enrolled in the Party School for a time. Deng Liujin had long made clear her determination not to marry and have children, but at the end of 1938 she was ordered to work in the south with Zeng Shan, who had been chairman of the Jiangxi soviet and who wanted to marry her. She bowed to this pressure and married him in early 1938 on the way south, producing three (or four) sons over the next few years. She continued with her work and studies in Zhejiang and Jiangsu despite substantial opposition from her husband and other male leaders who urged her to stay home and look after her children. In 1949 she was given the task of setting up a nursery in Ji'an for abandoned and orphaned children, and in 1960 was made deputy head of a State Department section where her work involved children's welfare and the establishing of kindergartens and nurseries. She was apparently criticised during the Cultural Revolution but resumed work in 1976, again in the area of kindergartens and nurseries. Despite the setbacks she suffered, Deng Liujin never hesitated to attribute her remarkable achievement of rising from illiterate peasant to public administrator to the support of the Communist Party. At the time of writing she was believed to be living in Beijing.[4]

DENG YINGCHAO, 1904–1992, was born in Guangxi Province, although she is described as a native of Henan Province, whence her family originated. She has always been held in the highest esteem in China for her lifelong commitment to the revolution and to the Communist Party, as well as because of her model, albeit childless, marriage to the urbane Premier Zhou Enlai. Deng Yingchao was born into an impoverished gentry family and educated in Beijing and Tianjin. She became politically active in the 1919 May Fourth Movement, and it was during this time that she met Zhou Enlai. She did not travel to France as a work–study student, as some sources suggest, but remained in China and continued her student activism. She joined the Communist Party in 1925, the same year as she married Zhou Enlai on his return from France, and held high-level positions in both the KMT and the Communist Party during the 1920s. She travelled to Moscow with Zhou Enlai in 1928. Deng Yingchao was suffering from tuberculosis when the Long March started and was therefore carried the whole way on a stretcher, apart from short periods when she rode a horse. During the Yan'an period she travelled extensively in north and central China as director of the women's work department and as an official representative of the Communist Party accompanied Zhou Enlai on lengthy sojourns in KMT areas, especially in Chongqing, during the second period of KMT–CCP unification. She went to Moscow for medical treatment in 1939, and in 1945 was elected an alternate member of the Central Committee; Cai Chang was at that time the only woman member of the committee. Deng Yingchao was elected in 1949 to the committee charged with planning the new republic and was the same year elected to the Central People's Government. She held many high-level positions until the Cultural Revolution, at which time her movements were severely restricted, even though she suffered no physical harm. After 1978 Deng Yingchao was made a full member of the powerful Politburo and appointed to several prestigious committees including president of the 6th Chinese People's Political Consultative Committee in 1982, although her role was often merely ceremonial. She made very few public appearances after June 1991, but was till the end of her life considered one of the Eight Elders (*balao*) whom the current leadership consulted. Less than a century ago, it would have been inconveivable that a woman could command such respect in affairs of state.[5]

GAN TANG, see *Han Shiying*

HAN SHIYING, 1910–1971, was born in Nanxi County, Sichuan Province. According to Helen Foster Snow, she was listed by Li Bozhao as 'Of uncertain origin', but she was in fact born into the merchant class. She taught school at some stage and attended university in Sichuan in 1926 but it is not clear whether she graduated. She joined the Communist Party in 1926 and was apparently not married when she set off on the Long March, during which she did political and propaganda work. Han Shiying was instructed to drop out of the Long March in Yunnan in the spring of 1935 with Li Guiying and several male comrades to act as partisans and work with local guerrilla groups. She was imprisoned by the KMT in the winter of 1936 and released in May 1937 into the custody of her father in Sichuan, but eluded him and worked as a teacher in Chongqing, where she renewed contact with the Communist Party. Han Shiying married Zou Fengping in 1938, and in 1940 they were sent to Yan'an where she attended the Marx–Lenin College for six months then the Party School for five and a half years. Han Shiying and her husband suffered some criticism during the 1942 Rectification Movement but after 1949 she was appointed to several women's organisations in Sichuan as well as becoming deputy director of the Sichuan People's High Court. During the Cultural Revolution, however, she suffered terribly and was finally 'persecuted to death'. She was arrested, labelled a traitor and humiliated by having matters of the deepest privacy exposed to the public view in big character posters. Her daughter admitted later that as a child she participated in the bullying by pelting her mother with gravel in the street. Han Shiying was required to report to 'the organisation' all visits and contacts she made, and she became frightened, reclusive and suicidal. The enormous political and psychological pressure she was under triggered bronchial problems and damaged her health. She was sent to cadre school, a euphemism during this period for labour camps for cadres and intellectuals, where she slept in a dormitory and was made to do menial physical work, including smashing stones with a hammer.

Upon her return home to Chengdu, she was ill and depressed. When she finally sought medical help for difficulty in breathing, she was refused treatment at a hospital because it was fashionable at that time to accuse 'capitalist roaders' such as she of feigning illness in order to evade their proper punishment. She died at home on 28 November 1971. She was rehabilitated in 1978. Had the revolution not erupted in China during her youth, Han Shiying would probably have lived a comfortable and secluded middle-class life as a wife and mother.[6]

HE ZIZHEN, 1910–1984, was born in Yongxin County, Jiangxi Province. Since members of her family had once been minor officials and she had received some education, she was considered to be of the intellectual class. He Zizhen joined the Youth League in 1925, the Communist Party in 1926, and met and married Mao Zedong on Jinggangshan in 1928. She bore him six children: two she placed in the care of others, two died, one she abandoned during the Long March and one was absorbed into Mao's extended family. When she and Mao separated in Yan'an in 1937 she went or was sent to Russia where she gave birth to her last child, who soon died, then spent several years in a sanitorium. After her return in 1948 she lived an isolated life in southern China, seeing few people and widely believed to be mentally ill. She died of natural causes in Shanghai on 19 April 1984.[7]

HO TZE-NIEN, see *He Zizhen*

HO TZU-CH'ÜN, see *He Zizhen*

HSIEH SHAO-MI, see *Xie Xiaomei*

JIN AIQING, see *Jin Weiying*

JIN WEIYING, 1904–1941?, was born in Daishan County, Zhejiang Province. Her family may have been gentry, but they were certainly progressive, and she was able to attend primary school, doing so well that she went on to teachers' college and taught for several years after that. Jin Weiying moved to Shanghai and became active in the labour movement, joining the Communist Party in 1926. She rose to the unusually high position for a woman of membership of the executive committee of the central soviet government in Ruijin. At some stage she married Deng

Xiaoping, who in 1978 succeeded Mao as China's paramount leader, but by 1934 she had divorced him and was married to Li Weihan (aka Luo Mai and Lo Man), secretary to the party's central organisation unit. It is believed that she bore Li Weihan a son who achieved prominence in the party during the 1990s. During the Long March Jin Weiying was a political instructor with the Convalescent Company, which also involved doing local work and organising food supplies. She worked in the Organisation Department of the Central Committee in Yan'an and then worked with students of the Anti-Japanese University and other institutions in Yan'an. She became ill, however, and was already separated from her husband by the time she left for, or was exiled to, Russia in the spring of 1938. She was consigned to a sanitorium in Russia and was presumed killed during German air-raids in late 1941.[8]

JIN ZHICHENG, see *Jin Weiying*

KAN SHIH-YING, see *Han Shiying*

KAN SHIYING, see *Han Shiying*

K'ANG K'E-CHING, see *Kang Keqing*

KANG KEQING, 1911–1992, was a peasant, born in Wan'an County, Jiangxi Province. She joined the Youth League in 1927 and the Communist Party in 1931. She met (1928) and married (1929) Zhu De on Jinggangshan. Before, during and for several years after the Long March Kang Keqing was active in the field with the Red Army, gaining considerable military experience and expertise. Although childless and previously uninterested in women's affairs, she was assigned after 1949 to head organisations devoted to child welfare and to the executive committee of the All-China Women's Federation. In both capacities she played an active and leading role. She was elected deputy chair of the Women's Federation in 1957. She was criticised and suffered indignities during the Cultural Revolution, but in 1977 was elected to the Central Committee. In 1978 she resumed the position of deputy chair of the Women's Federation and was elected deputy chair of the 5th Chinese People's Political Consultative Conference. She died in Beijing of natural causes on 22 April 1992.[9]

LI BOZHAO, 1911–1985, was born in the city of Chongqing, Sichuan Province. Her father was of the gentry, holding the position of county magistrate, but official Chinese sources describe her family as 'impoverished intellectuals'. In 1924 Li Bozhao enrolled in a women's teachers' college in Sichuan where Zhang Wentian and other revolutionaries taught, and joined the Youth League the following year; she joined the Communist Party in 1931. Expelled from college in 1925 for her revolutionary involvement, Li Bozhao went to Shanghai and taught briefly at a night school for female workers before being sent to Moscow in 1926 to study at what became Sun Yat-sen University. During her four years in Moscow, Li Bozhao studied literature and theatre, met Cai Chang and Zhou Enlai and, in 1929, married Yang Shangkun, who later became deputy director of the party's political department. Between 1930, when she returned to China with her husband, and setting out on the Long March in 1934, Li Bozhao worked in Shanghai and in Fujian doing propaganda and teaching, then in the Jiangxi soviet editing a newspaper and developing a theatre troupe for which she also wrote songs and plays. During the Long March her main duties revolved around raising troop morale and spreading propaganda through songs, dances, performances and 'living newspapers'. She was separated from the main march, and her husband, in September 1935 when she was forced to spend a year in Tibet with Zhang Guotao's 4th Front Army. Li Bozhao had a baby in Yan'an in September 1937, according to Helen Foster Snow, and for most of the Yan'an period was assigned to cultural, propaganda and theatrical activities. She spoke at the Yan'an Forum on Literature and Art, presumably following Mao's official line that all art must serve politics. After 1949 Li Bozhao became a professional dramatist, writing plays, short stories, novels and an opera entitled *The Long March*. She was appointed director of the People's Theatre of Beijing and vice-president of the Central Academy of Drama; she was also elected vice-president of the League of Dramatists. In 1966 her husband Yang Shangkun was arrested as a traitor and spent twelve years in prison. Li Bozhao was criticised, 'struggled' and made to clean toilets in a six-storey building, physically brutal work that virtually crippled her. After her rehabilitation she showed little rancour, however, resuming her work by writing a play entitled *Northward* about the Long March split between Mao and Zhang Guotao and attended its premiere in 1982. She died on 17 April 1985 of a heart attack in Beijing.[10]

LI CHIEN-HUA, see *Li Jianhua*

LI CHÜN-CHEN, see *Li Jianzhen*

LI GUIYING, 1911–1997, was born in Xunwu County, Jiangxi Province. A peasant, she was married out as a child bride at the age of seven but left this marriage, possibly when she became involved in revolutionary work. She joined the Youth League in 1930 and the Communist Party in 1933. On the Long March she carried out the same duties as the other peasant women: political instruction, hiring of bearers, occasional litter-bearing. At the start of the Long March, Li Guiying was married to Dai Yuanhuai, who held the title of special commissioner of south Sichuan, and in the spring of 1935 she and her husband were instructed to remain behind in Yunnan to act as partisans and work with local guerrilla groups. Han Shiying and several men were left behind with them. Dai Yuanhuai was soon killed, and Li Guiying married one of the other men, Yu Zehong, but he too was killed. She went to Sichuan, where she gave birth to a child in the beginning of 1936, apparently leaving the baby with relatives of Han Shiying so that she could return to revolutionary work. She was imprisoned by the KMT in the winter of 1936, released in October 1937 and went to Hankou in 1938 whence she reported to Deng Yingchao on guerrilla work in the south-west. In 1939 she married Luo Xiangtao, who was attached to the New 4th Army in Anhui, and worked in central China until 1949. After 1949 Li Guiying held various mid-level posts such as head of military supplies for the Huadong regional army, but was labelled a 'traitor' during the Cultural Revolution because of her imprisonment in the late 1930s. Her name was removed from the party register and she was not rehabilitated until July 1978, by which time she was totally blind and unable to work.[11]

LI JIANHUA, 1915–1936, was born in Gao'an County, Jiangxi Province. She was the first of The Thirty Women to die. Li Jianhua's real name was Tu Xiugen; she adopted the name Li Jianhua when she joined Peng Dehuai's division of the Red Army in 1930, at the age of fifteen. She joined the Youth League and the Communist Party in 1931. Born into a merchant family, she was educated to higher primary school level, and this degree of literacy earned her the classification of 'student' among the communists. She was sent to train as a telegraphist after the communists captured a wireless in early 1931, then assigned to headquarters as an apprentice wireless operator at the front in the Jiangxi soviet. She married 27-year-old telegraphist Yue Xia in August 1934 and, after the first few months of the Long March working as radio operators in separate units, she was transferred to Yue Xia's unit as his assistant. She became pregnant on the Long March but when and where her baby was born is not recorded; presumably the baby was abandoned. Li Jianhua and her husband were assigned in 1935 to Zhang Guotao's 4th Front Army, where she remained in contact with Kang Keqing during their year in Tibet. She is believed to have crossed the Yellow River with the Western Wing of the 4th Front Army (the Western Route Army) and been killed by Moslem cavalry.[12]

LI JIANZHEN, 1906–1992?, was born in Fengshun County, Guangdong Province, to a family of impoverished peasants. She was sold as a child bride to a merchant family which became involved in revolutionary activities in the Dongjiang area in the 1920s. Li Jianzhen joined the Youth League in 1926 and the Communist Party in 1927. Her husband was killed in 1930 and she appears to have left her only child of that union, born in 1925, in Guangdong when she was sent to Fujian to work with the women's bureau and in party administration. She came to the attention of Deng Yingchao, Zhou Enlai and Mao during this time and was transferred to the Jiangxi soviet to head the central women's bureau. Li Jianzhen was a political worker on the Long March, responsible for raising food supplies and confiscating money and valuables from landlords. At the end of 1935, when the communists reached Wayaobu, Li Jianzhen married fellow Long Marcher Deng Zhongming. She became director of the women's department of the Shaanxi–Gansu–Ningxia border region in Yan'an but in 1938 was sent back to the south with her husband to work in the Jiangxi–Zhejiang–Guangdong region. Deng Zhongming was killed in 1943. Li Jianzhen became party secretary at county level in Fujian in 1945, participated in 1949 in the Chinese People's Political Consultative Conference, and was elected the same year to the executive council of the All-China Women's Federation. She held various provincial posts, mainly in Guangdong, in the 1950s and by 1960 had risen to the powerful position of secretary of Guangdong party provincial committee. During the Cultural Revolution she was apparently removed from all positions, but in 1977 was elected as an alternate member of the Central Committee and resumed her duties as Guangdong provincial party secretary. It is not known when she retired, but she is believed to have died in 1992. She is one of very few women to have held the position of provincial party secretary, an achievement that is all the more admirable given her origin as an illiterate peasant.[13]

LI PO-CHAO, see *Li Bozhao*

LI SHAO-HUNG, see *Li Guiying*

LI XIAOJIANG, see *Li Guiying*

LIAO CHIH-KUANG, see *Liao Siguang*

LIAO SHIGUANG, see *Liao Siguang*

LIAO SHIH-KUANG, see *Liao Siguang*

LIAO SIGUANG, 1911–, was born in Huiyang County, Guangdong Province. She was one of the three women classed by Li Bozhao in 1937 as 'Of uncertain origins'. Liao Siguang was sold as a child bride at the age of three and was involved in underground revolutionary work in the Dongjiang area of Guangdong by the time she was seventeen. She joined the Youth League in 1929 and in 1930 married He Kequan, alias Kai Feng, with whom she travelled to Shanghai to carry out youth propaganda. They married and in the summer of 1933, just before being ordered to go to the Jiangxi soviet, Liao Siguang gave birth to a baby; she placed this child in a missionary hospital. She worked as an inspector with the Youth League in Ruijin and joined the Communist Party in 1934. She was about five months pregnant when she set off on the Long March, giving birth to and abandoning a boy baby in Guizhou. Her duties on the Long March included propaganda work and organising food supplies and funding. After reaching Yan'an she worked for several years with Deng Yingchao and, for a time, Liu Qunxian, developing the women's movement, in anti-Japanese activities and with orphaned and abandoned children in central China, especially in Wuhan and Chongqing. She attended the Party School in Yan'an for a period then in 1946 worked in land reform in the north-east. Liao Siguang was a delegate at the 1st National Women's Congress in Beijing in 1949, after which she was appointed to several municipal and provincial posts in Guangzhou. During the Cultural Revolution she was imprisoned and interrogated but refused to incriminate her comrades with written 'confessions'. She was rehabilitated after the Cultural Revolution and in 1986 was deputy chair of the Guangdong Chinese People's Political Consultative Conference. At the time of writing she was believed to be living in Guangdong.[14]

LIAO YUEH-HUA, see *Xiao Yuehua*

LIU CAIXIA, see *Liu Caixiang*

LIU CAIXIANG, 1915–1980?, was born in Gan County, Jiangxi Province, to a family of poor peasants who sold her as a child bride. She joined the Youth League in 1931 and the Communist Party in 1932, and had become head of Fujian–Jiangxi women's department by 1934. The same year she married Bi Zhanyun, chief of staff of the 1st Front Army's 9th Regiment. Liu Caixiang hired stretcher-bearers as well as carrying litters herself on the Long March. Little is known of her activities after the Long March except that she held several minor positions in Hebei and Henan; some time after 1947 she was deputy principal of a school for children of army personnel. She is believed to have died in 1980 of natural causes.[15]

LIU CHIAN-HSIEN, see *Liu Qunxian*

LIU QUNXIAN, 1907–1941?, was born in Wuxi, Jiangsu Province. She was classed as a 'proletariat', having started work at the age of nine and putting in sixteen-hour days in a silk factory by the age of thirteen. Liu Qunxian joined the Communist Party possibly in 1926 and became known as a labour leader among the women factory workers in Wuxi. In July 1927 she was sent to Moscow where she studied at the Sun Yat-sen University for three years and where she married her fellow student Bo Gu, who also acted as her interpreter at a labour conference in Moscow in 1928. Upon her return to China in 1930 she headed an organisation for women workers in Shanghai and continued this work when she moved to the Jiangxi soviet in 1933. She gave birth in Shanghai in May 1933 to a daughter whom she despatched for safekeeping to relatives in Wuxi and was recovering from a miscarriage as she set off on the Long March; she may have had a child in Moscow as well. During the Long March she captained the independent women's unit for a time and was a political worker with the General Political Department; in Zunyi she organised carpenters and other workers who then formed themselves into guerrilla groups; after that she carried out propaganda work as head of the women workers group. She apparently gave birth to a son in Bao'an, and worked briefly in Yan'an, according to Helen Foster Snow, as the 'Director of National Mines and Factories', but became ill and spent nearly two years in the south before going to Moscow in March 1939. Her marriage was over by this stage and there is speculation that she was exiled to Russia, where she is presumed to have died during German air-raids in mid 1941.[16]

LIU TSAI-SHANG, see *Liu Caixiang*

LIU YING, 1905–, was born in Changsha County, Hunan Province, to a gentry–landlord family; her original name was Zheng Jie. Her mother sent her to a private school despite her father's traditional view that girls should not be given an education. Liu Ying joined the Communist Party in 1925 and two years later was elected head of Hunan women's bureau and an alternate member of the provincial party committee. By 1927 she and Lin Wei, a fellow revolutionary who had studied in France, had become lovers. Lin Wei was killed in 1927 and one source says that Liu Ying gave birth to his child, although no further details are offered. After working in Shanghai, Liu Ying was sent to Moscow to study at the Central Workers' University. She returned to China in 1932 and was involved from then on with the Youth League. On the eve of the Long March she was alerted by Mao Zedong to return quickly to Ruijin, an act of kindness that may be explained by their status as fellow provincials. Liu Ying was a political fighter on the Long March, hiring bearers and on

occasion helping carry litters. In mid May she was also appointed
secretary-general of the Central Committee succeeding Deng
Xiaoping in this position, which she held for several months.
Towards the end of the Long March, Liu Ying married Zhang
Wentian, known then as Luo Fu, who was secretary of the Central
Committee and whom she had first met in Moscow. In Yan'an
she worked with the Youth League and may have given birth to a
baby, who died. Exhausted, ill and pregnant, she travelled to
Moscow with He Zizhen at the end of 1937, gave birth
to another child who died, and returned to Yan'an in March
1939. Liu Ying was appointed head of the secretariat of the
Central Committee then worked in the north-east between 1945
and 1949. She took charge of party affairs in Moscow from 1950
to 1954 while her husband was ambassador to Russia, then was
recalled to work with Zhou Enlai in the foreign ministry. When
her husband was labelled a 'rightist opportunist' in 1959, Liu
Ying was demoted to a modern history work unit. When her
husband was accused of treachery in the Cultural Revolution,
Liu Ying was subjected to harassment then confined under guard
for over a year before she and her husband were exiled, under
house arrest, in Guangdong for six years. Zhang Wentian died in
exile a few months before the end of the Cultural Revolution.
Liu Ying was rehabilitated in 1977 and appointed in 1978 to the
Central Committee's commission for inspecting discipline. The
major traumas of the 1960s and 1970s had neither fundamentally
disrupted the steady trajectory of her life from educated youth
to responsible bureaucratic position nor shaken her loyalty to the
Communist Party. At the time of writing, Liu Ying was believed
to be living in Beijing.[17]

OUYANG QUANYUAN, see *Wang Quanyuan*

QIAN XIJUN, 1905–1990?, was born in Zhuji County, Zhejiang
Province, to poor peasants who sold her as a child bride. Her
betrothed was an enlightened boy who rejected their arranged
marriage and became one of the founders of the Youth League.
Qian Xijun joined the Youth League in 1924, the Communist
Party in 1925 and was classed as a 'student' because she attended
school. In Shanghai she attended the same free school run by
the communists as the writer Ding Ling did, and went on to

further schooling, working with the underground between 1926 and 1931 publishing revolutionary materials. During this time Qian Xijun worked with and in 1926 married Mao Zemin, the youngest brother of Mao Zedong. When Mao Zedong's wife, Yang Kaihui, was executed at the end of 1930, Qian Xijun and Mao Zemin looked after her three sons for several months but upon being assigned to the Jiangxi soviet in 1931 they left the boys in Shanghai. Qian Xijun became a branch secretary of the central government and assisted Mao Zemin in his work as treasurer of the soviet bank. As an organiser and inspector during the Long March she did propaganda work, hired bearers and organised grain supplies and cash funds. She was assigned with Wei Gongzhi to smuggle a large sum of international aid money from Shanghai to Xi'an in 1937, a task that took four months and brought her to Xi'an just as her sister-in-law He Zizhen was passing through that city on her way out of Yan'an. Qian Xijun then spent four years (1938–1942) with her husband in Xinjiang, in the north-west. After Mao Zemin was executed there by a warlord who betrayed the communists, Qian Xijun returned to Yan'an, where she studied at various party schools. In 1945 or 1946 she married Zhou Xiaoding and went with him to Shanghai to organise strikes among the workers. No mention is made of her having had children. After 1949 she was made deputy head of the Food Bureau and of the general office of the Bureau of Light Industry, as well as being elected to the 3rd (1959), 4th (1965) and 5th (1978) Chinese People's Political Consultative Conferences. It is not known what happened to her during the Cultural Revolution, but she visited Wei Gongzhi in hospital some time between 1969 and 1973, and assisted Guo Chen in his research on the Long March in the mid 1980s. She is believed to have died in 1990.[18]

QIU YIHAN, 1907–1956, was born in Pingjiang County, Hunan Province. An intellectual, she joined the Youth League in 1926 and the Communist Party in 1929. She and Li Jianhua were part of Peng Dehuai's division of the Red Army in 1930 and worked with young people. Qiu Yihan was appointed in 1931 to head the Hunan–Jiangxi women's bureau, became an inspector in 1932 for the public health unit and taught at the Red Army University, in what subject is not known. Just before the Long March she was branch secretary of the Youth League at the Red Army University and a political instructor, but her activities must have been severely restricted during the March since she set out with a poisoned hand and her glasses (she was very short-sighted) were broken quite early on. When her husband Yuan Guoping contracted acute tuberculosis in Guizhou, Qiu Yihan was assigned to care for him in a separate medical unit. She was given the title of secretary and is said to have done political work. She went with her husband to work with the New 4th Army, where she was head of the political department of the Military University of East China. After 1949 she held the important posts of head of the organisation department of the City of Nanjing and head of the organisation department of Jiangsu Province. She died of natural causes in 1956.[19]

TENG LIU-CHIN, see *Deng Liujin*

TENG YING-CH'AO, see *Deng Yingchao*

TSAI CH'ANG, see *Cai Chang*

TU XIUGEN, see *Li Jianhua*

WANG CHIEN-YUAN, see *Wang Quanyuan*

WANG QUANYUAN, 1913–, was born Ouyang Quanyuan in Ji'an County, Jiangxi Province. Of peasant origin, she joined the Youth League in 1930 and the Communist Party in 1934. In August 1935, during the Long March, she was assigned to the 4th Front Red Army commanded by Zhang Guotao, was placed in charge of the Women's Vanguard Regiment in 1936 and crossed the Yellow River with what came to be known as the Western Route Army. One of the few survivors, she was captured by anti-communist Moslem cavalry but escaped after two years. Rejected by the Communist Party in Lanzhou when she tried to reunite with her comrades, she returned to Jiangxi where she was criticised and ostracised for many years as a traitor. She was not exonerated until the 1980s, when she was eventually accepted back into the party. She married four times and at the time of writing was living in Jiangxi near Jinggangshan.[20]

WEI GONGZHI, 1908–1973, was born in Xinyang County, Henan Province. She was classed as an intellectual since she came from a gentry family, and had received some education; she also had bound feet which she liberated in her early teens after the May Fourth Movement. She attended Kaifeng middle school, then enrolled in 1926 in the Wuhan branch of Whampoa Military Academy where she studied military matters; one of her classmates was Zhou Yuehua. She joined the Communist Party in 1926, worked as a nurse during the famous Canton Commune uprising of December 1927, and edited *Red Army Life* while living in the first Chinese soviet in Hailufeng in Guangdong Province, which was crushed in February 1928. It was possibly during this period that she met and married Ye Jianying, who later became chief of personnel of the Military Council and in 1975 was Minister of National Defence. Wei Gongzhi studied in Moscow from 1929 to 1930 and was appointed to various positions in charge of artistic and cultural activities in the Jiangxi soviet. She wrote many plays, dances and songs and, along with Li Bozhao, was credited with developing the artistic life of the early soviet. Nevertheless, in 1931 she was expelled from the party as a suspected Trotskyite, her name to be removed 'forever' from party records. Wei Gongzhi therefore embarked on the Long March as an 'ordinary person' (*laobaixing*), that is, not a cadre, and walked with the Cadres Unit, undertaking the same duties as the women political workers. She was reinstated at the end of the Long March, however, when Mao directed that everyone who had completed the Long March be awarded party membership. Wei Gongzhi was 'Director of the "Chinese People's Anti-Japanese Dramatics Society"' when Edgar Snow met her in Bao'an in 1936, and had just had a baby when Helen Foster Snow met her in September 1937 in Xi'an. In the meantime Wei Gongzhi had spent four months with Qian Xijun smuggling a large sum of international aid money from Shanghai to Xi'an in 1937. She returned to Hunan on party business in 1939 but was back in Yan'an at the Party School by 1943, when she was again accused, briefly, of political misbehaviour. She worked in extremely harsh conditions in the north-east from 1945 to 1949, and contracted tuberculosis, so that she was unable to work. Her death in 1973 'from natural causes' was no doubt hastened by her being sent to Hubei during the Cultural Revolution (in 1969) and not provided with proper medical care.[21]

WEI KUNG-CH'I, see *Wei Gongzhi*

WEI HSÜ-YING, see *Wei Xiuying*

WEI XIUYING, 1910–, was born in Ruijin County, Jiangxi Province. She was of peasant origin and although given away at the age of five as a child bride, she never married. Wei Xiuying ran away with the Red Army in 1930 and joined the Communist Party in 1932. Between then and the Long March she led political work among the local women and worked with Jiangxi provincial women's bureau. She was a 'political fighter' on the Long March, hiring bearers and many times carrying litters herself when bodyguards would not stoop to such work and hired labourers had fled. In Yan'an she was attached to the women's bureau before being sent back to the south in 1938 to carry out women's work and guerrilla activities in the dangerous Jiangxi–Guangdong region. Recalled to Yan'an in 1940, she attended the Marx–Lenin School and the Party School; she was elected in 1945 to the 7th Party Congress. Between 1945 and 1949 she held various posts at provincial level in Jilin in the north-east, and after 1949 was appointed to the Jiangxi provincial party committee, was secretary of the Jiangxi women's bureau, and deputy head of the rural workers office of the All-China Women's Federation. Wei Xiuying suffered criticism during the Cultural Revolution but was re-instated in 1978. She retired in 1983, retaining her seat on the Jiangxi Chinese People's Political Consultative Conference. She was still hale and hearty in 1986 and at the time of writing was living in Jiangxi. The Cultural Revolution had not destroyed her loyalty to the Communist Party, which she regarded as responsible for rescuing her from poverty, illiteracy and an unhappy marriage.[22]

WU FULIAN, 1912–1937, was born in Shanghang County, Fujian Province. She was the second of the Long March women to die. Wu Fulian was of peasant stock, given away by her widowed mother as a child bride. At the age of seventeen she left home and travelled about with communist propaganda teams, becoming head of the Young Pioneers (1929), a member of the Communist Party (1929), head of the local women's bureau (1931), a member of the county committee (1931) and a member of the provincial Fujian–Guangdong–Jiangxi Committee (1932). She worked on this last committee with Li Jianzhen, and a man named Liu Xiao whom she later married. She was sent to the Central Party School in the Jiangxi soviet in 1933 and headed a provincial women's bureau in 1934. After completing military training at the Central School with Wei Xiuying and Deng Liujin, she participated with them in the mass recruitment drive that preceded the Long March. Her duties on the Long March included political work with the field hospital and the Convalescent Company, hiring bearers, buying/confiscating grain and cash, seeking out billets and placing out direction markers for the marchers. Assigned to Zhang Guotao's 4th Front Army in August 1935, she was made head of a north-west women's bureau, then political commissar of the Women's Vanguard Regiment. She survived six months with the Western Route Army resisting Moslem cavalry in the Gansu Corridor, but was wounded, captured, and died in prison in April 1937.[23]

WU FU-LIEN, see *Wu Fulian*

WU HULIAN, see *Wu Fulian*

WU TSUNG-LIEN, see *Wu Zhonglian*

WU ZHONGLIAN, 1908–1967, was born in Yizhang County, Hunan Province. Although her family were described as 'urban poor', she attended school and went on to Hengyang Women's Teachers' College, where she joined the Communist Party in 1927 and became involved in underground work and propaganda activities. With her then-husband Peng Qi, about whose life and death nothing is known, Wu Zhonglian set up a local branch of the Communist Party, and in 1928 retreated to Jinggangshan; there she did organisation work with the Youth League. She left Jinggangshan at the same time as Kang Keqing and He Zizhen and participated in guerrilla activities in Jiangxi and Fujian before being assigned to teaching at the Red Army School in the Jiangxi soviet. Wu Zhonglian was an organiser on the Long March but, weakened from malaria, often had trouble keeping up. Because of her high level of literacy, she was nevertheless required to act as secretary of the Cadres Unit, writing out each night sheafs of marching orders for the following day. She had married Zeng Risan at some stage and was pregnant and in hospital by

July–August 1935. She was assigned to Zhang Guotao's 4th Front Army, and gave birth to a baby boy at Ganzi in Tibet in the spring of 1936. Wu Zhonglian crossed the Yellow River in September 1936 but survived the massacre of the Western Route Army; her husband was killed. Wu Zhonglian left her son with a couple in Gansu, but was herself twice captured by the Moslems. Twice she escaped but, in company with Zhang Qinqiu, was betrayed and captured in Xi'an by the KMT. Zhou Enlai negotiated their release from Nanjing and Wu Zhonglian reached Yan'an in August 1937. During the Yan'an period she acted as head and secretary-general of the organisation department of the Shandong Column of the 8th Route Army; then director of the political department and secretary-general of the 1st Column of the Jiangsu–Anhui Column in east China. After 1949 she lived in Hangzhou with her husband Jiang Hua, who was on the Zhejiang provincial party committee, and her son Wu Changzheng (Long March Wu), whom she brought back from the north-west. Wu Zhonglian rose to the position of president of Zhejiang People's High Court and was on the executive committee of the All-China Women's Federation. Her imprisonment by the KMT in 1937 was used against her during the Cultural Revolution, and she was 'persecuted to death' in 1967. She was rehabilitated in 1978, two years after her son Wu Changzhen was killed in an accident. Although she was educated, Wu Zhonglian would never have had the opportunity to fill her position on the high court had she not been a member of the Long March generation of women.[24]

XIAO YUEHUA, 1913–1983, was born in Dabu County, Guangdong Province. Her poor peasant family gave her away as a child bride, but she eventually ran away to Hailufeng, where she became involved in revolutionary activities. While working in western Fujian some time after 1927 she and her husband, whose name is not known, fell foul of a witchhunt within the communist ranks; he was killed but she survived, only to be ostracised. Li Jianzhen, who later went on the Long March, befriended her. Xiao Yuehua joined the Youth League in 1933 and was transferred to the Youth League office in Ruijin where she worked with Hu Yaobang. That same year she was chosen by 'the organisation' to be the sexual partner of the German Comintern agent Otto Braun

(Li De), her initial refusal countered by threats of dismissal from her job. She carried out the same duties as the other peasant women on the Long March of hiring bearers, finding food and caring for the wounded, although Ding Ling later told Harrison Salisbury that Xiao Yuehua had been an orderly for Dr Nelson Fu. Xiao Yuehua joined the Communist Party in May 1937, about the same time as she gave birth to Otto Braun's son and filed for divorce, and was employed in Yan'an as a despatcher in the Central Committee office. Little is known of Xiao Yuehua's life after this. She kept her son and apparently remarried, and in 1960 was made deputy head of the road maintenance office in the Hunan Communications Bureau. She may also have worked in Changsha. During the Cultural Revolution she came under suspicion but is said to have courageously offered refuge to several unnamed leaders who had been criticised. In 1983 she was diagnosed as having cancer. Hu Yaobang, with whom she had worked in Ruijin in 1933 and whose death triggered the demonstrations that were squashed in the Tiananmen massacre of 4 June 1989, arranged for her to be brought to Beijing for treatment, but she died not long after. Hu Yaobang ordered that the red flag of China and the flag of the Communist Party be draped over her coffin.[25]

XIE FEI, 1913–, was born in Wenchang County on Hainan Island, the tear-shaped island off the southernmost point of Guangdong Province: she was thus classed simply as a 'Cantonese' or 'Hainanese'. While her family may have been poor, she nevertheless attended school and enrolled in 1926 in Hainan No. 6 Teachers' College where she became very active in various revolutionary groups. She joined the Youth League and the Communist Party in 1927. The following year she did undercover work in Hong Kong and in 1929 was sent by the party to Singapore. During her three years in Singapore she was arrested only once, but several times ingested sensitive documents, boiling them first, to prevent them falling into the hands of the KMT; she had stomach problems for the rest of her life. Xie Fei spent a further two years doing undercover work in the coastal city of Amoy in Fujian Province and in 1934 was transferred to the Security office in Ruijin. During the Long March she was an organiser and in 1936 she married Liu Shaoqi at Wayaobu; Liu Shaoqi was then a member of the Politburo and later became the chief target of the Cultural Revolution. Xie Fei worked with Liu Shaoqi in Tianjin, returned briefly to Yan'an to attend the Party School, then in 1939 was assigned with her husband to the New 4th Army in central China. She became separated from him while crossing the Yangtze River and for several years led into battle an independent regiment of soldiers who called her Regimental Commander Xie. She never remarried. In 1945 she was assigned to head the organisation department and a women's alliance in eastern China, was made deputy director of Beijing's Huabei Revolutionary University in 1949, and in 1950 headed the training section of the Chinese People's University. Xie Fei then enrolled in a law course at the People's University at the age of thirty-nine and in 1956 was appointed deputy principal of the Central School for Political and Legal Cadres. She was targeted as a rightist in 1959 and sent to work on a pig farm for an unspecified period before being allowed to return to Beijing. Because of her brief marriage to Liu Shaoqi she was physically attacked during the Cultural Revolution and imprisoned under frightful conditions from 1968 to 1973; Liu Shaoqi died in prison at the end of 1969. Rehabilitated in 1978, Xie Fei was appointed deputy principal of the Central People's Security College, and also sat on several legal and security councils as well as the Chinese People's Political Consultative Conference. The successful academic career she had carved out in the second half of her life was due largely to her own efforts, but would not have been possible had she been entirely without the *guanxi* of having been a Long Marcher, despite the principle of equal access upon which the new nation was founded. At the time of writing Xie Fei was believed to be living in Beijing.[26]

XIE QIONGXIANG, see *Xie Fei*

XIE XIAOMEI, 1913–, was born in Longyan County, Fujian Province, to a family of shopkeepers who were deeply involved in revolutionary activities. She completed primary school and was thus classed as a 'student'. She joined the Youth League in 1929 and the Communist Party in 1930. She married Luo Ming, who was party secretary of Fujian, in 1930 and she was appointed secretary of Fujian provincial committee. Ten days before the

Long March, Xie Xiaomei gave birth to a daughter, whom she placed with a local communist family so that she could go with Luo Ming. When he was seriously wounded in Guizhou she devoted considerable time to caring for him. In March or April 1935 they were ordered to stay behind in Guiyang to agitate among the peasantry but they were betrayed, arrested and released repeatedly over the next few years in Guiyang, Shanghai and Nanjing. Because of Luo Ming's political past the party would not take them back but asked them to continue revolutionary work in Fujian: they taught school and spread communist and anti-Japanese propaganda in Xie Xiaomei's hometown for several years. In 1947 they went to Singapore to escape the death throes in south-eastern China of the KMT, and in 1949 returned to the mainland. Xie Xiaomei was appointed to various teaching and library posts, but was investigated during the Cultural Revolution because she had been arrested so many times in the 1930s, and was labelled a traitor. She was sent to cadre school in the countryside where she was required to perform manual labour for three years. She retired in 1973 in protest against the policies of the Cultural Revolution and was punished with a pitifully low pension. In 1981 she was rehabilitated and awarded the privileges and pension appropriate to an old Long March cadre. At the time of writing she was believed to be living in Guangdong.[27]

YANG HOUZENG, see *Yang Houzhen*

YANG HOUZHEN, 1908–1977, was born in Ruijin County, Jiangxi Province. Her feet had been bound as a child, but she 'liberated' them at some unspecified time. Her father was a teacher and she attended primary school but, instead of being classed as a student or intellectual, she was listed by Li Bozhao in Yan'an as a 'housewife', along with Zeng Yu; this is rather perplexing since at that time she appears to have been between husbands. Yang Houzhen joined the Red Army in 1929, when her husband, army commander Luo Binghui, defected from the KMT during the Ji'an Uprising. She was on Jinggangshan in late 1929, joined the Communist Party and attended the Red Army University in 1931, and was placed in charge of a cooperative of some sort in Fujian. Despite the dreadful handicap of her liberated feet, Yang

Houzhen walked almost every step of the Long March, although she does not seem to have been assigned duties. Harrison Salisbury says she gave birth to a child on the Long March but Chinese sources are silent on this point. She was, however, wounded during the same bombing raid as He Zizhen. She was separated from Luo Binghui when he was assigned to Zhang Guotao's 4th Front Army in August 1935 and their marriage appears to have ended then. Luo Binghui told Helen Foster Snow in Yan'an in 1937 that he had three children in Jiangxi and a son in Yunnan. 'I never could find out how many wives he had had,' she wrote; Yang Houzhen was not mentioned. In Yan'an, Yang Houzhen managed cooperatives and local factories run by families before her health gave out. She remarried and at some stage gave birth to a child, who she took with them when her husband Liu Zhengming was dismissed from the party, reason unclear. She opened a shop and supported the family until Liu Zhengming was cleared and reinstated in 1946. After 1949 she was employed by the Ministry of Culture as head of a sporting goods factory. No reference can be found of her experience during the Cultural Revolution and she is said to have died of natural causes in 1977.[28]

YANG HU-CHEN, see *Yang Houzhen*

ZENG YU, 1908?–1941, was born in Yizhang County, Hunan Province. She was one of two women classified in a list Li Bozhao compiled for Helen Foster Snow in Yan'an as 'housewife'; the other woman was Yang Houzhen. Zeng Yu was active with the communists on Jinggangshan and joined the Communist Party in 1928. Pregnant when the Long March began, she illegally joined the marchers in order to remain with her husband Zhou Zikun. As an unregistered participant she was not assigned duties, and abandoned her baby, the first to be born on the Long March, in November 1934 near Laoshan. There is no record of how long she spent in Yan'an, but she accompanied her husband to the south when he was appointed to the New 4th Army. In January 1941 she took her child, of which there are no details, home to her family in Hunan for safekeeping but she herself disappeared, presumed killed, while making her way back to the New 4th Army. She was the third of the Long March women to die.[29]

ZHENG JIE, see *Liu Ying*

ZHENG YU, see *Zeng Yu*

ZHONG YUELIN, 1915–, was born in Yudu County, Jiangxi Province. She was of peasant origin, given when she was eight years old to a progressive family which allowed her access to literacy and encouraged her to join with them in revolutionary activities. She joined the Youth League in 1931 and worked in youth and women's affairs in the Jiangxi soviet. During the Long March she was a 'political fighter' responsible for hiring bearers, carrying litters and organising food supplies. At the end of the Long March, in 1935, she joined the Communist Party and married Song Renqiong, who was political commissar of the Red Army Cadres Corps. She gave birth to a child in autumn 1936 in Bao'an, who died. Zhong Yuelin studied wireless communication and worked as a field wireless operator in north China with her husband until 1949. After 1949 she filled nominal positions that allowed her to remain with her husband as he held various high-level positions, including membership of the Central Committee and minister in the Ministry of Machine-building Industry. Zhong Yuelin suffered criticism during the Cultural Revolution while her husband was attacked repeatedly by Red Guards in 1966–1967. Rehabilitated in 1977, he eventually became a member of the Central Committee and the Politburo. At the time of writing, Zhong Yuelin was living in Beijing.[30]

ZHONG YULIN, see *Zhong Yuelin*

ZHOU YUEHUA, 1904–1977, was born in Guangji County, Hubei Province. Her father, a peasant who became successful as a tailor, taught her to read and write and she later attended Wuhan Free Normal School; she was thus classified as a 'student'. Her mother had bound feet, and Zhou Yuehua's feet were also bound but she liberated them, possibly during her teens. She joined the Communist Party in 1926 and the following year studied military matters at the Wuhan branch of Whampoa Military Academy; one of her classmates was Wei Gongzhi. Zhou Yuehua worked as a nurse during the famous Canton Commune uprising of December 1927 and in the first Chinese soviet in Hailufeng in Guangdong Province, which was crushed in February 1928.

During this period she met He Cheng, a medical doctor whom she married and worked with from then on; they had at least one child. Zhou Yuehua and her husband set up clinics in Wuhan and Shanghai which acted as covers for their underground work, and she was arrested several times over the next few years. Each time, she managed to walk free, protesting: 'I don't know what you are talking about, I am an illiterate housewife.' She worked as a nurse with the General Medical Unit on the Long March, walking most of the way, even though she was given a small white horse to whom she became very attached. Zhou Yuehua and her husband were assigned to Zhang Guotao's Left Column, but He Cheng slipped away to Yan'an on the pretext of securing medical supplies. By the time Zhou Yuehua reached Yan'an her husband had gone to Russia, and it was eight years before they were reunited. Zhou Yuehua undertook further study in Yan'an and was placed in charge of investigating security with regard to posts and telecommunications before travelling in 1945 to the north-east where she worked with He Cheng in public health. After 1949 she was a leading member of the Ministry of Public Health and held various associated positions. Her health gave out, however, and she retired in 1960. She was 'struggled' during the Cultural Revolution and beaten because she would neither confess to political crimes she had not committed nor write confessions accusing others. She died on 17 September 1977, of illness.[31]

NOTES

PART I PROLOGUE

1 Christina Gilmartin, 'The politics of gender in the making of the party', in Tony Saich and Hans van de Ven (eds), *New perspectives on the Chinese communist revolution*, M E Sharpe, Armonk, New York, 1995, p 34.

CHAPTER 1 LOVER, MOTHER, WIFE

1 Mid-autumn festival is the fifteenth day of the eighth lunar month. The longan is an autumn fruit, of Euphoria longan, a large evergreen tree native to China, and is related to the lychee; the English name 'longan' is derived from its common Chinese name *long yan* (dragon's eye).

2 Information on He Zizhen's early life, her relationship with Mao Zedong and experiences on the Long March has been garnered from the following Chinese-language materials: her biography 'Guangrong er kankede yi sheng' (A life that was honourable but full of tribulations) by Qiu Zhizhuo in Liaowang Bianjibu (ed.), *Hongjun nüyingxiong zhuan* (Heroines of the Red Army), Xinhua chubanshe, Beijing, 1986, pp 83–101; Liu Fulang, *The analysis of Mao Tse-tung's personality*, Union Press, Hong Kong, 1973; and Guo Chen, *Jinguo liezhuan*, Nongcun duwu chubanshe, Beijing, 1986.

3 Christina Gilmartin, 'The politics of gender in the making of the party', in Tony Saich and Hans van de Ven (eds), *New perspectives on the Chinese communist revolution*, p 43. This article provides a comprehensive analysis of how women were excluded from the formal power structure of the Communist Party in the early 1920s.

4 *Nüjie* (Precepts for women), written about 100 AD by a woman named Ban Zhao, counselled young women to spurn education and to remain submissive. It was the basic text according to which girls were brought up in traditional China. Ban Zhao herself, however, was a respected scholar and a forthright adviser to Empress Dowager Deng who ruled for fifteen years (106–121 AD) during the Han dynasty. For an analysis of Ban Zhao's life and work see Lily Xiao Hong Lee's 'Ban Zhao (c.48–c.120): Her role in the formulation of controls imposed upon women in traditional China', in her *The virtue of yin: Studies on Chinese women*, Wild Peony, Sydney, 1994, pp 11–24.

5 This account of their meeting is from a 1980 interview He Zizhen gave to Wang Xingjuan (see 'He Zizhen', in *Nüying zishu*, Jiangxi renmin chubanshe, Nanchang, 1988, pp 7–8).

6 Agnes Smedley, *The great road: The life and times of Chu Te*, John Calder, London, 1958, p 226.

7 Gong Chu published his article, 'Wo yu hongjun' (The Red Army and me), which included his conversation with the comrade who described this meeting of He Zizhen and Mao, in 1952. It is quoted in Liu Fulang, *The analysis of Mao Tse-tung's personality*, pp 62–63.

8 Yang Kaihui is considered to have been Mao's first real wife, even though, strictly speaking, she was his second. This is because he consistently disowned the marriage his parents had arranged for him when he was thirteen or fourteen to a young woman six years older, claiming to have not consummated this marriage. Edgar Snow records Mao's time in Beijing and marriage to Yang Kaihui as well as Mao's brief mention of her capture and execution (*Red star over China*, Victor Gollancz, London, 1937, re-issued 1963, pp 147–53; 173). Given that there is no record of her political activities, Edgar Snow's comment that Yang Kaihui was 'a youth leader during the Great Revolution, and one of the most active women Communists' seems to have been prompted out of respect for Mao (see *Red star over China*, 1963, footnote on p 153). Liu Fulang says she had little interest in politics (*The analysis of Mao Tse-tung's personality*, p 60). Christina Gilmartin quotes Luo Zhanglong, 'an early male member of the party', as saying Yang Kaihui undertook 'numerous political tasks' ('The politics of gender in the making of the party', in Tony Saich and Hans van de Ven (eds), *New perspectives on the Chinese communist revolution*, p 49).

9 Christina Gilmartin, 'The politics of gender in the making of the party', in Tony Saich and Hans van de Ven (eds), *New perspectives on the Chinese communist revolution*, p 43.

10 In ascending order of power the party hierarchy is the people, the

soviets, the Central Committee, from whose members are elected the Politburo (Political Bureau), from which is chosen the Standing Committee; the Standing Committee is thus the distillation of the party's power. Mao was elected to the Politburo in 1924 in Canton and according to Edgar Snow was also Chairman of the Party Front Committee of the 1st Division of the 1st Peasants' and Workers' Army in Hunan. The Central Committee stripped him of both positions in 1927 but he continued as Chairman of the Front Committee and made himself Political Commissar of the 4th Red Army. The Central Committee reinstated him in absentia at the 6th Party Congress in Moscow in December 1928 when they decided to approve his agrarian line. Edgar Snow, *Red star over China*, 1963, pp 162–68.

11 Agnes Smedley, *The great road*, pp 236–37.

12 Agnes Smedley has recreated a dramatic account of this period (*The great road*, pp 225–304). Edgar Snow also covered these events, although in much less detail, in his retelling of Mao Zedong's recollections (*Red star over China*, 1963, pp 165–69). The two versions sometimes differ slightly as to dates.

13 Edgar Snow, *Red star over China*, 1963, p 173.

14 Edgar Snow, *Red star over China*, 1963, p 119; Agnes Smedley, *China fights back: An American woman with the Eighth Route Army*, Victor Gollancz, London, 1938, p 153.

15 Harrison Salisbury, *The Long March*, Harper & Row, New York, 1985, pp 49–50.

16 Huang Changjiao, 'Buqude zhandou' (Indomitable fighter), in *Jiangxi funü gemingdouzheng gushi*, Jiangxisheng funü lianhehui, Beijing, 1963, pp 55–67.

17 Agnes Smedley, *The great road*, p 309. Smedley also quotes Zhu De as saying there were thirty-five women. The Chinese, however, generally talk of The Thirty Women who went on the Long March and Helen Foster Snow (*Inside Red China*, Da Capo Press, New York, 1939, 1977 reprint, p 174) says there were fifty women, twenty of whom were 'nurses and other women'. Since Helen Foster Snow is the only observer to mention these extra twenty women, it is possible this was a misperception that the twenty nurses would be women when in fact they were boys and young men.

18 The names of the fifteen wives (and their husbands) were: Cai Chang (Li Fuchun), Chen Huiqing (Deng Fa), Deng Yingchao (Zhou Enlai), He Zizhen (Mao Zedong), Jin Weiying (Li Weihan, aka Luo Mai, which Edgar Snow, Helen Foster Snow and Harrison Salisbury transcribe as 'Lo Man'), Kang Keqing (Zhu De), Li Bozhao (Yang

Shangkun), Liao Siguang (He Kequan, aka Kai Feng), Liu Qunxian (Bo Gu), Qian Xijun (Mao Zemin), Wei Gongzhi (Ye Jianying), Xiao Yuehua (Otto Braun, aka Li De), Xie Xiaomei (Luo Ming), Yang Houzhen (Luo Binghui) and Zhou Yuehua (He Cheng).

19 The four students, or intellectuals, were Li Jianhua, Liu Ying, Qiu Yihan and Wu Zhonglian; apart from the telegraphist Li Jianhua, no indication is given of what office they held at the time of setting off on the Long March. The eleven women of peasant origin were Deng Liujin, Han Shiying, Li Guiying, Li Jianzhen, Liu Caixiang, Wang Quanyuan, Wei Xiuying, Wu Fulian, Xie Fei, Zeng Yu and Zhong Yuelin.

20 The Chinese counterpart of the Western week is called a *xun*; this is a traditional term referring to a ten-day period. A month is made up of three *xun*: *shang xun* (upper, or first), *zhong xun* (middle, or second) and *xia xun* (lower, or third).

21 Exactly how many men set off, how many were lost (by death, desertion, replacement and dropout) and how many finally completed the march is not known. Harrison Salisbury's figures (*The Long March*, passim), which have been quoted in this account, give a good idea of the enormity of the losses over the various stages of the march.

22 This is Helen Foster Snow's description of 'Miss Liu Chien-hsien, Leader of the Proletariat' (*Inside Red China*, pp 185–86).

23 Guo Chen, *Jinguo liezhuan*, p 128.

24 The six women who were not part of the Convalescent Company were Cai Chang, Kang Keqing, Li Jianhua, Liu Ying, Wei Gongzhi and Zhou Yuehua.

25 Chang Kuo-t'ao, *The rise of the Chinese Communist Party: The auto-biography of Chang Kuo-t'ao*, The University Press of Kansas, Lawrence, 1972, vol. 2, p 180.

26 The German Cominterm representative Otto Braun reported this event in his memoir, written several decades later, saying he had insisted on the courtmartial because the commanding officer (whom he mis-identified as Xiao Jingguang; the man's name was Zhou Zikun) had acted with cowardly irresponsibility by escaping 'with the staff guard, leaving his troops to their fate. They were cut off and dispersed.' (*A Cominterm agent in China, 1932–1939*, Stanford University Press, Stanford, California, 1982, p 91). Harrison Salisbury also mentions this incident (*The Long March*, pp 98, 104).

27 Translations of songs and chants are by Sue Wiles. This song is from Guo Chen, *Jinguo liezhuan*, p 146.

28 The birthing episodes of Zeng Yu in December 1934, of Liao

Siguang in January–February 1935, of He Zizhen in early February 1935 and of Chen Huiqing in late April 1935 are from Guo Chen, *Jinguo liezhuan*, pp 49–51, 79–85. Harrison Salisbury has suggested Zhaxi as the location of the birth of He Zizhen's baby (*The Long March*, p 374, note 13); others say it was near the Red River.

29 Edgar Snow says Yang Houzhen had bound feet but does not mention her having liberated them: 'Mrs. Lo P'ing-hui, wife of a Red Army commander (and the only lily-footed woman who made the Long March)' (*Red star over China*, 1963, p 376). Guo Chen, however, says she had liberated her feet.

30 Chang Kuo-t'ao, *The rise of the Chinese Communist Party*, vol. 2, p 380.

31 Kunming's winter is very mild (9°C on average) and in summer the mercury stays around 20°C. Chen Huiqing's baby must have been born in the Guizhou–Yunnan border area: one report has her still within Guizhou just after the birth of her baby, another says she was about 80 kilometres from Kunming, which would place her in Yunnan (Guo Chen, *Jinguo liezhuan*, pp 13, 83).

32 This information, and the following two comments of his, are in Chang Kuo-t'ao, *The rise of the Chinese Communist Party*, vol. 2, pp 377, 405, 407.

33 The actual break-up of troops was that Zhang's Left Column retained his 9th and 31st Corps and took the 1st Front Army's 5th and 9th Corps plus some of the Central Column. Mao's Right Column retained his 1st and 3rd Corps plus the Red Army University and some of the Central Column and took the 4th Front Army's 4th and 30th Corps, but both of these rejoined Zhang when Mao folded his tents and silently stole away in the September night.

34 Agnes Smedley, *The great road*, p 337.

35 Agnes Smedley, *The great road*, p 338.

36 The shift to romanising Chinese in the *pinyin* system has made the names of provinces in the north somewhat confusing for Westerners. Kansu in the old system is now Gansu; Shensi in the old system is now Shaanxi (to differentiate it from its eastern neighbour Shanxi). Once the Right Column disentangled itself from Zhang Guotao its name was changed to the Shaanxi–Gansu Branch Force of the Anti-Japanese Vanguard Force of the Red Army to emphasise its new location and purpose, which was to oppose Japanese aggression in north China (Harrison Salisbury, *The Long March*, pp 281–82).

37 Agnes Smedley, *The great road*, p 337.

38 Harrison Salisbury, *The Long March*, p 296.

CHAPTER 2 NOT QUITE EQUAL

1 The elements of Wang Quanyuan's story are recorded in Guo Chen, *Jinguo liezhuan*, pp 180–90; in her biography 'Xueyu–xingfeng yi nüjie' (A heroine through foul winds and a rain of blood) by Luo Guojun in Liaowang Bianjibu (ed.), *Hongjun nüyingxiong zhuan*, pp 188–206; and in Dong Hanhe, *Xilujun nüzhanshi mengnan ji*, Jiefangjun wenyi chubanshe, Beijing, 1990, pp 17–59.

2 This description by Zhu De of conditions in Jiangxi and how the communists went about winning new areas is in Agnes Smedley, *The great road*, pp 204–5, 242.

3 This was how Deng Liujin said she joined the party at the laconic urging of her fellow villager Fu Caixiu (Guo Chen, *Jinguo liezhuan*, p 11).

4 The twelve women of the Women Workers' Group were: Li Bozhao; Deng Liujin; Han Shiying; Jin Weiying; Li Guiying; Liu Caixiang; Liu Ying; Wang Quanyuan; Wei Xiuying; Wu Fulian; Xie Fei; Zhong Yuelin (from Wang Quanyuan's biography in Liaowang Bianjibu (ed.), *Hongjun nüyingxiong zhuan*, p 192; Guo Chen, *Jinguo liezhuan*, passim). Dong Hanhe includes Wu Zhonglian in the Women Workers' Group (*Xilujun nüzhanshi mengnan ji*, p 26). These women probably set off on 10 October 1934.

5 Guo Chen, *Jinguo liezhuan*, p 21.

6 This song was sung to a folk tune of the Xingguo area in Jiangxi (Guo Chen, *Jinguo liezhuan*, pp 35–36).

7 The seven political fighters, or workteam members, were Li Guiying (the team's political instructor); Deng Liujin; Liu Caixiang; Wang Quanyuan; Wei Xiuying; Wu Fulian; Zhong Yuelin (Guo Chen, *Jinguo liezhuan*, pp 7–8, 18).

8 Guo Chen, *Jinguo liezhuan*, pp 8–9. Harrison Salisbury says it was Wei Xiuying's menstruation blood that confused a boy nurse during a river crossing; he does not mention Deng Liujin (*The Long March*, p 81). Perhaps the tale is apocryphal.

9 Agnes Smedley, *China fights back*, p 49.

10 The details of Wang Quanyuan's time in Zunyi, the work of mobilising the masses, her marriage, and the springtime crossing into Yunnan Province are from Guo Chen, *Jinguo liezhuan*, pp 24–25, 182, 42.

11 The women who 'introduced' the two Wangs into marriage in Zunyi were Li Jianzhen, Cai Chang, and Jin Weiying (Guo Chen, *Jinguo liezhuan*, p 182; Dong Hanhe, *Xilujun nüzhanshi mengnan ji*, p 27). Helen Foster Snow's interview with Wang Shoudao is in Nym Wales

(penname of Helen Foster Snow), *Red dust: Autobiographies of Chinese communists*, Stanford University Press, Stanford, California, 1952, pp 77–79.

12 The women involved in the pear episode were Xie Fei, Zhong Yuelin and Liu Caixiang. The pear, incidentally, did revive Wu Fulian (Guo Chen, *Jinguo liezhuan*, pp 42–44). The talc of the manure-heap wheat is also recorded by Guo Chen (*Jinguo liezhuan*, pp 58–59).

13 Edgar Snow, *Red star over China*, 1963, p 170. Edgar Snow wrote of 'the spirit, the training, the discipline, the excellent equipment, and especially the high political morale, of the regular Red Army' (*Red star over China*, 1963, p 266).

14 Chang Kuo-t'ao, *The rise of the Chinese Communist Party*, vol. 2, p 243.

15 Helen Foster Snow, *My China years*, William Morrow & Co, New York, 1984, p 279.

16 Qi Xu, 'Li jin qianxin zhi yu jian' (A will strengthened by hardship), in Liaowang Bianjibu (ed.), *Hongjun nüyingxiong zhuan*, pp 175–87).

17 Guo Chen, *Jinguo liezhuan*, pp 150–57.

18 Guo Chen, *Jinguo liezhuan*, p 183; Dong Hanhe, *Xilujun nüzhanshi mengnan ji*, p 28.

19 Chang Kuo-t'ao, *The rise of the Chinese Communist Party*, vol. 2, p 412; Harrison Salisbury, *The Long March*, p 371, note 20.

20 Agnes Smedley, *The great road*, pp 325–26.

21 Li Bozhao was the main collaborator on this song 'Two mighty armies join forces', which she wrote on the road after the 1st Front Army crossed the Snowy Mountains and sang at the 1st–4th Army reunion celebrations in Maogong in mid-June 1935 (Kang Keqing, *Kang Keqing huiyi lu*, Jiefangjun chubanshe, Beijing, 1993, pp 162–63). Li Bozhao was married to General Yang Shangkun, from whom she became separated when the Left and Right columns parted company in September.

22 Isabel and David Crook, *Revolution in a Chinese village: Ten Mile Inn*, Routledge & Kegan Paul, London, 1959, 1979, p vii.

23 Wu Zhonglian's husband, Zeng Risan, was killed during the massacre of the Western Route Army. Zhou Yuehua was married to Doctor He Cheng. Li Jianhua's husband's name was Yue Xia. Guo Chen, *Jinguo liezhuan*, pp 165–68, 174–79, 183, 192, 201–13.

24 Chang Kuo-t'ao, *The rise of the Chinese Communist Party*, vol. 2, pp 408, 424–25.

25 Chang Kuo-t'ao, *The rise of the Chinese Communist Party*, vol. 2, p 441.

26 Chang Kuo-t'ao, *The rise of the Chinese Communist Party*, vol. 2, p 439.

27 Guo Chen, *Jinguo liezhuan*, pp 184–85.

28 Harrison Salisbury, *The Long March*, p 265.

29 Edgar Snow, *Red star over China*, 1963, pp 319–22.

30 This and the following song are from Guo Chen, *Jinguo liezhuan*, pp 41, 42.

31 Agnes Smedley, *The great road*, pp 274–75.

32 Chang Kuo-t'ao, *The rise of the Chinese Communist Party*, vol. 2, p 351.

33 Ross Terrill, *The white-boned demon: A biography of Madame Mao Zedong*, Touchstone (Simon & Schuster), New York, 1984, p 141.

34 Chang Kuo-t'ao, *The rise of the Chinese Communist Party*, vol. 2 pp 460–61. The Western Route Army consisted of the 9th and 30th Corps of Zhang's 4th Front Army, and the 5th Corps of Mao's 1st Front Army, plus the Women's Anti-Japanese Vanguard Regiment. Its military commander was Xu Xiangqian, its political commissar Chen Changhao, and its political head Li Zhuoran. Chen Changhao's wife, Zhang Qinqiu, was head of its political organisation section (Guo Chen, *Jinguo liezhuan*, p 185; Dong Hanhe, *Xilujun nüzhanshi mengnan ji*, p 30).

35 Guo Chen, *Jinguo liezhuan*, p 185; Dong Hanhe, *Xilujun nüzhanshi mengnan ji*, p 31; Harrison Salisbury, *The Long March*, p 320.

36 Her telling of these events is in Dong Hanhe, *Xilujun nüzhanshi mengnan ji*, pp 30–35.

37 These messages were telegraphed on 12 March 1937 and the decision to split and scatter was made in the last ten-day period of that month (Dong Hanhe, *Xilujun nüzhanshi mengnan ji*, pp 34–35).

38 Guo Chen, *Jinguo liezhuan*, pp 174–78; Dong Hanhe, *Xilujun nüzhanshi mengnan ji*, pp 167–68.

CHAPTER 3   THE GIRL COMMANDER

1 Nym Wales (penname of Helen Foster Snow), 'K'ang K'ê-ching: A peasant partisan', in *Red dust: Autobiographies of Chinese communists*, pp 216–17; the original text uses a variant spelling—Chu Tê—for Zhu De's name, and in Helen Foster Snow's *Inside Red China* his name is spelt Chu Teh.

2 Helen Foster Snow, *Inside Red China*, p 187.

3 Nym Wales, 'K'ang K'ê'ching: A peasant partisan', pp 212–17. The main Chinese material used for this chapter is Kang Keqing's reminiscences, which were dictated over seventeen mornings in the summer–autumn of 1987 then researched and written up as a draft for her to correct before their eventual publication in 1993 (Kang Keqing, *Kang Keqing huiyi lu*, esp pp 1–206), and her biography 'Hongjunli de nü siling' (Red Army Girl Commander) by Bi Fang

in Liaowang Bianjibu (ed.), *Hongjun nüyingxiong zhuan*, pp 25–37. Her year of birth is given variously as 1910, 1911 and 1912, with 7 September 1911 cited in her obituaries as her date of birth.

4 Bi Fang, 'Hongjunli de nü siling' p 29.

5 Kang Keqing, *Kang Keqing huiyi lu*, p 32.

6 Agnes Smedley, *The great road*, p 2.

7 Agnes Smedley gives Zhu De's birthdate as '1886 December 12 (or November 30)' (*The great road*, p 445) and this is generally taken as the year of his birth. If, however, as Kang Keqing says in her reminiscences, Zhu De turned sixty *sui* on 1 December 1946 (*Kang Keqing huiyilu*, p 319) then he would have been born in 1887, since in traditional Chinese terms you are one *sui* old at birth.

8 Chinese sources give this woman's name as Wu Ruolan; Agnes Smedley transcribes it as Wu Yu-lan (*The great road*, p 223); Helen Foster Snow as Wu Yü-lan ('K'ang K'ê'ching: A peasant partisan', p 214).

9 Kang Keqing, *Kang Keqing huiyilu*, pp 54–62.

10 Nym Wales, 'K'ang K'ê'ching: A peasant partisan', p 214; *Inside Red China*, p 190.

11 Helen Foster Snow, *Inside Red China*, p 188.

12 Guo Chen, *Jinguo liezhuan*, p 15.

13 Helen Foster Snow, *Inside Red China*, p 184.

14 This comment about 'ganren' was an observation of Zhu De's (*The great road*, p 315); it is sometimes attributed to Mao Zedong. Three *li* equal one mile or about 1.7 kilometres; one *li* is about 0.5 kilometre.

15 Edgar Snow, *Red star over China*, 1963, pp 170–71. The present-day version of the Red Army's Eight Points for Attention reflects, among other things, an improvement in their sleeping arrangements: 1. Speak politely; 2. Pay fairly for what you buy; 3. Return everything you borrow; 4. Pay for anything you damage; 5. Don't hit or swear at people; 6. Don't damage crops; 7. Don't take liberties with women; 8. Don't ill-treat captives.

16 Agnes Smedley, *The great road*, p 231.

17 Harrison Salisbury, *The Long March*, pp 149, 372, notes 10 and 11.

18 Xiwangmu is also known as Queen Mother of the West. For a detailed study of the origin and development of the myths associated with Xiwangmu see Michael Loewe, *Ways to paradise: The Chinese quest for immortality*, George Allen & Unwin, London, 1979.

19 Quoted material in this section on Cai Chang is from Helen Foster Snow's biography of her in *Inside Red China*, pp 182–85; see also

the brief biography 'Yige weidade nüxing' (A great woman) by Hu Guohua in Liaowang Bianjibu (ed.), *Hongjun nüyingxiong zhuan* (pp 7–24). A substantial biography of Cai Chang (Su Ping, *Cai Chang zhuan*, Zhongguo funü chubanshe, Beijing, 1990) was published to commemorate her seventy years as a revolutionary.

20 Guo Chen, *Jinguo liezhuan*, p 54.

21 Guo Chen, *Jinguo liezhuan*, p 36.

22 *Kang Keqing huiyi lu*, p 152. The exact number of men who died taking Luding Bridge is uncertain, but it seems to have been between seventeen and fifty (see Dick Wilson, *The Long March 1935: The epic of Chinese communism's survival*, Viking Press, New York, 1971, p 174).

23 The story of how the women managed to transport their equipment and wounded across the bridge, and their song, is in Guo Chen, *Jinguo liezhuan*, pp 36–40.

24 Guo Chen, *Jinguo liezhuan*, pp 56–57.

25 Agnes Smedley, *The great road*, pp 331–32; Edgar Snow, *Red star over China*, 1963, p 203.

26 Harrison Salisbury, *The Long March*, pp 279–80, 391, note 6.

27 Agnes Smedley, *The great road*, p 347.

28 Kang Keqing's account is in her *Kang Keqing huiyi lu*, pp 171–201.

29 Chang Kuo-t'ao, *The rise of the Chinese Communist Party*, vol. 2, pp 423, 427.

30 Nym Wales, 'K'ang K'ê-ching: A peasant partisan', pp 211, 217–18.

31 Chang Kuo-t'ao, *The rise of the Chinese Communist Party*, vol. 2, p 441.

PART II PROLOGUE

1 See Maurice Meisner, *Mao's China and after: A history of the People's Republic*, The Free Press, New York, 1986, pp 33–41.

2 Chang Kuo-t'ao, *The rise of the Chinese Communist Party*, vol. 2, p 491.

3 Immanuel C. Y. Hsü, *The rise of modern China*, Oxford University Press, Hong Kong, 1975, p 711.

4 Their most influential works were: Edgar Snow, *Red star over China* (1937, 1963 re-issue; and 1968 revised edition); Agnes Smedley, *China fights back* (1938); Helen Foster Snow, *Inside Red China* (1939); Edgar Snow, *Scorched earth*, Victor Gollancz, London, 1941. Some years later Helen Foster Snow published two works based on her earlier notes: *Red dust* (under her pen name Nym Wales, 1952), and *My China years* (1984). Agnes Smedley's biography of Zhu De, *The great road*, was published posthumously in 1958. All of these

books have been used in preparing Part II of this book, on the Yan'an period.

5 Han Suyin, *Birdless summer* (Jonathan Cape, London, 1968), p 312.
6 Maurice Meisner, *Mao's China and after*, pp 41–42.

CHAPTER 4   COMMUNICATION BREAKDOWN

1 Edgar Snow, *Red star over China*, 1963, p 19.
2 Edgar Snow, *Red star over China*, 1963, p 22.
3 Edgar Snow, *Red star over China*, 1963, pp 79–84.
4 Edgar Snow transliterated He Zizhen's name in the Wade–Giles system of romanisation as Ho Tzu-ch'en or Ho Tze-nien, referring to her only in passing (*Red star over China*, 1963, pp 82, 83, 98, 107, 147, 374; 1968 edn, p 349). His trusting assumption about Mao's monogamous nature is on p 126 of the 1963 reissue of *Red star over China* but appears to have been deleted from the 1968 revised edition.
5 This is part of Edgar Snow's description of the 'wonderful loess lands' of north-western China, which includes the provinces of Gansu, Shaanxi, Ningxia and Shanxi where the main body of the Reds spent the decade or so after the Long March (*Red star over China*, 1963, p 40).
6 Janice R. MacKinnon and Stephen R. MacKinnon, *Agnes Smedley: The life and times of an American radical*, University of California, Berkeley, 1988, p 182. Otto Braun's description is from his *A Cominterm agent in China*, pp 190, 217.
7 Details of He Zizhen's life in Yan'an and Russia (Moscow and Ivanovo), her rescue and her return to China are in the main from Guo Chen, *Jinguo liezhuan*, pp 193–201, with some additional material from her biography in Liaowang Bianjibu (ed.), *Hongjun nüyingxiong zhuan* (pp 83–101).
8 Janice R. MacKinnon and Stephen R. MacKinnon, *Agnes Smedley*, p 195. This is an excellent biography of the fascinating and complex Agnes Smedley.
9 Helen Foster Snow, *My China years*, pp 261–63, 267, 275, 279, 284. Helen Foster Snow told Ross Terrill in 1981 that He Zizhen had hated Agnes Smedley (Ross Terrill, *The white-boned demon*, p 142, and p 433 (Reference note to p 146)).
10 Otto Braun wrote briefly of the break-up of He Zizhen's marriage and Mao's subsequent marriage to Jiang Qing, calling this scandal that touched on Mao's intimate life 'most distasteful and, of itself, insignificant' and an 'unpleasant episode' (Otto Braun, *A Comintern*

agent in China, pp 249–50, 253–54). Braun says this argument took place in winter 1937–38 but he must have meant early 1937 since He Zizhen left Yan'an before the 1937–38 winter; the timing of the events in this period is infuriatingly slippery, often varying from source to source.

11 Edgar Snow repeating Agnes Smedley's words, quoted by Janice R. MacKinnon and Stephen R. MacKinnon, *Agnes Smedley*, p 188.

12 Guo Chen, *Jinguo liezhuan*, p 194.

13 Helen Foster Snow, *Inside Red China*, pp 167–68.

14 Janice R. MacKinnon and Stephen R. MacKinnon, *Agnes Smedley*, p 188.

15 Helen Foster Snow, *Inside Red China*, p 189.

16 Helen Foster Snow, *Inside Red China*, p 178. She goes on to say that He Zizhen was also an active communist worker and had been a school teacher before marrying Mao. Liu Qunxian's touching request of Helen Foster Snow that she take care of her one-year-old son is recorded in *Inside Red China* (p 185).

17 Janice R. MacKinnon and Stephen R. MacKinnon, *Agnes Smedley*, pp 188–92. See also Ross Terrill, *The white-boned demon*, pp 142–45, 432 (Reference notes to pp 142–46).

18 See, for example, Cheng Wei, *Gongheguo diyi jia: Mao Zedong de hunyin yu jiating*, Jingguan jiaoyu chubanshe, Beijing, 1993, pp 166–75; and Guo Chen, *Jinguo liezhuan*, p 200.

19 See, for example, Ye Yonglie, 'Jiang Qing yu Mao Zedong jiehe neimu', *Zuojia wenzhai*, December 1992, pp 1–2. Jiang Qing's claim that she never met He Zizhen is from Roxane Witke, *Comrade Chiang Ching*, cited by Ross Terrill, *The white-boned demon*, p 147.

20 Janice R. MacKinnon and Stephen R. MacKinnon, *Agnes Smedley*, p 191; Otto Braun, *A Cominterm agent in China*, p 250.

21 Edgar Snow, *Red star over China*, 1968, p 468; Otto Braun, *A Cominterm agent in China*, p 250.

22 Helen Foster Snow had run into Deng Yingchao in Xi'an on 18 September (this was their first meeting). Deng Yingchao had just arrived from Peiping and it would have taken her another twelve days to get to Yan'an, so the earliest she could have left Yan'an with He Zizhen was 30 September.

23 Liu Ying's biography 'Fengyu zhengcheng liushi zai' (Sixty years of hard journeying) by Sun Xiaoyang is in Liaowang Bianjibu (ed.), *Hongjun nüyingxiong zhuan*, pp 38–52.

24 Guo Chen, *Jinguo liezhuan*, pp 138–43. Jin Weiying's first husband,

Deng Xiaoping, succeeded Mao as China's paramount leader in 1978. Her second husband, Li Weihan, was also known as Luo Mai (or Lo Man in Edgar Snow's *Red star over China* and Salisbury's *The Long March*).

25 'Liu Chien-hsien, Leader of the Proletariat' in Helen Foster Snow's *Inside Red China* (pp 185–86) is actually Liu Qunxian. Her husband Bo Gu was Secretary to the Central Committee, an ally of Otto Braun and leader of the anti-Mao faction. See Guo Chen, *Jinguo liezhuan*, pp 129–38.

26 Otto Braun, *A Cominterm agent in China*, pp 262–63.

27 Ross Terrill, *The white-boned demon*, p 149.

28 Edgar Snow says he was told when he visited Yan'an in 1939 that He Zizhen 'had gone, with her child, to live in Russia'. (*Red star over China*, 1968, p 468). Ross Terrill appears to follow Snow, saying that He Zizhen took Jiaojiao with her when she left for the Soviet Union (*The white-boned demon*, p 142), that Jiaojiao was 'in Moscow with He Zizhen' (pp 162–63) around the time Jiang Qing had her first child (1939?), that Jiaojiao 'had since Yanan days been brought up alongside Li Na, Jiang [Qing]'s own daughter . . .' (p 214), and that Jiaojiao was 'returning from Russia in 1945' (p 163). Kang Keqing claims Jiaojiao travelled to Moscow some time after October 1940 in company with one of Zhu De's long-lost daughters (a fourteen-year-old named Zhu Min who was found in Chengdu and is believed to have died in the air-raids in Russia in 1942–43) (*Kang Keqing huiyilu*, pp 316–17). Guo Chen states that He Zizhen went to Moscow alone, leaving Jiaojiao in Yan'an; the little girl was then sent to her at an unspecified later date around the time hostilities broke out between Russia and Nazi Germany, that is, mid 1941, and stayed with her in Russia until at least 1946 (*Jinguo liezhuan*, pp 194, 196).

29 Edgar Snow wrote of his visit to Moscow in the winter of 1942–43 in his *People on our side* (Random House, New York, 1944), saying that even though the capital was cheerless and dreary and life grim and tough it was better in Moscow than in some other Russian cities and towns (p 157). The 'perhaps bags' and details of the food rationing system are from this book (pp 161–62).

30 Guo Chen, *Jinguo liezhuan*, p 197.

31 Cheng Wei, *Gongheguo diyi jia*, pp 168–69.

32 Guo Chen, *Jinguo liezhuan*, p 198.

33 Guo Chen, *Jinguo liezhuan*, pp 198–99.

CHAPTER 5   OUTSIDE, LOOKING IN

1 Dong Hanhe, *Xilujun nüzhanshi mengnan ji*, pp 36–51. See also Guo Chen, *Jinguo liezhuan*, pp 187–90; and Liaowang Bianjibu (ed.), *Hongjun nüyingxiong zhuan*, pp 202–6.
2 Details of economic conditions during the war with Japan and the civil war between the communists and the KMT are from Lloyd E. Eastman, *Seeds of destruction: Nationalist China in war and revolution 1937–1949*, Stanford University Press, Stanford, California, 1984.
3 Edgar Snow, *Red star over China*, 1968, pp 506–7. The party papers in question are entitled 'Before the Sixth Party Congress' (Tony Saich and Hans van de Ven (eds), *New perspectives on the Chinese Communist revolution*, pp 316, 356). See also *Who's who in Communist China*, Union Research Institute, Hong Kong, 1966, pp 616–17.
4 *Lu Xun: Selected works* (translated by Yang Xianyi and Gladys Yang, Foreign Languages Press, Beijing, 2nd edn, 1980), vol. 1, pp 168–88.
5 Kang Keqing's biography in Liaowang Bianjibu (ed.), *Hongjun nüyingxiong zhuan*, p 30.

CHAPTER 6   THE RED AMAZON

1 Agnes Smedley, *China fights back*, p 97.
2 Chang Kuo-t'ao, *The rise of the Chinese Communist Party*, vol. 2, p 521.
3 Helen Foster Snow was in Yan'an from early May to 7 September 1937. She published part of her interview with 'The Red Amazon, K'ang K'e-ching' in the section titled 'Three women leaders' in *Inside Red China* (pp 186–91). This book includes a general introduction, written in her amusing if somewhat patronising 1930s style, that is an absorbing and perceptive description of the Yan'an women ('The better half of the Chinese revolution', pp 167–91).
4 Helen Foster Snow, *Inside Red China*, p 189.
5 Helen Foster Snow, *Inside Red China*, p 189.
6 Nym Wales, 'K'ang K'ê-ching: A peasant partisan', p 214.
7 Charlotte Furth 'Rethinking Van Gulik: Sexuality and reproduction in traditional Chinese medicine', in Christina K. Gilmartin et al (eds), *Engendering China: Women, culture, and the state*, Harvard University Press, Cambridge, Mass, 1991, pp 125–46.
8 Agnes Smedley, *China fights back*, p 89. *China fights back* consists of letters written by Agnes Smedley while at the anti-Japanese front in the Taihang Mountains from September 1937 to January 1938 and is a vivid eyewitness account of that time and place.
9 Agnes Smedley, *China fights back*, pp 86–87.

10 These comments by Kang Keqing about He Ying and about her own military ambitions are from Helen Foster Snow, *Inside Red China*, p 188, and Nym Wales, 'K'ang K'ê-ching: A peasant partisan', p 218.

11 Helen Foster Snow, *Inside Red China*, p 174.

12 Kang Keqing, *Kang Keqing huiyilu*, pp 209–10.

13 Kang Keqing, *Kang Keqing huiyilu*, p 222; Otto Braun, *A Cominterm agent in China*, p 247.

14 Chang Kuo-t'ao, *The rise of the Chinese Communist Party*, vol. 2, pp 521–2, 562.

15 Helen Foster Snow, *My China years*, p 279.

16 Otto Braun, *A Comintern agent in China*, p 248.

17 Agnes Smedley, *The great road*, p 4; Edgar Snow, *Red star over China*, 1963, p 363.

18 Kang Keqing, *Kang Keqing huiyilu*, pp 222–23.

19 Kang Keqing recalls the American medico Dr George Hatem setting off with her (*Kang Keqing huiyilu*, pp 224–25), but Helen Foster Snow says Dr Hatem farewelled her with a small gift when they left on 7 September and she ran into him a little later in the war zone (*My China years*, pp 282–83, 285). Helen Foster Snow's comment about Kang Keqing being 'determined' to go to the front is in *Inside Red China*, p 292.

20 Agnes Smedley, *China fights back*, pp 139–40.

21 Kang Keqing, *Kang Keqing huiyilu*, p 228.

22 Agnes Smedley, *China fights back*, p 175. The 8th Route Army was renamed the 18th Army in one of Generalissimo Chiang Kai-shek's reorganisations about this time, but the earlier name stuck and the Red Army of this period is usually referred to as the 8th Route Army.

23 Kang Keqing, *Kang Keqing huiyilu*, pp 234–35.

24 Agnes Smedley, *China fights back*, p 153.

25 Janice R. MacKinnon and Stephen R. MacKinnon, *Agnes Smedley*, p 201.

26 Agnes Smedley, *China fights back*, p 268.

27 Agnes Smedley, *The great road*, p 369.

28 Kang Keqing, *Kang Keqing huiyilu*, pp 276–77.

29 Kang Keqing related her experiences in Luoyang and Xi'an in *Kang Keqing huiyilu*, pp 277–80; 285–86.

30 Zhang Qinqiu (1904–1968) had studied in Moscow between 1925 and 1929; she assumed the name Gou Xiuying to avoid detection while working in the factory and a kitchen in Ningxia (Guo Chen,

Jinguo liezhuan, pp 177–78; Dong Hanhe, *Xilujun nüzhanshi mengnan ji*, pp 155–66).

31 Guo Chen, *Jinguo liezhuan*, pp 150–57.

32 Guo Chen, *Jinguo liezhuan*, p 81.

33 Ross Terrill, *The white-boned demon*, pp 21, 28, 62–64, 160.

34 For the life and times of Jiang Qing see Ross Terrill, *The white-boned demon*. It should be noted that Terrill's book is about Jiang Qing and that some of his comments about secondary characters such as He Zizhen are not reliable; for example, his statements about He Zizhen and her children need to be treated with some caution (pp 139, 142, 162–63, 214–15). His remark on p 142 that many of the Long March women had bound feet ('It is not easy to dance on feet that were once bound, as many of the Amazons' feet were') is untrue: just three of The Thirty Women had once had bound feet, long since 'liberated' but still partly crippled (Wei Gongzhi, Yang Houzhen and Zhou Yuehua).

35 Ding Ling, 'Thoughts on Women's Day 8th March' in Robert Tung, *Proscribed Chinese writing*, Curzon Press, London, 1976, pp 11–16.

36 See David E. Apter, 'Discourse as power: Yan'an and the Chinese revolution' in Tony Saich and Hans van de Ven (eds), *New perspectives on the Chinese Communist revolution*, pp 221–23.

37 Kang Keqing, *Kang Keqing huiyilu*, pp 304–5.

38 Barbara W. Tuchman, *Sand against the wind: Stilwell and the American experience in China 1911–45*, Papermac (Macmillan), London, 1991, pp 477–78, 486. See also Barbara W. Tuchman, 'If Mao had come to Washington in 1945' in her *Notes from China*, Collier Books, New York, 1972, pp 77–112.

39 Her biography in Liaowang Bianjibu (ed.), *Hongjun nüyingxiong zhuan*, p 30.

PART III PROLOGUE

1 Franz Michael, *Mao and the perpetual revolution*, Barron's Educational Series, Woodbury, New York, 1977, p 263.

CHAPTER 7   UNTOUCHABLE

1 Sources for the latter part of He Zizhen's life are her biography by Qiu Zhizhuo, 'Guangrong er kankede yi sheng'; Guo Chen, *Jinguo liezhuan*, pp 199–201; and Shui Jing's 'Wo pei He Zizhen shang Lushan jian Mao Zedong', *Jiating* 1992: nos 10, 11, 12. He Zizhen is mentioned in passing in the controversial book by Mao's doctor

Li Zhisui, *The private life of Chairman Mao: The memoirs of Mao's personal physician*, trans. Professor Tai Hung-chao, with the editorial assistance of Anne F. Thurston, Random House, New York, 1994, pp 56, 72, 79, 258, 382–84, and notes on pp 641, 642, 646.

2   Cheng Wei, *Gongheguo diyi jia*, p 174.

3   The gist of this note is given in her biography in Liaowang Bianjibu (ed.), *Hongjun nüyingxiong zhuan*, p 100.

4   Lucian W. Pye, 'Rethinking the man in the leader', *The China Journal*, issue 35, January 1996, p 107.

5   Shui Jing, 'Wo pei He Zizhen shang Lushan jian Mao Zedong'.

6   See, for example, the biographies of The Abandoned Empress, Empress Xiao Xian Donggo, Empress Xiao Xian Chun, Empress Ula Nara and Wanrong (Empress Xuan Tong) in Clara Wing-chung Ho (ed), *Biographical dictionary of Chinese women*, M E Sharpe, New York, 1998.

7   These inconsistencies appear in Li Zhisui, *The private life of Chairman Mao*, pp 56, 383, 659, 383. For a discussion of the historical accuracy of Dr Li's revelations and the standpoint from which he wrote his memoirs see Anne F. Thurston, 'The politics of survival: Li Zhisui and the inner court', *The China Journal*, issue 35, January 1996, pp 97–105. Dr Thurston edited *The private life of Chairman Mao*; hers is one of four articles analysing Dr Li and his book in that issue of *The China Journal*.

8   Li Zhisui, *The private life of Chairman Mao*, pp 382–84.

9   Anne F. Thurston, *The private life of Chairman Mao*, p 646 (note to p 397); Lucian W. Pye, *The China Journal*, issue 35, January 1996, p 107.

10   Li Zhisui, *The private life of Chairman Mao*, pp 109–10. The following three quotes from Dr Li are on pp 383–84, 349, 109.

11   Dong Hanhe, *Xilujun nüzhanshi mengnan ji*, pp 169–74; Lily Xiao Hong Lee, *The virtue of yin*, p 86.

12   Guo Chen, *Jinguo liezhuan*, p 156.

13   Li Zhisui, *The private life of Chairman Mao*, pp 120–21.

14   These snippets about He Zizhen's feelings towards Jiang Qing during the Cultural Revolution are from Guo Chen, *Jinguo liezhuan*, pp 199–201.

15   A journalist named Gao Shuli tracked Yang Yuehua down in April 1995 and wrote up her story as 'Yang Yuehua fangwen ji' (Record of an interview with Yang Yuehua); it was published in *Qianshao yuekan (Outpost monthly)*, September 1995, pp 49–50.

16   Li Fuchun 'slept with a woman colleague of his wife's and was

reprimanded [by the Party]', according to Ross Terrill, *The white-boned demon*, p 150.

CHAPTER 8   NEVER SAY DIE

1   Sources for the last part of Wang Quanyuan's story are Guo Chen, *Jinguo liezhuan*, pp 188–90; her biography 'Xueyu–xingfeng yi nüjie', Dong Hanhe, *Xilujun nüzhanshi mengnan ji*, pp 51–59; and Hu Yang's 'Yige nühongjun tuanzhang de chuanqi rensheng', *Jinan yuebao*, reprinted in *Beijing qingnian bao*, 5 August 1996, p 5.

2   [Miss] Peter Lum, *Peking 1950–1953*, Robert Hale Ltd, London, 1958, pp 103–6.

3   Dong Hanhe, *Xilujun nüzhanshi mengnan ji*, pp 54–55.

4   Hu Yang, 'Yige nühongjun tuanzhang de chuanqi rensheng'.

5   This is Dong Hanhe, who wrote *Xilujun nüzhanshi mengnan ji*; the photo is on p 55.

6   Hu Yang, 'Yige nühongjun tuanzhang de chuanqi rensheng'.

CHAPTER 9   ABOUT TURN

1   Kang Keqing, *Kang Keqing huiyilu*, pp 373–75; pp 319 ff of this book of her memoirs are the main source for this chapter.

2   The story of Li Zhen up till 1949 is not dissimilar to Kang Keqing's. She was born an illiterate peasant about 1908 in Hunan Province, joined the revolution in the late 1920s, and went to the Marxist School in Ruijin in 1933. In August 1934 she departed from Ruijin with the 6th Army Group for the Hunan–Hubei–Sichuan–Guizhou soviet base under He Long. She was aged twenty-six, pregnant and assistant head of the organisation department of the 2nd Front Army when it set off in November 1935 to follow the path of the 1st Front Army's Long March and meet the 4th Front Army in Tibet. The child she gave birth to in the Grass Lands appears to have died at birth. She served at the anti-Japanese battlefront in 1937 under He Long and briefly attended a school for female cadres, not, it seems, in Yan'an. After 1945 she served in the north-west then in Korea as a secretary in the political department during the Korean War. From 1957 she was a Deputy Prosecutor-General with the PLA. Because of her longtime professional relationships with Peng Dehuai and He Long, Li Zhen was confined for four years before being out of work for another six during the Cultural Revolution. She was already seventy by the time she was reinstated in 1978 but took on committee work with the General Political Bureau, the National

People's Congress and the All-China Women's Federation. She remained childless; her husband Gan Siqi died in 1964. See Li Zhen's biography 'Jiefangjun weiyi de nü jiangjun' (The only female General in the People's Liberation Army) by Gu Lanying in Liaowang bianjibu (ed), *Hongjun nüyingxiong zhuan*, pp 207–15.

3 *Zhou Enlai*, television documentary, jointly produced by Central Television of China and Chinese Communist Party Archival Research Unit, 1998.

4 Christina Gilmartin, 'The politics of gender in the making of the Party' in Tony Saich and Hans van de Ven (eds) *New perspectives on the Chinese communist revolution*, p 48.

5 Song Meiling was the youngest of the famous three Song sisters—their surname is often written 'Soong'. Song Meiling married the Generalissimo in 1927; she celebrated her hundredth birthday early in 1997, in Taiwan. Song Qingling, whose name is variously found as Soong Ch'ing-ling, Soong Ching Ling and Soong Ch'ing Ling, was the middle Song sister. She married Dr Sun Yat-sen in 1914, never remarried after his death in 1925 and died in China in 1981 at the age of 88.

6 This comment is in Nym Wales' (ie. Helen Foster Snow's) *Red dust: autobiographies of Chinese communists*, p 218.

7 A lucid analysis of the 'Let a hundred flowers bloom together, let the hundred schools of thought contend' movement can be found in Maurice Meisner, *Mao's China and after*, pp 167–203.

8 Mao Zedong, *On the correct handling of contradictions among the people*, quoted in Maurice Meisner, *Mao's China and after*, p 197.

9 An interpretation of just how Mao Zedong managed to confound all who opposed his romantic notion of perpetual revolution and destabilisation—'the elaborate charade in which the Chinese leadership and the Chinese masses concealed his errors in order to preserve a facade of solidarity and success'—is interestingly told by Dennis Bloodworth, who was Chief Far East Correspondent on the *Observer* at that time: Dennis Bloodworth, *The messiah and the mandarins: The paradox of Mao's China*, Weidenfeld & Nicolson, London, 1982.

10 Nym Wales [Helen Foster Snow], *Inside Red China*, pp 110–11.

11 Kang Keqing, *Kang Keqing huiyilu*, p 256.

12 Anne F. Thurston, *Enemies of the people: The ordeal of the intellectuals in China's Great Cultural Revolution*, Harvard University Press, Cambridge, 1988. Dr Thurston's comments about and quotes from the people she interviewed are in her article 'The politics of survival:

Li Zhisui and the inner court', *The China Journal*, issue 35, January 1996, pp 100–2.

13 Kang Keqing, *Kang Keqing huiyilu*, p 488.

14 Harrison E. Salisbury, *The Long March*, p 334.

15 See Wolfgang Bartke, *Who's who in the People's Republic of China*, M E Sharpe, New York, 1981.

16 Tani Barlow quoted in Tani E. Barlow (ed), *Gender politics in modern China: Writing and feminism*, Duke University Press, Durham, 1993, p 238.

17 Amnesty International estimated in August 1989 that 'at least 1,000 civilians, most of them unarmed, had been killed and several thousands injured by troops firing indiscriminately into crowds in Beijing between June 3 and June 9, 1989'. Cheng Chu-yuan, *Behind the Tiananmen massacre: Social, political, and economic ferment in China*, Westview Press, Boulder, 1990, p 138. Harrison Salisbury has also published an eyewitness account of the Tiananmen Incident: *Tiananmen diary: Thirteen days in June*, Little, Brown & Company, Boston, 1989.

18 Nym Wales [Helen Foster Snow], *Red dust*, p 218.

Appendix The Thirty Women

1 For the later periods of these women's lives see Lily Xiao Hong Lee, 'Where are the heroines of the Long March now? A survey of their lives and work after 1949' in *The virtue of yin*, pp 65–88.

2 Wolfgang Bartke, *Who's who in the People's Republic of China*, 1981, p 15; Guo Chen, *Jinguo liezhuan*, pp 90–94; Nym Wales, *Inside Red China*, pp 182–85; Harrison Salisbury, *The Long March*, pp 89–90; Hu Guohua, 'Yige weidade nüxing' (A great woman) in Liaowang Bianjibu (ed.) *Hongjun nüyingxiong zhuan*, pp 7–24.

3 Guo Chen, *Jinguo liezhuan*, pp 81–84; Nym Wales, *Inside Red China*, pp 29–30, 169.

4 Guo Chen, *Jinguo liezhuan*, pp 9–12; Zhao Yining, 'Fengxian chu shenhoude mu'ai' (The tribute of profound maternal love) in Liaowang Bianjibu (ed.), *Hongjun nüyingxiong zhuan*, pp 141–52.

5 Guo Chen, *Jinguo liezhuan*, pp 94–99; Nym Wales, *Inside Red China*, p 296; Zhao Wei, 'Zai wanli zhengtu zhong' (On the 10 000-*li* journey) in Liaowang Bianjibu (ed.), *Hongjun nüyingxiong zhuan*, pp 1–6; Wolfgang Bartke, *Who's who in the People's Republic of China*, 1981, pp 53–54.

6 Guo Chen, *Jinguo liezhuan*, pp 156–57; Nym Wales, *Inside Red China*, p 175.

7 He Zizhen's story is told in chapters one, four and seven of this book.

8 Guo Chen, *Jinguo liezhuan*, pp 138–43. When listing The Thirty Women, Helen Foster Snow fused Jin Weiying (who was also known as Ah Jin and who was married to Luo Mai/Luo Man) and Xie Fei (who was known as Ah Xiang and who was married to Liu Shaoqi) into one woman of whom she wrote 'Ah Ch'ing (Hsiang) (wife of Lo Man) was a "Cantonese" which is enough said': see Nym Wales, *Inside Red China*, p 175.

9 Kang Keqing's story is told in chapters three, six and nine of this book.

10 Guo Chen, *Jinguo liezhuan*, pp 120–27; Li Shangzhi, 'Changzheng ren pu changzhen ge' (Long Marcher composed Long March songs) in Liaowang Bianjibu (ed.), *Hongjun nüyingxiong zhuan*, pp 66–73; Harrison Salisbury, *The Long March*, pp 88–90, 99, 202, 240, 251–52, 334; Nym Wales, *Inside Red China*, pp XLIV–V, 27–29, 295–96.

11 Guo Chen, *Jinguo liezhuan*, pp 154–57; Wu Dongfeng, 'Zai qianglindanyu zhong lixian jingnan' (Undergoing great trials in a hail of bullets) in Liaowang Bianjibu (ed.), *Hongjun nüyingxiong zhuan*, pp 153–62.

12 Guo Chen, *Jinguo liezhuan*, pp 79, 85, 178–79.

13 Guo Chen, *Jinguo liezhuan*, pp 23–26; Liu Zhuo'an, 'Cong nüzhanshi dao shengwei shuji' (From woman fighter to secretary of provincial party committee) in Liaowang Bianjibu (ed.), *Hongjun nüyingxiong zhuan*, pp 53–65; Nym Wales, *Inside Red China*, pp 178–81, 192–96; Wolfgang Bartke, *Who's who in the People's Republic of China*, 1981, pp 177–78.

14 Guo Chen, *Jinguo liezhuan*, pp 48–52; Chen Wanwen, 'Xiangwang he xunqiu shuguang' (Longing for and seeking the dawn) in Liaowang Bianjibu (ed.), *Hongjun nüyingxiong zhuan*, pp 129–40; Nym Wales, *Inside Red China*, p 175.

15 Guo Chen, *Jinguo liezhuan*, p 21.

16 Guo Chen, *Jinguo liezhuan*, pp 128–38; Harrison Salisbury, *The Long March*, pp 87–88; Nym Wales, *Inside Red China*, pp 185–86.

17 Zeng Zhi, *Changzheng nü zhanshi*, Beifang funü ertong chubanshe, np, 1987, pp 13–27; Guo Chen, *Jinguo liezhuan*, pp 77, 92–93, 99–104, 138; Sun Xiaoyang, 'Fengyu zhengcheng liushizai' (Sixty years of hard journeying) in Liaowang Bianjibu (ed.), *Hongjun nüyingxiong zhuan*, pp 38–52; Harrison Salisbury, *The Long March*, pp 6, 33, 81, 88–90, 124, 143, 151–52, 173–75, 193–95, 277, 328, 371; Nym Wales, *Inside Red China*, p 178.

18 Guo Chen, *Jinguo liezhuan*, pp 28–34, 149, 194; Liu Jinghui and Mao Shucheng, 'Jiechu de Hongjun xuanchuanyuan' (Outstanding Red Army propaganda worker) in Liaowang Bianjibu (ed.), *Hongjun nüyingxiong zhuan*, pp 102–17.

19 Guo Chen, *Jinguo liezhuan*, pp 12, 73, 178.

20 Wang Quanyuan's story is told in chapters two, five and eight of this book.

21 Guo Chen, *Jinguo liezhuan*, pp 32–33, 143–49; Nym Wales, *Inside Red China*, pp 296–97.

22 Guo Chen, *Jinguo liezhuan*, pp 13–15; Huang Qizhuang, 'Yige nüzhanshide zuji' (Footprints of a woman fighter) in Liaowang Bianjibu (ed.), *Hongjun nüyingxiong zhuan*, pp 163–74; Harrison Salisbury, *The Long March*, pp 32, 36, 81, 88, 206, 237, 265–66.

23 Guo Chen, *Jinguo liezhuan*, pp 190–93.

24 Guo Chen, *Jinguo liezhuan*, pp 174–78; Dong Hanhe, *Xilujun nüzhanshi mengnan ji*, pp 155–74.

25 Harrison Salisbury, *The Long March*, pp 81–82; Guo Chen, *Jinguo liezhuan*, pp 69–71.

26 Guo Chen, *Jinguo liezhuan*, pp 44–47; Hu Guohua and Zhuang Jianmin, 'Bu pingfande lu' (An extraordinary path) in Liaowang Bianjibu (ed.), *Hongjun nüyingxiong zhuan*, pp 74–82.

27 Guo Chen, *Jinguo liezhuan*, pp 158–65; Qi Xiu, 'Lijin qianxin zhi yu jian' (A will firmed by undergoing great difficulties) in Liaowang Bianjibu (ed.), *Hongjun nüyingxiong zhuan*, pp 175–87.

28 Harrison Salisbury, *The Long March*, p 167; Guo Chen, *Jinguo liezhuan*, pp 201–3; Nym Wales, *Inside Red China*, p 125.

29 Guo Chen, *Jinguo liezhuan*, pp 79–81.

30 Guo Chen, *Jinguo liezhuan*, pp 4–6, 18, 26–7, 43, 58; Hu Guohua, 'Miandui jiannan shenghuode kaoyan (Tested by facing life's difficulties) in Liaowang Bianjibu (ed.), *Hongjun nüyingxiong zhuan*, pp 118–28.

31 Guo Chen, *Jinguo liezhuan*, pp 167–74.

BIBLIOGRAPHY

Barlow, Tani E. (ed.). *Gender politics in modern China: Writing and feminism*, Duke University Press, Durham, 1993.

Bartke, Wolfgang. *Who's who in the People's Republic of China*, M E Sharpe, New York, 1981.

Benton, Gregor. *Mountain fires: The Red Army's three-year war in south China, 1934–1938*, University of California Press, Berkeley, 1992.

Biographical dictionary of Chinese women: Qing period (1644–1911), M E Sharpe, New York, 1998.

Bloodworth, Dennis. *The messiah and the mandarins: The paradox of Mao's China*, Weidenfeld & Nicolson, London, 1982.

Braun, Otto. *A Comintern agent in China 1932–1939*, trans. Jeanne Moore [first published in German in 1975], Stanford University Press, Stanford, 1982.

Chang Kuo-t'ao [Zhang Guotao]. *The rise of the Chinese Communist Party 1928–1938: Volume two of the autobiography of Chang Kuo-t'ao*, The University Press of Kansas, Lawrence, 1972.

Cheng Chu-yuan [Cheng Chu-yüang]. *Behind the Tiananmen massacre: Social, political, and economic ferment in China*, Westview Press, Boulder, Colorado, 1990.

Crook, Isabel and David. *Revolution in a Chinese village: Ten Mile Inn*, Routledge & Kegan Paul, London, 1959 (3rd impression, 1979).

Eastman, Lloyd E. *Seeds of destruction: Nationalist China in war and revolution 1937–1949*, Stanford University Press, Stanford, 1984.

Fairbank, John K. and Reischauer, Edwin O. *China: Tradition and transformation*, George Allen & Unwin, Sydney, 1979, 1986.

Gilmartin, Christina K. et al (eds). *Engendering China: Women, culture, and the state*, Harvard University Press, Cambridge, Mass, 1991.

Han Suyin. *Birdless summer*, Jonathan Cape, London, 1968.

Hsü, Immanuel C.Y. *The rise of modern China*, 2nd edn, Oxford University Press, Hong Kong, 1975.

Lee, Lily Xiao Hong. *The virtue of yin: Studies on Chinese women*, Wild Peony, Sydney, 1994.

Li Zhisui. *The private life of Chairman Mao: The memoirs of Mao's personal physician*, trans. Professor Tai Hung-chao, with the editorial assistance of Anne F. Thurston, Random House, New York, 1994.

Loewe, Michael. *Ways to paradise: The Chinese quest for immortality*, George Allen & Unwin, London, 1979.

Lu Xun: Selected works, 2nd edn, trans. Yang Xianyi and Gladys Yang, Foreign Languages Press, Beijing, 1980.

Lum, [Miss] Peter. *Peking 1950–1953*, Robert Hale Ltd, London, 1958.

MacKinnon, Janice R. and MacKinnon, Stephen R. *Agnes Smedley: The life and times of an American radical*, University of California Press, Berkeley, 1988.

Meisner, Maurice. *Mao's China and after: A history of the People's Republic*, The Free Press, New York, 1986.

Michael, Franz. *Mao and the perpetual revolution*, Barron's Educational Series, Woodbury, New York, 1977.

Pye, Lucian W. 'Rethinking the man in the leader', *The China Journal*, 35, January, 1996.

Saich, Tony and van de Ven, Hans (eds). *New perspectives on the Chinese Communist Revolution*, M E Sharpe (An East Gate Book), New York, 1995.

Salisbury, Harrison E. *The Long March: The untold story*, Harper & Row, New York, 1985.

Salisbury, Harrison E. *Tiananmen diary: Thirteen days in June*, Little, Brown & Company, Boston, 1989.

Smedley, Agnes. *China fights back: An American woman with the Eighth Route Army*, Victor Gollancz, London, 1938.

Smedley, Agnes. *The great road: The life and times of Chu Teh*, John Calder, London, 1958.

Snow, Edgar. *People on our side*, Random House, New York, 1944.

Snow, Edgar. *Red star over China*, 1963 reissue, Victor Gollancz, London, 1937.

Snow, Edgar. *Red star over China*, first revised and enlarged edition, Victor Gollancz, London, 1968.

Snow, Edgar. *Scorched earth*, Victor Gollancz, London, 1941.

Snow, Helen Foster. *Inside Red China*, 1977 reprint [with a new preface and biographical notes by the author], Da Capo Press, New York, 1939.

Snow, Helen Foster. *My China years*, William Morrow & Co, New York, 1984.

Terrill, Ross. *The white-boned demon: A biography of Madame Mao Zedong*, Touchstone (Simon & Schuster), New York, 1984.

Thurston, Anne F. 'The politics of survival: Li Zhisui and the inner court', *The China Journal*, 35, January 1996.

Tuchman, Barbara W. *Notes from China*, Collier Books, New York, 1972.

Tuchman, Barbara W. *Sand against the wind: Stilwell and the American experience in China 1911–1945*, Papermac, London, 1991.

Tung, Robert, *Proscribed Chinese writing*, 2nd rev edn 1978, Scandinavian Institute of Asian Studies Monograph Series No 21, Curzon Press, London, 1976 [text in Chinese].

Wales, Nym [pen name of Helen Foster Snow]. *Red dust: Autobiographies of Chinese communists* [as told to Nym Wales], Introduction by Robert Carver North, Stanford University Press, Stanford, Calif, 1952.

Who's who in Communist China, Union Research Institute, Hong Kong, 1966.

Wilson, Dick. *The Long March 1935: The epic of Chinese Communism's survival*, Viking Press, New York, 1971.

CHINESE SOURCES

Cheng Wei. *Gongheguo diyi jia: Mao Zedong de hunyin yu jiating* (First family of the Republic: The marriages and families of Mao Zedong), Jingguan jiaoyu chubanshe, Beijing, 1993.

Dong Hanhe. *Xilujun nüzhanshi mengnan ji* (Women soldiers of the Western Route Army fall into enemy hands), Jiefangjun wenyi chubanshe, Beijing, 1990.

Dong Peiyan (Robert Tung). *Zhongguo xiandai wenxuan* (Proscribed Chinese writing), Bei'ou yazhou wenti yanjiusuo, Xianggang, 2nd rev edn 1976, Scandinavian Institute of Asian Studies Monograph Series No 21, Curzon Press, London, 1978.

Gao Shuli. 'Yang Yuehua fangwen ji' (Notes on an interview with Yang Yuehua), *Qianshao yuekan*, 1995, no 9, pp 49–50.

Guo Chen. *Jinguo liezhuan: Hong Yifangmian Jun sanshiwei changzheng nü hongjun shengping shiji* (Biographies of brave women: 30 women soldiers of the 1st Front Red Army), Nongcun duwu chubanshe, Beijing (or Niulanshan), 1986.

Hu Yang. 'Yige nühongjuntuanzhang de chuanqi rensheng' (A legendary female Red Army regimental commander), *Jinan yuebao* (Jinan monthly), reprinted in *Beijing qingnianbao* (Beijing youth), 5 August 1996.

Huang Changjiao. 'Buqude zhandou', in *Jiangxi funü gemingdouzheng gushi*, Jiangxisheng funü lianhehui, Beijing, 1963, pp 55–67.

Kang Keqing. *Kang Keqing huiyi lu* (Reminiscences of Kang Keqing), (issued posthumously; Foreword by [Long Marcher General] Yang Shangkun), Jiefangjun chubanshe, Beijing, 1993.

Liaowang Bianjibu (ed.). *Hongjun nüyingxiong zhuan* (Heroines of the Red Army), Xinhua chubanshe, Beijing, 1986.

Liu Fulang. *The analysis of Mao Tse-tung's personality*, Union Press, Hong Kong, 1973, pp 59–65.

Nüying zishu, Jiangxi renmin chubanshe, Nanchang, 1988.

Shui Jing. 'Wo pei He Zizhen shang Lushan jian Mao Zedong' (I took He Zizhen to Mount Lu to see Mao Zedong), *Jiating*, 1991:10, 11, 12.

Ye Yonglie. 'Jiang Qing yu Mao Zedong jiehe neimu' (The inside story of the union of Jiang Qing and Mao Zedong), *Zuojia wenzhai*, December 1992, pp 1–2.

Zeng Zhi. *Changzheng nü zhanshi* (Women fighters of the Long March), Beifang funü ertong chubanshe, np, 1987.

Zhou Enlai, television documentary jointly produced by Central Television of China and Chinese Communist Party Archival Research Unit, 1998.

INDEX

* The Thirty Women

301